T0354752

Pastor Is
a Verb

Pastor Is a Verb

LIFE BEYOND SUNDAY

KEITH PREKKER

ARCHWAY
PUBLISHING

Copyright © 2024 Keith Prekker.

All rights reserved. No part of this book may be used or reproduced by any means, graphic, electronic, or mechanical, including photocopying, recording, taping or by any information storage retrieval system without the written permission of the author except in the case of brief quotations embodied in critical articles and reviews.

This book is a work of non-fiction. Unless otherwise noted, the author and the publisher make no explicit guarantees as to the accuracy of the information contained in this book and in some cases, names of people and places have been altered to protect their privacy.

Archway Publishing books may be ordered through booksellers or by contacting:

Archway Publishing
1663 Liberty Drive
Bloomington, IN 47403
www.archwaypublishing.com
844-669-3957

Because of the dynamic nature of the Internet, any web addresses or links contained in this book may have changed since publication and may no longer be valid. The views expressed in this work are solely those of the author and do not necessarily reflect the views of the publisher, and the publisher hereby disclaims any responsibility for them.

Any people depicted in stock imagery provided by Getty Images are models, and such images are being used for illustrative purposes only.
Certain stock imagery © Getty Images.

ISBN: 978-1-6657-6045-4 (sc)
ISBN: 978-1-6657-6046-1 (e)

Library of Congress Control Number: 2024910565

Print information available on the last page.

Archway Publishing rev. date: 06/24/2024

CONTENTS

EPIGRAPH

"My job is not to solve people's problems or make them happy, but to help them see the grace operating in their lives."

— Eugene H. Peterson,
The Contemplative Pastor:
Returning to the Art of Spiritual Direction

FOREWORD

"I never saw them again."

This is the refrain in many of Keith Prekker's stories, and it is worth a slow visit. The life of a congregation, from the outside at least, seems staid and stable. If the church is surrounded by a cemetery, the names on the tombstones show a significant overlap with the names on the membership rolls. People sometimes tell jokes about dead people voting when issues involving change are being considered. "I know Mother wouldn't like this…," someone says, and the vote is decided.

Keith Prekker knows that reality.

But what makes these stories so delightful is his awareness of the fuller reality of the varied life of a congregation. Real life is a fast-flowing stream that sweeps the past away and spins people into a future they could not have imagined. This is as true in rural communities in far northern Minnesota as it is in urban Colorado. A congregation exists as an eddy, a swirl in that stream. It meets in a building built by people who have been swept away, and it meets for purposes that continue to change, attempting to adapt. It draws in people who need help, or a safe haven, or the blessing of tradition applied to their life relationships. Prekker tells stories of ministry with these people who are drawn into the eddy, and the stories ring true, even when – perhaps especially when—many of these stories end with the words, "I never saw them again."

Prekker seems to have always listened to these people, and when he didn't, he is honest about it. That trait alone makes this book a delight. He served congregations that were exploding with growth, and he served congregations that were shrinking. In his half-century of ministry he made breakthroughs and mistakes; he succeeded and failed. And in all of this, he lets us see the truth, even when it is painful. One of the things I most appreciate is that his stories of mistakes and failures are not set-ups for stories of a hero-pastor rising yet again from the ashes. Prekker tells true stories, and true stories do not always work out.

True stories do not always work out, but they are always worth thinking about. Prekker began his ministry in 1969, in a post-WWII world that was struggling to make sense of societal changes and a war in Southeast Asia. He served new congregations and old ones, small congregations and large, and in all of his service, he listened to the people who found themselves swirled into the changing work of the church. The stories he tells in this book let us listen, too, and that is a great gift.

The stories are short, and they can be read one-by-one, or in blocks. They are arranged in chronological order, grouped by the congregations that Prekker served, but they can be read in order or out of order. Any way you read them, each story gives you a glimpse of what the ministry of a congregation actually is, what the life of a pastor actually involves. And we get to see all of this through the eyes of a perceptive pastor who paid attention to what was essential.

These are stories of actual life, actual ministry, and they give me profound hope for the lives of congregations even as the stream of history sweeps through the world around them, changing everything.

Thank you, Pastor Prekker. Your stories delighted me, and puzzled me. Sometimes I nodded my head in recognition, and sometimes I just rolled my eyes. But always I was thankful to be in the company of a pastor and of congregations who were working steadily to carry out their call with determination and integrity. I will read this book more than once.

Richard W. Swanson
Professor of Religion, Philosophy, and Classics, Augustana University, Sioux Falls, SD
Director of the Provoking the Gospel Storytelling Project

PREFACE

"Just what do you actually do during the week?"

That question was posed to me at the conclusion of a visit from relatives one summer early in my ministry. We had known for some time of their planned visit and I had worked hard to clear my schedule that week in order to have free time with them; we'd enjoyed plenty of visiting and sightseeing together. Now their visit was at its end, and amid the laughter and tears and farewells, his question crystalized what I had suspected for a long time: Beyond what they see on Sundays, most people really don't know or understand what is involved in serving as a pastor in a congregation.

This book is an attempt to give an idea of what a pastor "actually does during the week" between Sundays.

In my Lutheran tradition, as in many denominations, the process of becoming a pastor usually involves an educational journey of completing a four-year undergraduate degree from an accredited college or university, plus an additional four-year degree from an accredited theological school or seminary. I went through that academic process.

After over fifty years of ordained ministry in the Lutheran church, it is my contention now, however, that a pastor's education has only just begun when graduation from formal seminary/theological education takes place. It continues in the myriad aspects of a pastor's work, and mostly during the week between Sundays.

I have assembled some of my more memorable "educational" encounters over the years in an attempt to share that.

All of these stories are true, and are written down as best as I can remember them, and as many as possible in consultation with the people involved. Most of the names have been changed to protect privacy; I have retained a few real names, either because the individual is a public figure, or the story particularly honors them.

Whether their real names appear here in print or not, the "professors" in the ongoing pastoral education process are varied: congregational members, other clergy, unwitting passersby—anyone and everyone. The classrooms are church buildings, hospitals, courtrooms, homes, and city streets.

Learning from them all, I tell these stories to share some of what a pastor actually does.

ACKNOWLEDGEMENTS

Many thanks to all who contributed real-life experiences to this book all these many years along the way and to those who encouraged the recording and sharing of these stories.

Thanks, also, to my many mentors over the years—from seminary faculty to fellow clergy to co-workers on various church staffs who helped me to understand and clarify the sometimes-shrouded dynamics at play in many situations. Foremost among my mentors are the lay people in and around the congregations I have been fortunate to serve. The patience, understanding, and wisdom you have showered on all of us who have served in your congregations and intersected with your lives have been blessings beyond compare.

Special thanks to my wife Pam Faro who has listened to these stories multiple times over the years, and patiently assisted with putting them down on paper in readable and organized form. When a book covers fifty years, with numerous locations, literally hundreds of people, and sometimes delicate and sensitive situations, the task of editing can be overwhelming. Pam thoughtfully worked through all this material, calling on her own experience as a storyteller and writer, a trained theologian, and a worship leader/choir director of many years, making order out of the chaotic collection of remembrances, recollections, and ramblings that were presented to her. I am deeply grateful.

And to my family, many thanks for your support and love through the rocky places that inevitably come in all lives but are often accentuated in the lives of those in "the helping professions."

INTRODUCTION

The education of a pastor doesn't end when he/she walks out the door of the seminary. To the contrary, it is only beginning. In my case, the education has continued for more than fifty years.

The stories that follow are all true. They represent real-life "continuing education" experiences in the life of one pastor. Though these specific stories are of my particular experiences, and a few may be somewhat unique, I believe that together they demonstrate the depth and breadth of pastoral ministry in general. My guess is these experiences could be affirmed, amplified, and expanded upon by most parish pastors. All the formal education in the world is only a preamble to the education one receives in dealing with real-life people in real-life situations.

There are "regular" expectations and responsibilities for a pastor in congregational life—the preparing and leading of worship being the most obvious. Weekly sermon preparation can require from several to many hours; the seminary recommendation to new graduates of one hour of preparation for each minute preached may seem like a lot, but for the first few years it can be pretty accurate. For one thing, reading the various commentators on any text can be helpful but is definitely time-consuming. Once a direction for the sermon is decided upon, searching for good quotes or illustrations is essential. The homiletics professor at my seminary titled each of his classes, "The Art of Sermon Illustration," and required us to set up a file of good illustrative materials. This was helpful, but illustrations from a file can become dated very quickly, so wide and ongoing reading of culturally varied materials is essential for finding good relevant illustrations. Then all the pieces need to be put together, and practiced out loud for sharing with the congregation on Sunday.

Sermon preparation is only one aspect of parish ministry, however. There are also administrative responsibilities in the parish. While the congregational governing board (in most Lutheran churches, the Church Council) has the main decision-making authority, the pastor is responsible for meeting with and advising/directing this group. The same is true for each of the several committees within the church.

And those worship services people see the pastor at? Worship planning involves plenty more than just sermon preparation. Regular meetings with the music folks and others—volunteer and/or professional—are essential to providing a meaningful worship life for the congregation.

Most congregations have one or more Bible studies that the pastor is expected to supervise if not lead. Lutheran churches also usually have a two- or three-year confirmation program of weekly instruction with congregational youth.

Pastors are expected to and generally desire to be a part of the larger community in which the congregation is located. This often entails serving on civic committees and/or being available in community crises. Involvement in local school activities, from classroom discussions of the theory of evolution or community ethics to fund-raising events, are often part of a pastor's ministry.

Pastoral care within the congregation includes regular hospital visitation, and bringing the sacrament of Communion and a "ray of sunshine" to the shut-in members. Depending on the number of homebound folks, and their conditions or needs, this can be a big part of a pastor's life.

(At one point in my second parish, I was requested by the church council to keep track of my hours for a month. The suggestion was that I was being overpaid. I kept track over the span of several months; it turned out I was averaging sixty-five hours per week. The concern about overpayment was dispelled, and the decision was made to call a second pastor to the staff.)

It is in the nitty-gritty of daily experiences that the gospel of God's love, grace, and mercy comes to life. The "types" represented in the characters of the biblical stories become real people, in real situations, needing the love and grace of God brought to them in the caring of God's people—God's church.

This book is an attempt to bring the routines of a parish pastor to life for the reader.

It is divided into sections, each referring to a congregation or setting in which I served as a student or pastor. The length of time I was in one setting or another varied from one to ten years, so of course there were more occasions for memorable experiences in some settings than in others. Hence the wide differences between the number of stories you'll find in each section.

My hope is that you will find these stories real and compelling. That you see in them the ongoing education of one called to serve in the church, and also the hand of God working through the imperfect efforts of one who tried his best to respond to the myriad aspects of ministry, in the pulpit and beyond.

I also hope that the reader will become more aware of the needs and therefore the service opportunities all around, because, in the simple but profound words of the children's Sunday School song:

"I am the church / You are the church / We are the church together.

All who follow Jesus / All around the world / We are the church together."

SEMINARY

The Seed Is Sown

Mt. Carmel Lutheran Church in Northeast Minneapolis sits at the intersection of Ulysses Street and St. Anthony Boulevard. It is in many ways your typical neighborhood church. Situated in a middle-class neighborhood, its membership as I was growing up there in the 1950s was made up mostly of working-class folks, a few cops and firefighters, some office workers, and a few professional people.

In those post-WWII years, Mt. Carmel was teeming with kids. Growing up there was great. Most of our neighbors attended as well. Our scout troop was sponsored there. It was half a block from our house so we walked to church. It was ideal.

Our Luther League high school youth group would often host thirty-five or forty kids for special outings and events. A highlight of most of our regular evening meetings would be the snacks. One night the snack was chocolate cake—wonderful, rich chocolate cake with gooey chocolate frosting. For some reason, the tables were arranged in a large square that night and as luck would have it I was seated directly across the square from my best friend. We started making faces at each other and taunting each other and wouldn't you know?—One thing led to another and pretty soon I had rolled my piece of cake up into a ball and when none of the moms who were supervising was looking I delivered a perfect throw right into the face of my friend.

However, before I had completed the follow-through on my throw, the pastor, who had come into the room behind me and seen the whole incident, had me by the nape of the neck, lifted me out of the chair, and half pushed, half carried me out of the room, up two flights of stairs to his study and deposited me, unceremoniously, into a chair. It had happened so fast that I hardly knew what had happened.

He went to his desk, took off his suit coat, put it on the back of his chair, and sat down. As I waited, anxiously, for what was to come, he said, "Keith, you need to think about going to seminary."

"Why, do they throw cake at the seminary?" was not the reply he expected or wanted. He said, loudly and firmly, "Get serious."

1

He went on to explain the educational process required to pursue ordination, and, more astonishingly to me, to talk about the things he saw in me that he thought might be pointing in that direction (the throwing of chocolate cake notwithstanding). Not wanting to be in any further trouble with him and wanting to get out of there as quickly as possible, I assured him I'd think about it and escaped as fast as I could.

But the seed had been sown.

Seminary Entrance Interview

While I was a student at the University of Minnesota, lots of struggle, sleepless nights, some scattered reading, visits with some dynamic young pastors I had known at camp and other places, and a deep stirring within, all eventually led me to apply for admission to Northwestern Lutheran Theological Seminary (NWLTS), a seminary of the United Lutheran Church in America. (The ULCA would eventually be merged into the Lutheran Church in America [LCA], and then subsequently into the present-day Evangelical Lutheran Church in America [ELCA]. Lutheran alphabet soup.)

But, applying does not equal being admitted. Once my application was reviewed and approved, there followed the FACULTY INTERVIEW—Yikes! I hadn't experienced a FACULTY INTERVIEW at the U of M where I'd done my undergraduate work! Why in the world would the faculty *interview* me? I approached the seminary in southwest Minneapolis with more than a little apprehension.

NWLTS was housed in the former Pillsbury mansions in South Minneapolis. The Pillsbury milling family members had lived in two grand homes from another era. Charles Pillsbury's home had been converted into the seminary's classroom and office building. Charles' uncle, John Pillsbury, had lived right next door in another fabulous residence complete with secret passages and fake walls. That home became the seminary library—though to call these two buildings "homes" is a bit like calling the Queen Mary a rowboat.

Walking in the front door of the main building I was overwhelmed by the grandeur of the place. The first floor was two stories in height. The walls were rich, dark wood, taken from a castle in England and imported to adorn this American abode. I felt totally insignificant as I waited to be invited into "The Library" for the interview. The library room of this building (not to be confused with the actual seminary library in the building next door) had been Charles Pillsbury's personal library, replete with the same rich wood walls as found upon entering the building, plus fireplace, bookshelves, and a long table. That day, the long table had eight or ten faculty members seated around it, with the seminary president at one end and an empty chair at the other. The empty chair was for me. If the purpose of this setup was to scare the living daylights out of me, it was very effective.

The interview began with the inquiries one might expect: Where are you from, where did you go to school, why did you decide to attend seminary? The questions were asked, seemingly randomly, by various faculty members, while the rest studied folders, presumably containing my admission documents. I don't remember the other specific questions but there was a real concern that, since I had graduated a quarter early from the university, I had completed only two of the three quarters of required Greek instead of the full course. I sat quietly as they argued over the importance of the third quarter of Greek, and their assumption that the Greek taught at the U of M was probably Classical Greek as opposed to the Koine Greek used in writing the New Testament. I was happy to let them debate this issue, hopefully assuming it was using up lots of the time allotted for my interview.

The discussion turned to a question about my home congregation. When they realized that I was from Mt. Carmel Lutheran Church in northeast Minneapolis, that was it. It turned out that my pastor was the son of a former president of the seminary, and in fact, the residence hall in which I would eventually rent an apartment was named for him.

Interview over. Welcome to the seminary family!

Later on, when I worked as a janitor for work-study, I found it ironic that that imposing library room which had so intimidated me at the beginning actually became a welcome refuge—I had the keys to the entire building and would occasionally use the quiet, stately room for my work break.

As they say, context matters.

Getting Started

Starting seminary was intimidating. The building was intimidating. The faculty was intimidating. The process was intimidating. My fellow students were intimidating. The decision to "give it a try" had been hard. For a math/science kind of person like me, the concept of studying theology was daunting.

I had gotten married after graduation from the U of M; my wife and I moved into married student housing and began to adjust to seminary life. The class schedule was arranged so that classes took place in the mornings with the afternoons free for study or work. Because of my experience working as a substitute janitor at the Minneapolis courthouse during college, I was hired to serve on the cleaning crew for the classroom/office building. My supervisor was another student, a seminary senior named Larry.

Speaking of intimidating, Larry was tall, square-jawed, with a crew cut and a muscular physique that stretched his t-shirt to the extreme. When I reported for my first day of work, my new boss looked me up and down, asked about my experience, and asked if I had ever run a floor buffer. He explained that our first task before classes began was to wax and buff the gorgeous teak floors of the classroom building. So, we set about moving the furniture out of the way. Once that was accomplished, I was taken to the basement storeroom and shown the five-gallon buckets of wax. Larry picked up one of the buckets, held it straight out to the side of his body, counted to thirty, and set it gently back down. "Now you do it," he ordered.

If you've ever lifted a five-gallon bucket of anything, you know how heavy it can be. Floor wax is extremely dense—hence, very heavy. I was able to barely lift the bucket at all, much less hold it out to the side. As the bucket went crashing to the floor, Larry said, "Close enough, let's go."

Returning to the second floor, I was treated to an amazing display of floor buffing expertise. He ran the buffer forward and back, side to side. He ran it around in circles. He spun himself around 360 degrees, transferring the handles deftly from right hand to left hand while keeping the buffer moving in its regular path. The *coup de grâce* was when he sat on the head of the buffer and reached up to the controls on the handle to run it while riding like a bronco buster.

"Now you try."

I confidently stepped to the handle and took the controls. Immediately upon depressing the "go" switch, the buffer slammed into the wall.

I muscled it away from the wall a few feet, but when I stopped moving it sideways with all my might, it slammed back into the wall. My new boss said, "That's great! You're a natural. I'm going downstairs to the coffee bar. Keep going, I'll be back shortly." After what seemed like an eternity, my arms trembling from the exertion and sweat streaming from every pore, I was thrilled to see the boss man when he came back. I told him I was exhausted.

Laughing with a roar that filled the large hall Larry said, "Oh yeah, I should have mentioned that if you push the handle down, the machine moves to the left, and lifting the handle moves the buffer to the right," and more laughter ensued, from both of us.

In the course of the next year, we became good friends and he became a valued mentor.

He did remain, however, somewhat intimidating.

Meet the Faculty

I mentioned I found the faculty intimidating. Each an expert in his field (they were all men in those days, as was the student body), they led us through Old Testament and New Testament, church history, homiletics, Greek, Hebrew, pastoral counseling, philosophy, Christian education, systematics, and more. Coming from the University of Minnesota with its forty-thousand-plus students, being a part of a graduating class of just twenty-eight was a big adjustment for me.

At the U of M, if you had a question you made an appointment with a teaching assistant and went to his/her office at the appointed time. At the seminary, it was standard practice for a professor to just find you at coffee hour to discuss some point in a paper you had written. Or, in my case as a janitor, to stop me while I might be mopping a floor and ask how I was coming on an assignment. Having been used to having no oversight and no individual connections with professors in college, the degree of personal involvement with the teaching staff at the seminary felt more intimidating than supportive to me. I found myself thinking, "Hey—leave me alone. I'm a big boy. I know the assignment and the deadline. I'll take care of this!"

The faculty was an interesting amalgamation of different personalities and personal experiences. The seminary president was an attorney and pastor who had previously served as a synod president. Our homiletics prof had been a running back for the Yale football team. The son of a former president of the seminary taught us systematic theology. Pastoral care was taught by a prof who had studied under a world-renowned author who was himself a Nazi prison camp survivor. The church history professor's father-in-law (in his eighties) had been coaxed out of his third retirement from other seminaries to teach Hebrew; many of his scholarly biblical and theological books are still available on Amazon. These teachers, and all the rest, approached each of their areas of expertise with an eye on parish ministry, since most if not all had previous parish experience to call upon.

Over the four years of seminary education, I came to understand the new-to-me level of supervision was intended to help, encourage, and support. But I never did completely get over a hint of discomfort with the "intrusiveness" of the well-intended personal contact with professors.

A Surprise at Lunch

Throughout northern Minnesota, there are literally hundreds of small rural Lutheran parishes. These parishes are often linked so that two or three—sometimes even more—are served by one pastor. Typically, each pastor has four weeks of vacation every year. This means there exists a need for many supply (fill-in) preachers in the area. Having seminary students fill these vacant pulpits makes sense on two fronts: 1) someone is in the pulpit during the pastor's absence, and 2) it's good experience for the students.

During the first year of seminary, we students were required to purchase a black clergy shirt and white clerical collar. When we made hospital calls as a required part of Pastoral Care 101, wearing these made us easily identifiable by hospital staff and patients alike, and gained us easy admittance to patient rooms. Those same "clerical uniforms" were expected to be worn whenever providing pulpit supply.

One of the first Sundays I was filling in, I had to lead services in two churches. Due to the long drive involved I had to be underway quite early that morning (4:30 a.m.). That meant "reveille" at 3:30, quick shower, quick breakfast, one last sermon run-through, and off to the North Country. The first service was at a church in a very small town. Got through that okay. This being long before cell phones, Google Maps, or GPS coordinates, I got detailed oral directions to the country church from one of the members of the town church.

I got to the country church in time and completed a second service there. Afterward, totally drained from the experience of early awakening, long drive, unfamiliar leadership experience, finding my way by directions involving local sites, and now facing a long drive home, I realized I was really hungry and needed some lunch.

Stopping at a roadside diner, I hurried in. Seeing that everyone seemed to take notice of me, I realized that I still had my clerical collar on. Oh, well.

The diner had one of those serving counters that ran the length of the room but curved with "horseshoe bulges" so that more people could be seated at the counter, and a waitress could serve more folks from inside the horseshoe-shaped counter with less walking. I sat down and started to look over the menu. The fellow directly across the horseshoe from me had been there some time already, had ordered, and was waiting for his food to be served. Shortly after I sat down, the waitress came with his meal, asked the routine questions about needing anything else, and left. As I glanced around the room, I saw the customer grab his knife and fork and start cutting and arranging his food. With a big mouthful balanced on his fork, he started moving it toward his mouth.

He happened to look up and saw me there with my black suit and collar. He paused, angrily put the fork down, gave me a dirty look, bowed his head for a table grace, and only then resumed his feast. He managed to continue his scowling at me with intermittent glances the entire course of the meal.

I was able to enjoy my lunch only after he left.

That's the day that I learned that the clerical collar can have unexpected effects.

Mistaken Identity

"Father!...Father!"

I realized the woman was calling out to me.

I was making some hospital calls at University Hospital as part of my Pastoral Care 101 class assignment, wearing the required clerical collar so that hospital staff could easily identify me in order to grant me patient access, and in case my assistance was needed.

Not having encountered this situation before and very unsure of myself, I explained that I wasn't a "Father," a Catholic priest, but rather a Lutheran seminary student. Undaunted, this woman said, "Do you know that psalm— you know—'The Lord is my shepherd?'"

After assuring her that I did know that psalm, I was hit with the big question, "But do you know the *real* one?" She went on, "A hospital chaplain was just in my mother's room and when we asked him to say that psalm he read from his Bible, but it wasn't the *real* psalm. Mother hardly recognized it."

Apparently, the chaplain had read from one of the newer Bible translations that didn't sound at all like the King James translation previous generations had learned to know and love. I thought I could remember the King James Version I had learned as a kid in Sunday School, and so off I went to attempt to recite the 23rd Psalm to an elderly dying Catholic woman surrounded by a roomful of emotional family members.

When I had finished, the woman with whom I had first spoken thanked me with tears in her eyes. "Thank you so much, Father. You don't know how much that meant to her and to all of us."

Though not a father in any sense of the word at that point, I was glad to have helped. (And was made painfully aware of the challenge of updating older translations that are found wanting by ongoing biblical scholarship, yet loved by former generations).

Choir Tour

Seminary was thrilling. After a bit of a shaky start, it was exhilarating to be ushered into a whole new expansive world of broader horizons, deeper understandings, and richer approaches to scripture, faith, and life.

There were exciting events beyond the study and learning, as well. In my first year, the seminary choir was planning a tour to the West Coast. They would fly to Portland, and then travel by bus up the Pacific Coast to Seattle. The tour would continue on into Canada with several concerts in British Columbia before returning to the US to conclude with a concert in Billings, Montana. The trip back to Minneapolis would be by train.

I had never been on an airplane. I had never sung in a choir. Why not combine the two new experiences? Wanting to give the impression of a large and vital institution of the church, the choir director was willing to take anyone. I volunteered and was accepted.

The "uniform" for our all-male choir was a black suit and shirt with the white clerical collar. Rehearsals were great fun and there was a real sense of *esprit de corps* as we prepared for the big tour.

The flight was really a "two-fer." Flying commercial, of course, we flew in two legs—Minneapolis to Seattle and Seattle to Portland. It was great.

After a couple of concerts, the director pulled me aside, thanked me for my enthusiasm, and then asked that on two of the more difficult songs I just move my lips and not actually make any sounds. Apparently, my attempts at music-making were detrimental to the overall effect of the choir. But even this indignity honestly didn't diminish the thrill of being a part of this fun group.

As with most college and seminary choir tours, a congregation would host the event and invite people from other neighboring congregations and the community at large to attend the concert. The sponsoring congregation would put on a meal for the choir before the concert, and afterwards host families would take one or two of the choir members to their homes for the night, returning them to the church after breakfast the next morning. Visiting with the host families was among the highlights of the tour. The questions we students would be asked ranged from "How does that 'collar thing' stay in place?" to "How did you decide to attend seminary?" to even some deep theological questions that reflected a lot of study and deep thinking on their part.

In Tacoma, Washington, the second-to-last stop on the tour, our bus ran into a tremendous snowstorm. There was some question as to whether that night's concert would even happen. If it were canceled, however, what would become of the lodging arrangements? But indeed, the show did go on! When the choir filed into the sanctuary and took its place on the chancel steps, we looked out on a nearly empty church. The few people in attendance were the faithful folks who had signed up to host choir members. Standing out—no, leaping out—from the small gathering were two very attractive blond women in the front row. During the intermission break offstage, there was a lot of speculation among the all-male choir members about who would be housed with these striking women.

At the conclusion of the concert, we all went downstairs to pick up our luggage and come back up to meet our respective hosts. The first hosts to step forward were these two women (mother and daughter, it turned out) and my tour roommate and I were assigned to their home. We smugly walked out of the sanctuary with these beautiful women, and were ushered into the back seat of a brand-new white Cadillac. We couldn't resist gloating as we drove past the rest of the choir members getting into "lesser vehicles" with "ordinary" people as hosts.

Less than a mile from the church the Caddie had a flat tire and my roomie and I had to get out in the raging snowstorm to change the tire in the snow and water and cold and mud, as the rest of the now-smug-themselves choir members and their hosts drove past us in warm comfort.

"The first shall be last...."

Hell's Heaven's Angel

One of my seminary classmates was a motorcyclist. Since the single students' housing was just one block from the seminary, having a car really wasn't necessary. His bike was a BMW—one might call it the "Cadillac" of motorcycles. Smooth and quiet, made in Germany...even to a non-cyclist it was a thing of elegant, refined, quiet beauty.

After we graduated a number of us kept in touch, and I knew that this classmate was called to serve a congregation in suburban Minneapolis. Still single at the time and with a sense of adventure, he continued to see no need for a car.

One day, a couple came into his parish wanting to get married. He invited them to sit down and talk about it.

It turned out they were "bikers." As they worked their way through the series of pre-marriage counseling sessions with my former classmate, they formed a friendship. They admired his sleek BMW bike, and he was somewhat in awe of their raised-handlebar, decked-out Harley "hogs."

Arrangements were made for the wedding. It was to be in a park near the church, with a reception at a nearby biker watering hole.

My former classmate made his way to the park on his BMW and was warmly greeted by a crowd of bikers—ready to witness a wedding and then go celebrate. The trappings were different from a "normal" church wedding, including the groom having a six-pack of beer hanging from his belt. But for the most part, a hushed silence of respect was observed by all once the ceremony began.

When the wedding service was completed and the many motorcycles were being started for the procession to the "reception hall" (local bar), the groom came over to my classmate and said, "I've never driven a BMW before. How about we swap bikes for the ride to the reception?" The switch was made, and the celebratory procession began to wend its way through the suburban streets.

According to my classmate, there were many, many wide-eyed pedestrians who stopped to watch the sight, the highlight of which was either the bearded, leathered biker dude riding the fancy BMW, or the clergyman in his black suit and clerical collar riding the "hog" low-rider motorcycle with the high handlebars and low suspension!

Fast forward many years to when I was retired in the summer of 2010, in which I had the opportunity to serve as a guest pastor for two weeks at the Wittenberg English Ministry in Wittenberg, Germany. This being the Martin Luther "holy site" where Luther started the Protestant Reformation by nailing his famous Ninety-Five Theses to the door of the Castle Church, the tourist traffic is almost overwhelming. Tour buses jockey for parking spots, tour guides lead groups of earnest sightseers, and restaurants and souvenir shops proliferate.

During my orientation, the site manager for the Wittenberg English Ministry was filling me in on my responsibilities. There was to be an English devotional service every afternoon (highlighted, of course, by the lusty singing of Luther's famous hymn, "A Mighty Fortress") and an English-language worship service each Saturday evening, alternating weekly between the Castle Church and the Town Church, both of which are still standing from Luther's day in the 14th century.

Learning that I was originally from Minnesota, my supervisor told me that one of the organists in the Castle Church was a young woman from Minnesota. She had met and married a German fellow while they were both studying organ at an American university. He suggested I should be sure to try to meet her before the service on Saturday where she would be playing and I would be preaching. As my wife and I toured Wittenberg a little and wandered up toward the Castle Church we could hear organ music, so went on in and climbed to the organ loft. I introduced us and told her of my Minnesota connection. "Really!" she exclaimed. "I wonder if you know my dad?" And she told me his name.

Her father was my former classmate of the motorcycle fame.

After I had brought my laughter under control, I explained about the classmate situation and then asked her if she had ever heard the story of the cycle-swapping wedding. She hadn't, but got just as much delight out of hearing it as I got from the telling. She said, "I can hardly wait to talk to my dad!"

Small world.

Wanted: Cross-Cultural Experience

When I was a fifth grader my parents rented out a room in our house to an exchange teacher from Melbourne, Australia. Mr. Clarke was an affable Aussie with a charming way and an engaging wit. He became more than "just a renter," always sharing breakfast with our family and often other meals as well. He was an avid golfer and scoffed when we explained that no one played golf in the winter in Minnesota. "We play year-round in Australia," he proudly declared. "If it snows, we use orange golf balls." After the second or third ten-inch snowfall, he finally conceded that even orange golf balls would not be enough to enable year-round golfing in more than two feet of Minnesota snow.

Ever since that wonderful year of getting to know and appreciate someone from a different culture, it had been my dream to be an exchange student in some faraway place. It had almost happened in my junior year of high school. When Hawaii was becoming a US state, it sponsored a program in which there would be a direct student exchange with every other state. I was chosen to represent Minnesota and would live in the home of a student from Hawaii for that junior year, while that student would come and live with my family in Minneapolis. But just the week before I was to leave, the Hawaiian legislature chose to not appropriate the money to fund the exchange.

Carrying the long-pent-up desire for more intercultural experience along with the deep disappointment from the Hawaiian debacle, during my second year of seminary I learned of a new exchange program being tested by the Lutheran World Federation (LWF). For years German seminary students had been coming to the US for their "*Vikar* year" (internship year). Now the LWF was proposing a similar program in reverse: for an American student to be selected to spend his internship year in Germany.

I applied, writing an essay on why I wanted to participate, citing among other reasons my family's experience with the exchange teacher—and happily, I was the one chosen to go.

What a life-changing experience I had in store.

INTERNSHIP IN GERMANY

The Adventure Begins, Part I— It Seemed a Good Idea at the Time

Towards the end of our second year, my classmates were all receiving their official internship assignments—but frustratingly the seminary was holding off on making a final decision for me, since the unusual possibility of an overseas internship loomed on the horizon. Finally, after what seemed like forever, confirmation of approval by the Lutheran World Federation (LWF) was received, my official assignment was given, and I could start making real plans to serve my internship year in Germany.

One of the first things to be done was to buy a car for use in Germany. Volkswagen had a "European Delivery Plan" (no longer in existence with VW, but still available with several other European auto manufacturers) in which a person in the US could purchase a car long-distance, pick it up at the VW factory in Wolfsburg, Germany, or one of several other pick-up centers, and drive it while in Germany. When ready to head back, you could then drop it off at a specified harbor shipping center, have it shipped to the US, and pick it up at a US harbor to drive home. Perfect!

So, I sold the Volkswagen I owned in Minneapolis, plus the Vespa motor scooter I had driven all through college and the first two years of seminary, purchased a new VW Beetle (for $1,300—it was 1967) to be picked up in Wolfsburg, Germany, and was ready to roll.

The airplane ticket provided by the LWF for getting over to Europe was from New York to Luxembourg on Icelandic Airlines. We had to get ourselves to New York.

To do that my wife and I, accompanied by a seminary librarian who was also traveling to Europe, signed up to drive and deliver a car from Minneapolis to New York. It was a private car belonging to an executive in Minneapolis who was being transferred. We were given a full tank of gas, twenty-five dollars in gas money (1967, remember), and an address in mid-town Manhattan where the vehicle was to be delivered.

The plan was to drive straight through to New York (twenty-four hours) with the driving shared by all three of us in two-hour shifts. But as we left Minneapolis, the librarian fell ill. Lying on the back seat, she was out of the driving rotation. Not much farther into the trip my spouse also fell ill, so I drove almost the entire distance, stopping to nap in the vehicle once or twice.

We arrived in New York City after more than twenty-four hours on the road, almost exactly at noon. Wrong time to drive into New York (if there ever is a right time). For a kid who grew up in the much smaller city of Minneapolis, the traffic was brutal. Plus, the car we were delivering was a 1967 Chrysler New Yorker. Over eighteen feet long and four thousand pounds, it totally dwarfed the VW I was used to driving, which was about five feet shorter and weighed half a ton less.

Dropping the women off at the hotel, I drove to the mid-town address listed on the paperwork, double-parked the car, and ran into the office. They told me I had to deliver the car to the shipping dock. Adamantly refusing, I showed them the paperwork that instructed me to deliver to their address. Since no one in the office had a driver's license (not unusual in NYC), they asked me to park it in an adjacent parking ramp. That done, I found my way back to the hotel.

My wife and I slept the afternoon away, both exhausted.

The Adventure Begins, Part 2— You Couldn't Make This Up

Having conked out for the afternoon in our New York hotel, we rose in time to get a taxi to JFK airport for our midnight flight to Luxembourg, with a planned one-hour layover in Reykjavik, Iceland. The waiting area at our gate in JFK seemed quite crowded. Indeed, it *was* crowded—with everyone who was ticketed for our flight, plus all the passengers from the midnight flight of the night before. There had been an equipment problem on that flight, and they had been rescheduled...to "our" plane.

After an hour of two-planes-worth of people waiting together, passengers on our flight were informed that the airline was going to put us up for the (remainder of) the night at a nearby hotel, and that buses were on their way to take us there. So instead of boarding for our midnight flight, at 1:30 a.m.

we were herded aboard buses and shuttled to the hotel. It was 2:30 a.m. when we finally had our room and were able to crash. (That might be a bad word to use in these circumstances.)

At 4:00 a.m. the room phone rang and we were instructed to get dressed and report to the hotel lobby to await transport back to the airport. At 6:00 a.m. we were all invited from the lobby into the hotel coffee shop for a quick breakfast. Breakfast hurriedly eaten we were ushered back to the lobby to wait for the surely-imminent bus to transport us back to JFK.

At 12:00 noon we were informed that the airline would be buying us lunch, so back into the hotel coffee shop we went. One bite into my sandwich, the airline representative came and hurried us all out and onto the bus (the no-eating rule on the bus was dispensed with, since most of us were clutching half-eaten sandwiches). We got back to the airport, waited another hour or so, and boarded the plane which taxied immediately to the end of the runway— where we sat for over an hour, waiting our turn to depart.

Our DC6 propeller craft was finally airborne at 3:00 p.m.—fifteen hours late.

We arrived in Reykjavik in the middle of the night, and were very glad to get off the plane for the hour layover. The turbulent ride on the plane had been like riding in a cement mixer, plus the air-conditioning on the plane was malfunctioning—it couldn't be turned off! A thorough search of the craft had turned up a total of three blankets, which had been distributed to the old and infirm. Thankfully, the gift shop at the Reykjavik airport was opened and we could huddle together there for a while for some warmth.

Our arrival in Luxembourg was somewhat anticlimactic. The airport terminal looked like a barn. And it wasn't open. We were able to glean from others that there were buses out front to connect to various cities in Europe. We chose the Frankfurt one, climbed aboard, and headed to Germany. The bus was warm! We did more sleeping than sightseeing on the many-hours-long ride to Frankfurt.

The bus deposited us on the sidewalk outside the city's train station. In our planning for this adventure, we had acquired the travel guide, *Europe on $5 a Day*. Disheveled, exhausted, and overwhelmed, we staggered across the street to a not-even-close-to-$5 hotel, got a room, and slept for many, many hours. WONDERFUL!!

An Unexpected Touch of Home

Having arrived in Europe a few weeks before the start of the language course we had signed up for, my wife and I were free to travel during that time and so we made good use of our new German car, visiting several different European countries. It was exciting, and exhausting.

On a swing into Switzerland, we found ourselves in Geneva on a Sunday morning. Our list of English-language churches in Europe showed an international congregation in the city, and we found it in time for worship. The pastor was an American, Pastor Clarence Nelson.

At the start of the service Pastor Nelson asked if there were any visitors. We were among several people who identified themselves as such. Each was asked by Pastor Nelson to introduce themselves—where they were from, etc. When it was our turn, I shared that we were from Minneapolis, Minnesota, and why we were in Europe.

Following that morning's service, we were approached by a woman who told us she was the pastor's wife and that they were both from Minneapolis as well. We chatted some and she invited us to their home for supper that evening. She very graciously phrased the invitation that we would be doing them a "favor" by helping them get caught up on things back home.

We learned that prior to their current assignment in Geneva, they had spent the previous two years serving a congregation in Saudi Arabia on the grounds of a large American oil company. She explained that Christian churches weren't allowed in that country, but in that American enclave where many American families lived (while making lots of money for the Saudis) an exception had been made.

Arriving at their apartment that evening, we were put instantly at ease by Mrs. Nelson's gracious hospitality. She insisted on first names, and explained that she had guessed that after some weeks on the road eating European food (most of which we didn't know the name for), we might enjoy some "real" burgers and corn on the cob. Did we ever! Looking back, I have no idea where she might have found all the items and ingredients we enjoyed that evening, many of which were not readily available in Europe at that time.

Not only was the meal fantastic, but the stories of their adventures in Saudi Arabia and around the world were amazing as well. As we were starting to take our leave, my eyes fell on some mail on a small table. It was addressed to our hostess: Ruth Youngdahl Nelson. And then I realized who she was.

She was the sister of Luther Youngdahl, former governor of Minnesota, and Reuben Youngdahl, former Senior Pastor of Mt. Olivet Lutheran Church in Minneapolis, the largest Lutheran church in the US. Another brother, Oscar, was an attorney and had been the 5th District Congressman from Minnesota from 1939 to 1943. Her brother Carl was head of the music department at Augustana College in Sioux Falls, South Dakota, and Benjamin Youngdahl, another brother, was head of social work at Washington University in St. Louis. Still another brother, Peter, was a lawyer in California.

Yes, she was sister to many well-known brothers, but she was a renowned speaker and author in her own right; titles include *God's Joy in My Heart, A Grandma's Letters to God,* and *You Can Make a Difference.* It was wonderful, years later, to see her in a recording of a lecture she had given at a national gathering. In it, I could see her arm was in a sling—despite her being seventy-eight at the time, she had broken her arm waterskiing. To her dismay, she said, the cast prohibited her from playing in her volleyball league game.

This highly accomplished and (at least in Lutheran circles of the day) famous woman took on the role of hostess to an unknown seminary student and his wife who were experiencing foreign travel for the first time, and gave the tired couple a little touch of home in a strange and foreign land.

Ruth Youngdahl Nelson: Rest in peace, you good and faithful servant of the Lord.

Learning German at *"Das Institut"*

Since I spoke very little German (high school German class was a distant seven or eight years prior), to prepare for my year of internship I signed up for a crash course in the language.

The Goethe Institute is a respected institution in Germany. Well-known for its rapid but thorough language education, it operates in several locations throughout the country. The city of Iserlohn was the location of the branch in which I was enrolled.

Once in Iserlohn, finding the institute was an adventure in itself in that time before Google Maps. Having found it, my wife and I went in and were greeted in German by a very nice lady. I explained that we spoke only English and she, in German, explained that there was only German spoken in the school (at least I think that's what she said). With hand signs and a few German words I could muster, I pointed out our names on the class list. She handed me the address of the lodging that had been arranged and motioned for us to go there, get settled, and be back the next morning at 8:00.

We found the address, which was a small neighborhood store. Upon entering, the proprietors (a woman, her mother, and her daughter) ushered us to our room in the back, in the residential part of the store. Our room was one of two that they rented out to students at the institute. The other was occupied by a Paraguayan fellow who we never really got to know. We went out to get a bite to eat that evening, and returned to the institute for breakfast the next morning.

That was to be pretty much the routine for the next two months. Breakfast at the school. Class all morning. Lunch at the school. Class all afternoon. Dinner on our own at one of the local *Gasthauses* or neighborhood restaurants that would accept the scrip we received as part of our tuition. Fall into bed with head swimming in garbled German/English, only to arise the next morning and do it all over again. Yikes!

The first day of class our teacher walked into the room smiling and held up a pencil. "*Was ist das?*" she asked. She went to each of us and asked the same question. She then went to the center of the room, held up the same pencil and answered her own question, announcing triumphantly, "*Das ist ein Bleistift!*" She then circulated around the room, saying to each of us individually as she held up the pencil, "*Das ist ein Bleistift!*" Going back to the center of the room, she once again asked the class, "*Was ist das?*" and in unison we responded proudly, "*Das ist ein Bleistift!*" And so it went, moving from single vocabulary words to simple sentences until we were (sort of) speaking German.

Vocabulary words and simple sentences led to short little stories to memorize. Little stories led to more complicated stories, each with new words and more complicated sentence structure. For two months this continued. It's surprising how much language one can learn in two months, and how confident one can become.

Graduation from the institute meant going to the site of my internship. That, in turn, meant learning how much more there was to learn.

German vs. *Schwabisch*

The Goethe Institute program we attended upon arrival in Germany was outstanding and provided a very good basic German language education. Upon leaving the Institute we traveled south to Leonberg-Ramtel, a suburb of

Stuttgart, where I would be serving my internship. We didn't realize, however, that the German we learned at the Institute was what is known as High German (or Standard German), but the German spoken day to day there in the Stuttgart region was a dialect called Swabian, or *Schwabisch*.

There are dialects in the US to be sure. And while "y'all," "howdy," and "soda-pop," would be examples of what we might call dialectic words, American dialects seem to be primarily distinguished by pronunciation than by entirely different vocabularies. Southern drawls might be called dialects. The "Bah-ston" inflections of John F. Kennedy's speech were called a dialect.

There may be nothing, however, in the US that directly corresponds to the German dialects. Each area of Germany has its own. Vocabulary, pronunciation, and grammar are so different in Germany's various regions, that people who speak different dialects often cannot understand each other.

A good example: If you live in Berlin, a breakfast roll is called *Schrippe*; in the *Schwabisch* dialect it is *Wickeln*. Hence the usefulness of having a common denominator of High German (which is *Brotchen*, for breakfast rolls). But sometimes even that doesn't help.

One of the first mornings in Leonberg, my pastor-supervisor invited us to breakfast in the parsonage. Seated at the table, I, quite proud of my (supposed) facility in the language, asked if someone would please pass the *Brotchen*. The pastor's five-year-old son went on a tirade because he had no idea what I was asking for (as I had not asked for *Wickeln*). His mother had to translate my High German request into *Schwabisch* for him before he would pass the rolls down the table. Even then he muttered under his breath, and I caught enough to know he was not being complimentary about the ignorant foreigner in their midst who didn't even know how to ask for a breakfast roll (much to the consternation of his mother).

My German Pastor-Supervisor

Internship is a time of experiencing the practical world of church life, and trying to connect it to the academic world of theological study that the pastor-to-be has been immersed in for two years. Having long wished for a cross-cultural experience, I was eager for this new opportunity that opened up for a Lutheran seminary student to serve an internship abroad. I served my year as a *Vikar* (intern) in the *Evangelische Versohnungs Kirche* (Evangelical Reconciliation Church) in Leonberg-Ramtel, Germany.

My pastor-supervisor was Pastor Paul-Gerhardt Seitz. He was a tall, imposing figure in his mid-thirties. A graduate of the prestigious theological department of the University of Tubingen, he was well-versed in the latest theological understandings of biblical literature. Not just any graduate, Pastor Seitz had been the valedictorian of his class. That meant not only had he excelled in the classroom, but he also had had to give his valedictory address three times—in German, English, and Greek.

Despite being incredibly brilliant, he was very personable and approachable. He always had time for me and my questions, and was willing (no, make that eager) to go over my sermons to correct the German, critique the content, and aid in preparations for the delivery.

In this inaugural/experimental program of a Lutheran seminary student serving his internship year in Germany, I was fortunate to have him as my supervisor.

Warm memories of Pastor Seitz and his caring, helpful nature came rushing back to me when, two years after graduating from seminary, I was in my first parish in Pierre, South Dakota, and I got a phone call from him. He had been contracted by the Lutheran World Federation to give a series of lectures on ecumenical relationships at different locations across the US. His first lecture was in Sioux Falls, South Dakota, and so he was wondering if he could bring his wife and two small children along and have them stay with us in Pierre for two weeks while he traveled the country presenting his lectures. "Of course!" was the answer and so the plans were made.

Their whole family flew first to New York. Pastor Seitz remained there for briefings and planning, and his wife and children continued on to Minneapolis. Meeting them there after their long and exhausting international travel, I piled them into my 1968 Chevrolet and drove them the eight additional hours to Pierre. When we arrived they all collapsed into bed and slept much more than the usual eight nighttime hours. Upon return to consciousness the next day, Frau Seitz asked to see a map of the route we had taken, and saw the length of the eight long hours we had driven just from Minneapolis to Pierre compared to the size of the whole country.

Later in their stay, when Pastor Seitz had concluded his lectures and rejoined his family with us in Pierre, he got up one morning, explained that a member of his congregation who worked for IBM had been working in Los

Angeles for a time, and wondered if we could make a run out there to "say hello." Once again the maps came out and I tried to explain that LA was a two- or three-day drive away. *"Mein Gott,"* Herr Seitz said, "This is a GIANT country!"

We passed on the trip to LA.

Frau Hahn

Frau Hahn was a 60-something woman. Always smiling, she was very active in the life of the *Evangelische Versohnungskirche* congregation, plus she was a member of the church council.

She never missed Sunday worship, and remained after the service each week to chat with anyone and everyone around. Always looking to make people feel welcome and involved, shortly after we arrived she invited my spouse and me to dinner at her home.

We arrived at the appointed time with the obligatory bouquet of flowers, were greeted warmly and then ushered into the apartment. She introduced us to her husband, whom I had not yet met. We went to the living room and sat down for a little chat. Frau Hahn then excused herself to tend to the dinner that was smelling so good.

Herr Hahn was not as good a conversationalist as his wife, so the chatter kind of lagged. I took the opportunity to look around the room a little. Everything was very neat and tidy. I looked at the artwork on the wall: nice mountain scenery, apparently some family photos, etc.

Glancing to my immediate left, I noticed a photo on the coffee table. It was not large, so I had to edge a little closer to make it out. It was a picture of a much younger Frau Hahn, dressed in a uniform, standing on a reviewing stand as a formation of soldiers passed in review. She wore a Red Cross armband on one arm, and a swastika emblem on the arm that was outstretched in the Nazi salute.

Somewhat taken aback, I had to ask her about it when she returned to the room. "Oh yes," she explained. "I was an official in the Red Cross and in order to maintain my position I had to join the Nazi Party. As a Red Cross official, part of my duties included reviewing parade units including military units."

Sweet little gray-haired lady. Very active church volunteer. Red Cross official. Nazi parade reviewer.

It took me a while to get over the shock. She must have sensed the disconnect in my mind, because she made an appointment and came in a few days later to talk about it. It was a moment of insight for me into the distorted world of pre-war Germany and how, even after the war, the German participants saw it all as quite normal and had a hard time understanding those of us who didn't.

"It was a different time…," they all would say, with a kind of far-away look in their eyes.

Surprise at My Door

The parsonage of the church I was assigned to was a nice single-family dwelling right next door, where my pastor-supervisor and his family lived. The pastor's study was attached but separate with its own external entrance. The study was very large with its own kitchenette, and a bathroom with a tiny tub—and it had been made over into a cozy one-room apartment for us.

The presence of the American *Vikar* was widely known in the community, as was the housing rearrangement, so no one ever came to the study/apartment door by mistake—with one notable exception.

One day the doorbell rang. This had never happened before. I went to answer it with some trepidation, and upon opening it found a young man dressed in a short-sleeved white shirt with a name badge that said, "Elder _____."

Yup, a Jehovah's Witness.

I thought, "This is too rich to be true," but stood and listened to him struggle through his introductory comments in some of the worst German I had ever heard. (It was even worse than mine.) I listened for a while, and then, interrupting him, I said, "You know, this is going to be a lot easier if we speak English."

His face lit up like a light bulb, and all of a sudden, I had a new best friend. I invited him in and we chatted for a while. True to his mission, he offered to meet with me in the coming week to explain the teachings of the Jehovah's Witnesses, and was a little hurt when I declined. He then asked if we could just meet to talk, but I declined that as well—I was pretty overwhelmed with work.

It *was* nice to be a bright spot in someone's day, fleeting (and unusual) though it might have been.

Herr Jauss

The janitor at the *Evangelische Versohnungs Kirche* in Leonberg-Ramtel during my internship there was Herr Jauss. He was a very friendly fellow who spoke more than passable English. We would chat regularly; it seemed as though he was seeking me out. He usually started speaking German, but fairly quickly would break into English.

One day we sat down to have a more extended visit and I got his story. He had been a POW during World War II. He jokingly claimed to be the "first German captured by Americans in North Africa." He and his fellow prisoners were shipped by boat to New York City and then by train to Texas (hence his rather unusual "German-Texan"-accented English). When they had arrived in New York, the irony of passing the Statue of Liberty as prisoners of war was not lost on them.

With very little understanding of US geography, the POWs had no idea of the length of the journey they were undertaking when they got on the train. They also assumed they would be riding in cattle cars, like how POWs in Germany were transported. They were astonished as they were escorted onto passenger cars with upholstered, cushioned, reclining seats.

When he was a boy, Herr Jauss told me, if he had been naughty his mother would always say, "I'll send you to Baltimore," as a threat of punishment. During one night on the journey to Texas, he awoke as the train slowed to go through a town. Imagine his amazement as the sign on the train station wall proclaimed "Baltimore." His first letter home told of "being sent to Baltimore."

That's not where he stayed, however. After several days the train bearing the POWs arrived in Texas. They were herded into brightly lit, shiny new dorms inside the barbed wire enclosure and were again astounded by the quality and basic comfort of the prison in which they were being held.

Herr Jauss was assigned to kitchen duty. The prisoners, under the supervision of a head cook and GI guards, cooked and served meals to the staff and the other prisoners. He told me that the Germans were again stunned that, even as POWs, they ate the same food as the guards and staff.

Toward the end of the war, the letters from home were becoming more and more dire. There was great suffering in Germany. Rationing was becoming stricter and more intolerable. Herr Jauss told about the day his family reported near-starvation conditions in their town…while the American GI guards coming through the food line where he worked would throw the eggs they were served in the trash if not cooked to their liking. He cried as he related the scene to me.

After the war he was shipped home by the US, and he became a confirmed "*Ami*-lover." He would often speak to me in very hushed tones in his almost comical Texas-German accent, giving me little bits of background information about the congregation, or the German outlook on something, or tips on the German language he thought might be helpful to me.

We were *Kameraden*—that is, "pardners."

Tour Guide

The *Evangelische Versohnungs Kirche* I served in was built after World War II in the "New Settlement" of Leonberg-Ramtel—a community built to house refugees from Eastern Europe who had been displaced by the war and its aftermath.

The building was very modern in style, a striking contrast to the traditional medieval churches that are found throughout most of Germany. According to the pastor, the architect had designed it to look like a tent, to symbolize the "church underway"—that is, always on the move to serve God's world. But as it was built of poured concrete and set into a hillside, the people of the community—both the congregation and the surrounding neighborhood—came to realize that it looked more like the mighty fortress of Martin Luther's hymn than any kind of an easily moveable tent.

Be that as it may, the building's unusual architecture and the concept of the "church of tomorrow" that the pastor and congregational leadership tried to develop and to promote extensively through various publications in both the secular and the church press, made it a destination for many congregational and civic groups from all over Germany. The pastor was regularly called upon to give tours of the building including the sanctuary, classrooms, and the walk-out basement teen gathering place and dance hall.

One day the pastor's wife came to my door in a panic because there was a bus pulling into the church's parking area and a group which had scheduled a tour was disembarking. The pastor had run an errand into Stuttgart and had not yet returned. I had to lead the tour.

I had followed along on a couple of previous tours the pastor had led, so I felt somewhat confident undertaking this task. I started with the classroom area and proceeded to the offices, the lower-level youth center, the central courtyard with its giant chess board, etc.

The last stop was the sanctuary. Starkly modern, several stories high, and with unadorned poured concrete walls, it was shocking in its breaking with traditional German churches. Instead of pews before a traditional altar, there were individual chairs facing a large modern square table. Suspended above it was a large piece of abstract art made of metal rods and bars welded together in a free-form creation approximately thirty feet across, four feet deep and four feet high.

The size and starkness of the sanctuary always caused me and, I noticed, most others, to be hushed and reverent. Maybe overwhelmed might be a better word. The tour group I was leading had that same reaction. After silently perusing the sanctuary individually they gathered in front of the altar/table. One of them asked what was the symbolism in the hanging sculpture. I had never heard an explanation, but had always assumed it was the crown of thorns placed on Jesus' head during the crucifixion, so I told the group, "It's the crown of thorns."

Just then the pastor came into the sanctuary, out of breath and full of apologies for being late for the tour. The group's leader accepted the apology and explained that the *Vikar* had done a fine job of leading the tour. One of the older ladies, a little hard of hearing and not having been present with the rest of the group during my earlier explanation, asked the pastor about the suspended sculpture above the altar/table. He went into a long explanation of the artist's rendering of the dove descending at Jesus' baptism.

I left as quickly and quietly as possible.

A Different Perspective

The town of Leonberg had another *stadtteil*, or subdivision, besides Leonberg-Ramtel where we lived (which was often just called Ramtel). Its name was Leonberg-Eltingen. It was often described to me by the locals as the "original" Leonberg (as evidence, there is a breed of dog that had been developed in the Eltingen area that was called a *"Leonberger Hund"*). While Leonberg-Ramtel where we lived consisted mostly of new buildings (lots of apartments and multiple-family dwellings), older Leonberg-Eltingen looked like the picture postcard of the traditional German village.

One Sunday I was invited to lead worship in the church in Eltingen. The old building with its traditional architecture was well maintained, but creaked a little when people walked on its ancient floorboards. I was shocked when I went into the old building to see that the pulpit was mounted on the wall. The preacher had to climb a staircase into the pulpit, which was on the same level as the balcony that ringed three sides of the sanctuary. This was a traditional German church layout that I had not encountered before. I found it to be a most uncomfortable experience to be speaking to the tops of the heads of the folks on the main floor while looking at the "balcony sitters" straight on.

However, that shock was minor compared to the jolt when, after worship, one of the genial members took me outside to the original cornerstone of the building: It read, "1492."

Obviously, the building had been rebuilt sometime (probably several sometimes) in the intervening years, but that congregation member thought the visiting American should see a cornerstone with the same year as when Christopher Columbus had sailed for America. I found it truly jarring.

No wonder the Germans were amused by Americans' pride over our then-recent US Bicentennial celebration! And they were fairly dumbfounded when I would speak of being proud of one-hundred-year-old church buildings in my part of the country—the Midwest being a more-recently settled-by-Whites part of the US than the East Coast, where the United States had been created two hundred years back.

"Merely" two hundred years, to the Germans.

Gast Arbeiter

The race riots of the summer of 1967 in Newark, Detroit, and other places in the US, were front-page fodder for newspapers across Europe as we arrived to start the internship. Once settled into my internship site in Leonberg and beginning to gain a bit of visibility and acceptance, the questions started to flow, slowly, gently at first, but then at a greater and more forceful stream at me. From "What is happening in America?" to "Why are Black people treated so poorly?" to "What is wrong with White Americans that they can treat a group of people so badly?"

We had now been away from home for six months and were getting what news we could from German television news reports and newspapers—in German, of course. Needless to say, I didn't always understand everything I heard or read. But the Germans could see what was happening in the US. And they were right.

The question in my mind was if they could see what was happening in Germany. Something along the same lines was happening in their own country—and right in our congregation.

Following World War II, with much of Europe ravaged from that horrendous conflagration, the United States had poured out billions of dollars worth of aid for reconstruction via the Marshall Plan. The program was so successful that unemployment was reduced to the point of labor shortages being created. One of the attempted solutions for the shortages was the importation of laborers from other countries, particularly from Turkey.

These immigrant laborers were primarily young men, for the dreadful toll of WWII had created a shortage of young German men. The totally predictable outcome was a burgeoning number of romances and marriages between the so-called *Gast Arbeiter* ("guest workers") and German women. One such romance occurred between a Turkish worker and a young woman from our church. This woman, formerly at the core of the congregation's life, was so harshly ostracized that she left the congregation. Her darling Turkish-German child was not accepted by the community.

My attempt to point out that the situation of this couple and their non-acceptance by the community was similar to the racial situation in the United States was not, shall we say, well received.

A Few Cultural Tidbits

When my October birthday rolled around my wife had arranged with her family to send over a box of cake mix for a birthday cake, as there were no cake mixes available in the German stores. This was 1967 and convenience foods were neither available nor much desired by the German people. The cake was baked. The pastor-supervisor and his family were invited to a makeshift party. There were *ooohs* and *aaahs* about the delicious cake. Lots of questions followed about the recipe and how my wife had assembled all the ingredients, etc. When we talked about the boxed cake mix that had come by mail (we even had to go to the trash to reclaim the box to prove it), the pastor and his spouse were amazed! They couldn't imagine that a cake that good had come from a cardboard box.

We hunted in vain for peanut butter. There was none to be found. Whining to contacts back home resulted in a postal gift from the sky. Concerned that a glass jar might break in transit (1967—no plastic peanut butter jars), a clever classmate painstakingly took a glass jar of the precious brown stuff, removed the contents, and lovingly stuffed it all into a couple of plastic baby bottles for shipment. It arrived safely, but alas, our German friends did not like peanut butter as much as chocolate cake.

On a more serious note: The war in Vietnam at that time was front-page news. Pictures of protests in the US with riots and cities burning were on the TV daily. Some of the people in our congregation who had befriended us thought we should remain in Germany for our own safety rather than returning home just before the Democratic National Convention. They had no concept of the vast distances between the locations of the riots and the home in the Midwest we'd be returning to.

Thanksgiving Turkey

An American holiday, Thanksgiving is of course not observed in Germany. But as homesick Americans, it felt important to my wife and to me that we should have a Thanksgiving dinner, even if the people around us didn't. So we started to assemble the ingredients as best we could. Most of the items, or reasonable substitutes, were readily available with a few exceptions. The biggest problem was the turkey, and we had also not found any celery for the stuffing.

We looked at several *Fleischmarkte* (meat markets) to no avail. Finally, as the day drew nearer, we decided to try a new "supermarket" that everyone was talking about in Stuttgart itself. I drove the fifteen miles to the site and found a smallish grocery store that was being visited by a few shoppers. At that time most Germans preferred to shop traditionally in separate small shops, one each for the various types of foods (butcher shop, bakery, etc.).

I started to wander about the store. The area with the meats was easy to find but I could see no turkey, so I moved on to the vegetable area. The vegetable assemblage was amazing. There were very few canned veggies, almost everything was fresh. I could smell celery but could not see any. Hunt as I might, the celery was not to be found. Finally, a store employee wandered by and I summoned the courage to ask. He looked at me incredulously. I think he thought I was joking. He asked me to step aside, reached for a low shelf right where I'd been standing, and picked up a large oblong whitish thing a little larger than a softball. He handed it to me with a look of condescension mixed with amusement. It was the root of the celery plant, there were no long leafy green shafts around at all. I managed to describe these shafts to him, and his incredulity grew to complete amazement. "Here in Germany, we cut that off and throw it away. You'll find that in the garbage," he explained.

Since I had already displayed my stupidity to this guy, I decided to forge ahead with him. Thanking him for the celery lesson, I tried to ask about turkey. Not knowing the word for turkey, I tried describing one. I'm not sure if it was my attempt at description, or my lack of facility with the language, but he found my efforts hilarious. I tried and tried with no success. Finally, I resorted to bending my arms into simulated wings and walking around going "gobble-gobble."

When he managed to pull himself together from his debilitating laughter, he pointed me to the small freezer across the room. It was almost empty, but down at one end I found the one turkey in the store (maybe even in Stuttgart, or in all of Germany, for all I knew). It was quite small and bore the label: "Jennie-O—Willmar, Minnesota, USA."

I'm from Minnesota. My grandma lived in Willmar.

I went home with a frozen turkey I was almost related to, a big, white, softball-sized chunk of celery root that I felt I knew personally, and a huge helping of thankfulness that I'd probably never again see the people I had so thoroughly amused at the "supermarket!"

Norwegian Hill

Norwegian Hill is a storied spot in Minneapolis. As the highest spot in the City of Lakes it was for many years the site for the annual Soap Box Derby. "The Hill" is approached from the west by a fairly-gently-rising and winding St. Anthony Boulevard, and the boulevard's eastern descent is a straight down one-block-long "hair-raiser"—perfect for the Derby!

Coming home after World War II, my dad bought one of the few houses available: a small, quirky, two-bedroom house that had been added on to at least once. It was on the plateau at the top of Norwegian Hill, four or five doors away from St. Anthony Boulevard. In the Minnesota winters, I learned to walk downhill on ice and snow to go anywhere, and uphill on ice and snow to get home. I learned to ride my bike on ice and snow on steep hills throughout town. In the summer between fourth and fifth grade, our family built and moved into a new home at the bottom of the steep side of Norwegian Hill, still considered by my high school classmates as "The Hill" area. I grew up living with ice, snow, and hills—lots of each.

As I grew older...think Minnesota cold...snow...ice...walk...DRIVE. Driving on ice and snow requires different techniques from driving on dry pavement, but when ice and snow are what you learn to drive on, it becomes almost second nature to deal with these hazards. Driving on ice and snow that has accumulated on hills—steep hills—well, that's a subset of a subset. That's a skill I learned from my first bicycle to my first driver's license.

Stuttgart, Germany, has a much milder climate than that of Minneapolis and is situated on much flatter terrain. The drivers in Leonberg-Ramtel are generally not so familiar with snow *or* steep hills, and certainly not the combination of snow *on* hills, as someone from Norwegian Hill in Northeast Minneapolis would be.

During my year in Leonberg-Ramtel, there was a mild snow event. I had to make a couple of calls that day, and at the end of the day returned home to the parsonage which sat atop a small rise—the highest point in Ramtel. I drove up the "hill" (rise) and parked my car in the usual spot. A short time later there was a knock on the door. It was the neighbor across the street. Somewhat hesitantly he noted that he had seen me drive up the hill. His car was at the bottom of the hill because he had been unable to navigate the icy road and he wondered if I would be willing to walk down the hill with him and drive his car up to his house. I did that and accepted his thanks, and refused the remuneration he offered.

This was followed by two more trips down and up with other neighbors' cars.

Who would have thought that all those snowstorms in Minneapolis would prove to be evangelism tools in Germany, and that Norwegian Hill would be a gift to some stranded Germans?

Car License Snafu

The Volkswagen Beetle that I drove in Germany in 1967-68 was bought in a "buy it and drive it in Europe and then ship it home" program. These programs were quite popular at the time. Not only did you not have to rent a car while in Europe, but the buyer then had a European car at a much lower price once they got it home.

In order for such a car to be exported to the US it must meet US laws, which sometimes required modifications to be made. In the case of my Volkswagen, it had to be equipped with an anti-theft locking mechanism on the steering column, and other things not standard on cars sold in Germany. In fact, that locking device required by US law was illegal in Germany.

These "buy-use-ship" cars were fitted with large, football-shaped license plates to make them easily distinguishable to authorities. The oversized, unusual license plates were valid for one year, and allowed one to drive a car with any such modifications legally.

But since my total stay in Europe was to be about fifteen months, my license plates would expire before I shipped the car back home…

When the one-year expiration of my car's license was approaching, I went on down to the German equivalent of the Department of Motor Vehicles. By this time, I was relatively conversant in German, but my accent clearly identified me as an American. Additionally, it turns out that government legalese is as unfriendly in German as it is in English—as is bureaucratic nonsense.

Since the special one-year license was non-renewable, I was told I would have to get a German license plate. But in order for me to license the car (that had been built with the modifications to meet US requirements) with a German plate for driving while still living a few more months in Germany, I would have to pay to have the steering rebuilt (doing away with the anti-locking modification required by the US) to meet German licensing standards. But then in order for me to ultimately import the car to the US at the end of my internship time, the steering would have to be "RE-rebuilt" to meet the US standards for which it was built in the first place.

I tried patiently to explain the craziness of this conversion/reconversion process to the government official, but he either couldn't or wouldn't understand. I sighed, told him I had left my checkbook in the car, and left the government office—never to return.

It was probably going to be cheaper, if it were ever discovered, to pay the possible future fine than to endure the cost, the inconvenience, and the headaches involved in the conversion/reconversion process.

I did, however, drive very carefully and with both hands firmly on the wheel for the remaining few months of my stay in Europe.

On the Way to School

Bad Cannstatt is one of the oldest *Stadtteile* (city districts) in the city of Stuttgart. As part of my internship, I was assigned to work with a hospital chaplain based out of the *Martin Luther Kirche* in Bad Cannstatt, and so my wife and I moved from the parsonage in Leonberg-Ramtel to the new site. Housing was provided in an apartment building owned by the state church.

One of the other residents of this apartment building was another *Vikar*, who was a German and somewhat older than I. We got to chat with each other occasionally as we passed in the hallway of the apartment building. I always sensed an uncomfortable "air" from him, but couldn't quite put my finger on it.

One day we had a chance for a more extended conversation. He wanted to tell me about his wartime experience with Americans. I was expecting to hear stories of GIs passing out candy bars to the kids, or playing Santa at a party after the war, or something of that nature.

Instead, I heard him recount being sent to the countryside with many other children, to live with relatives in a rural setting to avoid the heavy bombing in Stuttgart. He then went on in a more personal vein...

One day he was walking down a country road all by himself on his way to school. He had just gotten a new pair of trousers, a rare experience for a German child during the war. His brand-new pants still had the crease in the pant legs, and he was really proud of those trousers and that crease.

Suddenly a single fighter plane appeared overhead. According to his account, the pilot spotted him walking on the dirt road all alone and proceeded to make several strafing passes up and down the motorway. He was the only thing moving on that road.

The American pilot was strafing a little kid on the way to school.

He jumped into the ditch hoping to avoid being hit. But still concerned about his new pants, he maintained a "push-up" position in the ditch to try to keep the pants clean and neatly pressed. Tears accompanied his telling of that event.

We maintained a cordial "Good morning, how are you" relationship in the apartment hallway, but I saw him differently thereafter. He had lived something I could hardly imagine.

Pillbox

Towards the end of my internship my parents traveled to Germany, and we had a chance to do some sightseeing with them. One day my dad and I were walking down a street in a town. As we turned a corner, my father suddenly reacted as if hit by a baseball bat. He had turned pale and was visibly shaken. He had to go over to a bench on the street to sit down.

"Dad, what's the matter?"

"What is that purple building over there?" he asked. Down the street was a narrow four- or five-story building, with small, narrow windows. The purple was very bright and garish, and the German lettering on it announced it as a furniture store.

I explained the type of store it was and he said, "Oh, no—that's a 'pillbox.' We saw those all across Germany as we fought to end the war."

My dad had been a member of the US Army in WWII and had served in the field artillery. He went ashore on D-Day Plus 3 and fought his way with the Allied forces all the way into Germany, sustaining a head wound in the Battle for the Hurtgen Forest which earned him several weeks of rehab with a Dutch family, and a Purple Heart.

After he had caught his breath and his composure sitting on the bench, he explained that the German military had constructed those concrete "pillbox" bunkers as defensive measures at many key locations leading into and across Germany. His extreme reaction to seeing one of them, which he recognized immediately despite its being painted a strange color and having been repurposed into a commercial establishment, resulted from a traumatic experience he had had.

At one point in their advance, US Army General Patton's troops had been pinned down by snipers operating from one of these structures. The American troops had the structure surrounded, but the German snipers would not surrender. Dad's unit was ordered to bring their cannon up and aim it directly at the structure. The Germans inside were ordered to surrender or be blown up. They refused, and the order was given to fire. My dad was the one who had to pull the trigger. The concrete structure was blown to pieces, and among the pieces scattered about were body parts of the German defenders.

That memory had haunted my father all those years. He had never shared that with me before (actually, he never talked much about the war at all). I wonder if he had ever shared that with anyone. I wonder what other war horrors he kept bottled up inside.

Bier Stueble

One of the members of our congregation had just finished his basement where he had created what he called his *bier stueble,* or "little beer hall." When he had learned that my parents were coming to visit, he invited our family to his home to "christen" the *stueble.*

This was very kind on the one hand, but also a little awkward… I knew that my mother, as the daughter of a Women's Christian Temperance Union member who had been a staunch pietist from the Lutheran Free Church, was uncomfortable with the consumption of alcohol. Also, I knew our German host was a WWII veteran and had served in the Field Artillery, like my father—but that he of course had served with the Nazis. I was a bit apprehensive about how the evening would go.

The appointed evening arrived and we went to the home of our German host. The German fellow and his wife spoke no English; my mother spoke no German, and my dad spoke only a very little *Plattdeutsch* (a dialect from northern Germany, very different from the *Schwabisch* dialect our hosts spoke), so I became the interpreter/conversation facilitator.

After polite exchanges and explaining where Minnesota was in the US, the genial conversation turned to other things, and I was happy to see that even my mother seemed to be having a pleasant enough time while in the little beer hall.

Finally, inevitably, the conversation turned to WWII. The war had been a horrible experience for both men. It was ironic that both former soldiers had served in the Field Artillery, they agreed. Further conversation brought out that they had also been in all the same battles across France and Germany, including the Battle for the Hurtgen Forest where my father had been badly wounded.

At one point the German fellow pulled up his pants leg and showed his scar from where he was wounded by American shrapnel. My dad then showed his scar from where German shrapnel had pierced his helmet and caused his head wound. They talked and reminisced and laughed, and speculated on whether they might have wounded each other in the conflict.

At the end of the evening our host accompanied us out into the street in front of his home and the two former enemies shook hands, embraced, and returned to their own worlds—richer, perhaps, for putting a face on the former "enemy."

I left definitely richer for having witnessed that historic and touching encounter.

Prague Spring

The end of my internship was approaching. My supervisor had promised a trip to mark its completion. His mother was about to have her eighty-fifth birthday and it was decided that these two celebrations should be combined into one trip, all together. The pastor's mother was given her choice of destination between Vienna or Prague. She chose Prague.

On the day of departure Pastor Seitz and his mother and my wife and I all piled into the pastor's VW Beetle, and off we went for the three-hundred-mile trip. The drive was pleasant. At that point in 1968, the border to the Czech Republic was open, the autobahn was well cared for and we made good time.

Along the way the talk ranged over many topics, and Germany's recent past was part of the conversation. Grandma Seitz made it a point to show us all the good things that Hitler had done. "See that building over there? That's a hospital. Hitler built that." "This autobahn has really improved travel throughout Germany—Hitler built these autobahns, you know." "Don't get me wrong, Hitler did some bad things, but he also did some wonderful things for Germany, you know."

This was a refrain we would often hear from Germans in conversation.

Prague was a beautiful city, but a city still recovering from the ravages of the war. Having been under Soviet Russian control, it hadn't recovered as fast as West Germany. The overall impression was of a city that was at its core very elegant, but in need of a good cleaning and refreshing. We were there during what was called the Prague Spring, when Alexander Dubcek had introduced reforms that "liberalized" communism and relaxed the strict military control exercised under the previous Russian puppet dictator. Several times people, seeing from our clothing and mannerisms that we were

Westerners, approached us offering to exchange money at up to double the official exchange rate so that they would have German marks or, better yet, US dollars to use if they could get across the border to freedom.

After several days of sightseeing, one of our last stops was the Jewish cemetery. Walking through the grounds we noticed the Jewish tradition of placing a small rock on the headstone of a grave someone had visited. Many of the headstones had large piles of these rocks. I marveled at the dates on the headstones going back to the 17th century.

In the center of the cemetery there was a small open chapel. Upon entering you were in a totally bare space—no furnishings at all. Though dimly lit, if you went close to the light gray walls you soon discovered that they were not really gray at all, but white and thoroughly covered with small script. The script listed names in neat, precise lines, with each person's birth date, death date, and the concentration camp in which that person died. The whole interior of the chapel was lined with these remembrances—making the white walls appear gray.

I watched as Grandma Seitz came into the chapel, walked around a little, glancing here and there, and then approached a wall. As she got close enough to the wall to read the inscriptions, it apparently dawned on her what those inscriptions represented, and she blanched. She turned quickly, glanced around the whole chapel including the ceiling one more time, and realizing the enormity of what was represented there, went immediately to the car to wait for the rest of us.

When we got to the car she was softly weeping. We drove in silence for a time until she said, "It makes one ashamed to be a German."

Two weeks after our departure from Prague the Russian tanks rolled in. It was 1968. The Prague Spring was over for the Czechs.

But the powerful impact of that experience has lasted all these years for this American visitor.

It Had Been Wonderful, and Yet...

The internship year of seminary instruction is twenty-five percent of the education timewise, but in terms of actual usefulness it is generally far more than twenty-five percent valuable. That is to say that, while classes for learning Hebrew and Greek help pastors to understand some of the nuances of biblical interpretation, and most certainly contribute to a better understanding of the

Jewish and Christian scriptures; and while familiarity with great theologians and their writings is enriching and helpful to a well-prepared pastor; most of the day-to-day situations that pastors will have to face are not encountered in the classroom. Internship is intended to help connect the theoretical and the practical, providing real-life preparation for real-life ministry.

Internship in a foreign culture, however, where the language, the cultural norms, and the ecclesiastical practices are quite different from "back home," is of less purely practical value than would be an internship in the culture in which one is going to serve.

For example, when I had asked my German internship supervisor for experience in hospital calling, he explained, "Pastors here don't make hospital calls. That's what hospital chaplains are for." When I had asked about pastoral counseling, the response was, "Pastors don't do that here. We have 'Dear Abby' in the newspaper." Weddings were performed by the civil government with an occasional "church blessing" afterward. Funerals were often held in the church, but my limited language skills didn't lend themselves to participation in that kind of sensitive ministry.

Basically, my internship was a wonderful opportunity for personal growth, reading, and experiencing a different culture. It was also an opportunity to try to explain (and in some cases defend) American culture to people only tangentially familiar with the *Ami* (as they referred to Americans) way of life, mainly through their exposure to 1960s TV shows and American movies (they loved Westerns).

At the end of my internship year, I returned home with wonderful, lifelong memories and experiences—but with little practical parish experience to prepare me for my first call. I had preached just six times during the year, while my classmates interning in the US had been required to preach monthly or even more frequently. Most had been required to officiate at a funeral or two. Many had been involved in pastoral counseling of one kind or another. All had had front-row seats for parish administration duties. All were required to prepare and present monthly reports to their church councils and attend the council meetings. In Germany, I had had to attend the council meetings, but my only responsibility had been to open up the building, have the beer and wine ready for the start of the meeting, and put up with the jokes about having to have Coca-Cola on hand "for our *Ami* friend."

When writing my evaluation at the end of the year, which went to the seminary and to the Lutheran World Federation, I was asked to comment on the future of the program. My recommendation was to discontinue it. Though it had been a truly wonderful cultural, personal, and growing experience for me, the lack of practical, hands-on learning made me worry that I was not as prepared specifically for parish ministry in the US as I would have liked to have been.

So, the good people of my first call in Pierre, South Dakota, were more than parishioners—they became "adjunct faculty" in my ongoing education!

RESURRECTION—PIERRE, SOUTH DAKOTA

Getting My First Call

It was spring of our senior year in seminary, the final year of classes after the internship year.

Excitement was high because we were expecting our first calls to congregations as full-fledged pastors. We were nearing the end of the four years of seminary education on top of our four-year college degrees—tired of "preparing," and anxious to get out and try our wings.

The procedure was for the synod president (jurisdictional equivalent of a bishop in the Lutheran polity of the day) to collect our paperwork which included personal histories, seminary records, and our requests for geographical preference and congregational setting (whether to be a solo pastor, associate/assistant pastor, in specialized ministry, etc.). Our names would each then be matched and submitted for consideration to a specific congregation, which would subsequently decide if they wanted to interview us.

Regarding the congregational setting preference, I had requested to be considered for a solo pastor position in a small rural parish. I made that request because my internship in Germany had been so unusual. Though the international experience had been wonderful, because of the language barrier and the different practices between German and American churches, I felt that I could really benefit from the additional formative experience that being "on my own" in a smaller parish would provide.

When the matches came out, I was surprised to learn that my name had instead been submitted to a large city congregation in Minneapolis where I was to be the youth pastor—getting none of the additional and more comprehensive pastoral-learning experience I felt I still needed. But being still within the seminary process, I felt I had to comply and so went to meet with the senior pastor there to discuss the position.

One area in which I needed more experience was preaching. But in the proposed situation, I would preach only four times a year, when the senior pastor was on vacation. Another area of inadequacy from my unusual internship, in my opinion, was parish administration—which was not to be in my portfolio. And counseling?—none of that, either.

I would be responsible for Sunday School, youth ministry (aka a two nights per week "coffee house"), and "other duties as assigned." It seemed like this was not the right setting at all for me, so I called the synod president and asked if I could have my name withdrawn from the Minneapolis congregation and submitted elsewhere. He told me I could either stick with his first suggestion and try to negotiate a job description that I found more attractive, or I could go to a different synod (geographical area) altogether.

"OK," I said, maybe too hastily, "I'll go to another synod."

The next day I went to see my seminary president and explained that I thought I had made a mistake. He laughed and explained that the synod president was the uncle and godfather of the Minneapolis pastor I had apparently offended. He looked over all my paperwork and said he knew of a parish in a neighboring state, hence a different synod, that might be a good match for me.

The president from the neighboring synod called me later that same day, came to visit within a week, arranged for me to go to an interview with the church council—and on July 1st of that year, I started as a solo pastor in my first small parish in South Dakota.

Just the Spark We Needed

One's first parish is a thrill. Mine was in Pierre (pronounced "Peer"), South Dakota—state capital, town of 10,000, middle of the state, out on the prairie. The congregation was just five years old and was listed as having three hundred baptized members.

But after getting to know the place a little, it turned out the membership—men, women, and children all together—was really just eighty-five.

Even though I was "green as grass," it was readily clear to me that the congregation must grow, or die.

There was a brand-new building, small but adequate. The debt was huge for a supposed three-hundred-member congregation (three hundred had been the expected membership at that point, projected at the time of its organization five years prior). It was staggering debt for the actual membership of eighty-five. The answer, of course, was to grow the congregation. To that end I started an intensive program of home calling.

I knew that the congregation's founding pastor had already originally called on every home in Pierre. When I learned that one of our church members worked in the city utilities department and had access to a list of all the new electrical meter hook-ups, I knew where to make my calls: There were roughly ten new residents moving into Pierre per week. (The newly elected governor reflected a change in party affiliation from the previous administration, and so there were new political appointees moving to town to staff the government.)

After several weeks of calling faithfully on all the new arrivals to town, I realized I was not the only pastor using this strategy. I would sometimes pass one of the other clergy leaving a door as I was approaching it, and pass a third on their way to the door as I was leaving. Three months of this routine left me very discouraged and with not one new member of the congregation to show for my efforts.

Then one Sunday morning there was a visitor in church. *A VISITOR!* She was alone, and it was clear she was familiar with the Lutheran liturgy and hymns. Standing at the door to shake hands with the worshipers following the service, I could hardly wait until she came by. When she did, she asked if she could speak to me privately when I was done greeting worshipers.

In our conversation I learned she was indeed new in town. Her husband had been transferred to Pierre by his company, she was an elementary school teacher, they had a school-aged son, they were life-long Lutherans, and they had moved into one of the rental units right across the street from the church (so no new electric meter hook-up, and so I hadn't known to call on them). Mary informed me that they were members of a different branch of the Lutheran church, but that we used the same hymnal and she had discerned no difference in the worship service.

I explained the historical reason for different Lutheran denominations to her satisfaction, and she was inclined to join our congregation, but she explained they had already had their letter of transfer sent to the large Lutheran church right across the street from the state capitol. Assuring her I could talk to the pastor there about her joining our congregation instead, she presented me with one condition: she had to be able to start a children's choir. I agreed, no arm-twisting required.

The next Sunday, Mary was back with us with her husband and son. The

Sunday after that it was Mary, husband, son, and a neighbor couple—and this routine of expansion continued weekly.

Just before Christmas that year we received a group of new members that increased the size of the congregation by nearly fifty percent!—all due to Mary.

The next spring, at our Synodical Assembly (covering North Dakota, South Dakota, and Northwestern Minnesota) we were recognized as the fastest-growing congregation in the entire synod.

I started getting calls to see if I wanted to move to another parish, even though I hadn't been there quite a year yet.

The growth wasn't due to me.

One of My Best Teachers Never Attended Seminary

"So, Pastor, what are we going to do for stewardship this year?"

It was September of 1969. I had started there at my first parish in July. The summer had been a blur of new people, new community, new house, new state, new role, new responsibilities, new baby close to arrival. Overwhelming!

Stewardship. I knew the term. We had talked a little about it in seminary. Wise management of one's own resources and the church's resources as well. Money.

"What are we going to do for stewardship this year?" The question hit like a punch in the gut. I hadn't given it one thought.

The questioner was Milt Hanson. He was Director of Child Welfare for the State of South Dakota, an active lay member of the congregation, father of three teens and, I was to learn, one of the finest theologians you can imagine.

My stammering search for an answer obviously confirming what he had already suspected, Milt said, "I'd be happy to head up this year's stewardship campaign, if you want me to. There's only one condition. It has to be an every-member-visit campaign." It was not a hard decision to agree to that condition. I had a vague idea of what that meant, but I would have agreed to almost anything at that point, since I hadn't a clue of any kind of an alternative.

Milt set about organizing the campaign. He enlisted several congregation members who would contact, make appointments, and visit other members in their homes, going through a booklet Milt would develop. The booklet would highlight 1) the various ministries and programs the congregation and the church at large offered, 2) the present budget to accomplish these activities, and 3) the needs that were going unmet in the present budget, and possible improvements and/or additions to the current programs if giving to the congregation would improve.

Over the next month, Milt would drop in from time to time to keep me up to speed on the progress: booklet was done and looked great, home visitors were all lined up, dates were determined. Then it was time for launch. We commissioned the volunteer visitors on a Sunday morning during worship. After church that morning, Milt informed me that the first call is always made on the pastor. Would we be home that afternoon? With a brand-new little daughter, my answer was obviously "yes."

Milt arrived with no great fanfare. After the appropriate amount of "ooh-ing and aah-ing" over the baby, Milt sat down with us and ran through the booklet. He then produced the pledge card and said, "I took the liberty of calculating what a tithe (ten percent) would be on your salary." He matter-of-factly stated my base salary of $5,460 per year, added in the value of our parsonage housing, car allowance, insurance, and retirement, totaled it up and said, "Ten percent of that amounts to $17.86 per week."

We had been giving $5 per week, and thinking we were doing quite well at that. (Before comparing to what you might currently think is an appropriate amount, do remember that it was 1969.) The thought of budgeting more than triple that amount was stunning. I'm sure that the silence that followed told Milt what was going through our minds. He said, "Well, you don't have to decide this right now. I'll leave the card and pick it up later. How about tomorrow?"

Wow, this time the gut punch was personal. My wife and I talked earnestly that evening. We calculated and recalculated. We prayed and, yes, we cried. But we decided to give it a try.

Milt stopped by the next morning on his way in to work. He tucked our pledge card in his pocket without looking at the amount, visited briefly, thanked us, and was on his way.

The stewardship campaign that fall was great. I don't recall the exact numbers, but we were not only able to keep that tiny congregation afloat, we even increased some of the programming we were doing.

But then it was a year later, September of 1970. Still feeling harried with all the responsibilities of a bustling little congregation, I was in the office one afternoon when Milt Hanson stopped in. "What are we going to do for stewardship this year, Pastor?" he asked. Aarggh. The thought hadn't crossed my mind. Once again Milt offered to head up a campaign, and it had to be another every-member-visit. Once again his preparation was thorough, the visitors were enlisted and trained, and the pastor's family was to be the first family visited.

This time I was ready. In fact, I was excited for his visit. When Milt arrived for the visit, I hardly let him get settled in. "We did it Milt!" I exclaimed. "We did the ten percent and no one starved, no bills went unpaid. It was a real joy to be able to support the great work that we as a congregation and the synod and national church are doing!"

"Wonderful!" Milt exclaimed. "Now...you got a raise, didn't you?"

I thank God every day for Milt Hanson, his commitment, his vision, and his wisdom. He's been gone for some time now, but his legacy and vision live on in countless people who have heard his story from me, and in so many others whose lives he has touched in so very many ways.

Real-World Lessons Continue

I was twenty-five years old and overwhelmed. First call. First time being called "Pastor." First time living as a married adult in a single-family dwelling. First child arriving. First everything!

And I was beginning to realize that many learning experiences after seminary were challenging—some were even pretty unpleasant.

The folks at my first church were wonderful—warm, welcoming, encouraging. That is to say, most of the folks were. There was a fellow— early sixties, a doctor, short and bristly, dapper dresser, poorly-dyed thinning hair—who, as a member of the church council and call committee, had told me during my interview that he didn't think the congregation really needed a pastor. He and his thirty-five-year-old wife had been leading Sunday School during the yearlong vacancy and it had been going just fine, thank you.

This fellow was active in the community, especially the local Masonic Lodge. As a member of the executive committee of the lodge he had hit upon a plan he said would benefit both the lodge and our congregation. The Masonic executive committee had a monthly breakfast meeting at a local restaurant. Wouldn't it be a wonderful idea for that meeting to get moved from the restaurant to our church! They had been paying three dollars each (1969 dollars) for breakfast and would be happy to continue that payment. Our ladies' group, who would serve, could certainly use that money, he declared.

When I reminded him of what he knew, that there was no "ladies' group" in our congregation, he suggested that the term was just a technicality—I could enlist several "gals" to come in and make breakfast for his team. I explained to him that we were a congregation of young families and that mornings for most of the women in the congregation were a madhouse of getting everything organized, lunches made, kids off to school, and husbands and (more often than not) themselves off to work. I also explained that there was, in addition, a real conflict being played out in our denomination over the relationship of the church to the Masonic Lodge.

The doctor erupted. "We'll see about this at the next church council meeting," he sputtered.

At church council meetings he was often outspoken with off-the-wall ideas, but also often not listened to (which may have contributed to a sense of aggrievement that powered his combative attitude). Sure enough, at the next council meeting he brought up his suggested project. I spoke against it for the reasons I'd stated to him. Once again, an explosion erupted from him accompanied by his storming out of the meeting. I could see from the window that he went and sat in his car and did not drive away.

When the meeting adjourned and everyone else had left, he stomped back into the building and began to upbraid me for all my many shortcomings. He got so angry that he backed me up against the wall, got up on his tiptoes and screamed into my neck, "You're not a pastor, you're a dogmatic goon!!!"

Where I grew up, the proper response to such an attack was physical. But I knew that was not going to be appropriate now, as a pastor, so I managed to restrain myself.

He then informed me that he was leaving the congregation.

He had previously committed to purchasing two tables for the fellowship hall and said he would put a check in the church mailbox to pay for those. The remainder of his pledge, however, would be canceled and he would let me know where I could transfer his church membership.

What you need to know is that he was one of just three tithers in the congregation, and his pledge contributed about *one-quarter to one-fifth of the total church budget.*

After a sleepless night, deeply hurt, scared to death at the prospect of the congregation losing so much of its budget support, and now REALLY overwhelmed, I went to see Pastor Ed, the other Lutheran pastor in town who was my unofficial mentor. He said, "Oh, *that* guy. I wonder where he'll go next. He's been a member of every mainline congregation in town, including this one, and for one reason or another has left in a huff from each one. Don't get too upset about it. It was bound to happen."

One of the leading members of the congregation heard about this from my mentor and came to see me. "Don't worry about it. He has alienated almost everyone in the congregation. You'll get lots of support in this situation," he said.

I learned later that the combative doctor joined the Seventh Day Adventist church. Our giving as a congregation went up. Peace and tranquility returned.

So, what did I learn? Ugliness happens, even in churches. It can be faced, and in ways I hadn't thought of before. And most importantly, we don't need to be fear-based, we can trust in God.

But I was still feeling overwhelmed.

First Wedding

It was the first wedding I had ever officiated. It was beautiful, and traditional. In the early 1970s, not many people had the "audacity" to tamper with wedding traditions, and it seemed that everyone knew how it was "supposed to go." Several assorted girlfriends, aunts, and some obscure other relatives of the bride were all at the rehearsal to make sure it was done right.

The day of the wedding progressed, everyone was properly attired, and finally the moment was at hand. I stood at the front, facing the congregation. The groom and groomsmen marched toward me down the side aisle of the sanctuary and formed a line to my left at the base of the steps to the altar, facing the rear of the church. The bridesmaids, holding bouquets, came individually down the center aisle to musical accompaniment and lined up to my right, also facing the rear of the sanctuary. Next came the ring bearer, about seven or eight years old, and the flower girl, probably four or five. They positioned themselves to the outside of the best man and maid of honor, respectively. Perfection!

As the bride was escorted down the aisle by her teary-eyed father, the congregation rose and smiled/cried appropriately. Dad shook the hand of the groom, placed the hand of his daughter into the crook of the groom's arm, and retreated to his wife's side while the attendants and the bridal couple turned to face me.

After beginning with the traditional words of the Trinitarian formula, "In the name of the Father and of the Son and of the Holy Ghost," I invited the congregation to be seated. In the silence after everyone had sat down came the small, but nevertheless loud and clear, voice of the ring bearer, "Holy Ghost? What's a Holy Ghost?"

Being pretty sure this was not the time or place for a lecture in theology, I just went on with the wedding as planned, resolving to avoid using the words "Holy Ghost" again—the terminology "Holy Spirit" was in those days beginning to be used more; I would say that instead.

Things went extremely well. The soloist was lovely. The friends who read the scripture passages had practiced as I had encouraged. The attendants all unobtrusively wiggled their toes and flexed their knees to keep the blood circulating as per my instructions. Even my three-and-a-half-minute homily proceeded without a hitch.

The couple managed to get through their vows with a minimum of tears. After the vows, I asked them to kneel as I pronounced them husband and wife "in the name of the Father and of the Son and" (totally forgetting my earlier resolve) "of the Holy Ghost." At that point the ring bearer, who was a cousin of the bride, walked over to her, put his nose right in her face (she was still kneeling), and said in a very loud voice, "Norma, what the hell *is* a Holy *Ghost*?"

The horrified silence lasted for a long moment—and then laughter rang out through the church. I took the boy's arm and scooted him back to his place beside the best man. It was hard to tell if the bride's tears during the bridal kiss were tears of joy, of humiliation, of anger, or of hilarity.

I stopped using the term "Holy Ghost" that day. It was "Holy Spirit" from then on.

Legislative Stooge

Pierre is the capital of South Dakota. Its population was about 10,000 in 1970 when I was serving there. It sits on the bank of the Missouri River and is connected by a bridge to Fort Pierre, a much smaller community on the other side. Interestingly, the river in that area is the time zone dividing line—Pierre is on the east side of the river in Central Time; west of the river, Fort Pierre is in Mountain Time.

Pierre was chosen as South Dakota's capital because it is centrally located in the state. Since its two large population areas are in the far western (Rapid City/Black Hills) and the far eastern (Sioux Falls) parts of the state, and the distance between these population centers is so great (350 miles), it seemed a logical choice for the capital to be in between. Hence, Pierre.

The distances involved made it impossible for legislators to commute daily, so that meant that when the legislature was in session, the state lawmakers resided in town and the population of Pierre increased dramatically. During legislative sessions, the clergy of Pierre were asked to support the work of the legislature by serving as chaplains, plugged into a schedule to serve on an occasional basis. The responsibility of that volunteer position consisted largely of opening the day's session with prayer.

During the opening proceedings, the chaplain was seated on the dais with the presiding officer. Once the opening prayer was completed and the presiding officer called the legislators to order, the chaplain was expected to remain on the rostrum for a "respectable" period of time. Once things were underway, the chaplain was allowed to quietly get up and leave.

One morning when I was serving as chaplain, after the opening there began a spirited debate on the floor about protected status for the prairie sage grouse. This seemed like an opportune time for me to slip out. Suddenly one of the more bombastic legislators wanted me, in the middle of his speech advocating protection of the birds, to confirm that indeed there were prairie sage grouse in the Bible and that Noah had welcomed them onto his famous ark. He did this by making that as a statement of fact and then pointing to me (at that very moment trying to "get outta there" unobtrusively) and bellowing: "Ain't that right, Chaplain?" I froze in place.

Thankfully I had no access to a mic, and all he needed from me was my prop value. He went on to his next flourish, and I managed to complete my getaway.

Being used as a prop by some wild-eyed legislator on the floor of the South Dakota legislature…yikes! They hadn't covered that one in seminary.

Painful Mistake

I was walking on air over the birth of my first child.

I'm so old that in my day, in the hospital I had to wait in the "Fathers' Waiting Room," could only view the baby through the window in the hospital nursery, and was not even allowed to be in my wife's room when the baby was present. After a full seven days(!), mother and child were released from the hospital and we went home, and I was able to hold my precious daughter, Karen, for the first time.

Those are wonderful days. Those are humbling days. Those are "floating on air" days. The sleepless nights that follow, the dirty diapers, the crying fits that can't be figured out... None of that takes away the thrill of that new baby.

There was a woman named Jenny who had been visiting our congregation for a while. She was pregnant. I was still in the rarified air of new parenthood, and we would talk each Sunday about her progress and about the exciting things that were happening at my house: my baby actually grasping my finger, laughing out loud, etc.

One day while making a hospital visit to a different congregation member, I noticed Jenny's name in the Clergy Patient Registry notebook which the hospital provided visiting clergy. She was on the maternity ward, but there was no room number listed. I hurried excitedly up to that area, asked for her room number at the nurses' desk, and rushing into the designated room I blurted out, "Oh, Jenny! Boy or girl?!"

She was lying on her side, her back to the door. The room was dark. As she turned to face me, I saw she had been crying. "The baby was stillborn," she quietly told me, and started to cry again.

Shocked, and whiplashed from my terribly inappropriate excitement, I waited long moments and then asked, "Could we share a prayer?"

"No," came the muffled answer as she turned back toward the wall.

I waited silently for what seemed like a long time, then left.

When I went back the next day, she had been discharged.

I never saw her again.

I'll never forget her—or that horrible, rash mistake of mine. I've prayed that she was able to eventually find peace, and hopefully even joy.

Wedding from Nebraska

"Watch out for late-night calls from the bars."

That was a piece of advice I got from several other pastors of all denominations when I began serving at my first parish. It just so happened that Pierre, as the state capital, was the only place in South Dakota where a couple could get a marriage license and the required blood test in the same day. An all-too-frequent occurrence, according to my more experienced fellow pastors, was for a couple to come to town early in the day, start to celebrate, get their blood test, celebrate a little more, pick up the test results, celebrate, apply for the license, celebrate, celebrate, pick up the license, really, really celebrate, and at 10:30 or 11 p.m. call a local pastor from the bar they were at and want to get married right then.

There were variations of the above scenario, but all involved a one-day, "never see 'em again" kind of marriage mill. My informal mentor, Pastor Ed, had advised me that the way to sidestep this kind of occurrence was to have a policy firmly in place requiring three counseling sessions, each one week apart, prior to any wedding. I took his advice.

One morning I got a call from the church secretary of a neighboring parish, where I was on call for the pastor there who was on vacation. It so happened that it was his policy, I was told, to go ahead and officiate at such same-day weddings—and a couple from Nebraska was there wanting to be married that day. Would I come on over and perform the wedding, please? I went over to the church to meet with the couple, planning to hold the line on my own policy.

This couple was delightful. They were in their early thirties (older than I was), both well-established in their careers, obviously in love, and wanting to "tie that knot." I explained my policy and they suggested a compromise. "How about if we do the counseling sessions in one day? Three sessions—late morning, early afternoon, and late afternoon, with an evening wedding?" I gave in and agreed to the plan.

We met for three thoroughly enjoyable sessions. They had been dating for several years, were very mature, deeply in love, and were an absolute joy to be with. I had to scuttle about to find an organist, someone to sing and someone to be a witness. (The first two items were requests that they made; the third, of course, was a legal requirement.) That evening we had a beautiful wedding. The witness even provided some tears. No one had thought to get some rice to throw, but other than that it was a very touching experience. So much for hard and fast rules.

Ten years later I got a thank you letter on this couple's anniversary. They were the proud parents of a son and a daughter. The wife was the Sunday School Superintendent in their large church in Omaha. The husband had just completed his term as church council president.

My education continued.

A Different Approach

Because our congregation had received recognition at our annual regional conference for being the fastest-growing congregation in our territory, I started getting phone calls from churches asking if I was ready to move—even though I'd not even been in Pierre for a full year yet—presumably to perform "church growth miracles" in *their* settings. One such call was from a large church in a neighboring state which televised its services throughout a five-state area. This church had several pastors on staff but wanted to interview me in light of the rapid growth of my church in Pierre (which had nothing to do with me, but rather was the result of the amazing outreach of one very special woman—please read her story in "Just the Spark We Needed").

I knew of the congregation and the senior pastor by reputation only and was really not enthused by the prospect of relocating to that community or of working with that pastor. I sought the advice of my bishop, who said, "I can't tell you that you have to move there, but I *can* tell you that you have to go and interview there." So, I went.

The church was a rambling one-story structure with a very impressive modern-looking sanctuary at its center. Entering through the door labeled "Office," I was greeted by a larger-than-life picture of the senior pastor welcoming me to the place. (Looking back, I think this could be considered an early expression of the personality-driven "TV Preacher" genre, albeit in a typically understated Lutheran way.)

Soon joined by the chair of the Call Committee, I was ushered into a Sunday School classroom and seated on a plastic chair at a table. So much for my vision of an impressive conference room with comfortable reclining high-backed chairs surrounding a spacious table.

The five men in the room explained that they were the Call Committee, but that they couldn't start without the senior pastor being there. They assured me that he had telephoned and was on his way but would be a little late. We chatted and chatted. When I had just about given up hope, in rushed the senior pastor with his retinue—he was accompanied by both his driver and his personal secretary.

Quickly calling the meeting to order, he explained the situation: There were several other pastors on the staff; each had his own portfolio; my portfolio would be evangelism. They hadn't been growing much for the last several years, and since my current congregation had received the award for fast growth, he wanted me to move there and repeat "the miracle." To encourage said miracle, the pastor informed me that I would be paid X number of dollars "per head" for each new member I "brought in."

It wasn't hard to stand up, thank everyone for considering me for the position they were creating, and tell them exactly what I thought about "paying per head" and their whole concept of evangelism. When I had finished that, I went on to express other unasked-for opinions about that congregation, that pastor, and the position they were proposing.

Turning on my heel, I exited the room filled with righteous anger and self-satisfaction.

I called the bishop the next day. My anger had subsided, and I felt more than a little foolish about the whole episode. When he came on the line, I apologized profusely and began to tell the story. He cut me off and, laughing loudly, said, "I've already gotten a report on your interview from the pastor. I've been laughing ever since we hung up. Good for you! I've been hoping for a long time that someone would put that guy in his place. Thank you for that!"

Joyful Generosity

Mrs. Anderson was an older woman, incredibly kind, and very hard of hearing. She was officially a member of another congregation in town, but never attended services because of her hearing loss. I had met her when her pastor moved away and asked me to continue his practice of bringing Holy Communion to her and her husband who was homebound and dying of cancer.

After several Communion visits to her small immaculate white home surrounded by a white picket fence, I received a phone call from her, announcing (loudly) that "he's gone." She asked if I could come down to the funeral home to help plan the service. This being my second funeral ever, I was more than a little nervous driving to the meeting. Mrs. Anderson met me at the door of the funeral home and presented me with a check to "do with as you please." A little embarrassed, I thanked her and put it in my pocket without looking at it. The service planning was easy. "You just do it right," was her directive, and the meeting was concluded.

On the way home from the mortuary, stopped at a red light, I took the check from my pocket to take a look at it. It was for $250, and the "Pay to the order of" line was left blank. Sitting there, I recalled that Mrs. Anderson had told me I could complete it with either my name or the church's name. I had told her, to her apparent dismay at the time, that I would give the money to the church. But now, seeing the amount of the check, I was painfully tempted to follow her suggestion that it should go to me personally—$250 in 1970 dollars translates to more than $1,700 today! I solved this moral dilemma by hurriedly writing "Resurrection Lutheran Church" on the designee line then and there in the car.

The funeral service went well, but on a subsequent visit to Mrs. Anderson I was scolded. "I saw that you made my check out to the church," she said. "I really wanted that to go to you. I do want to support the church too, so I want you to come to visit me on January 15, April 15, July 15, and October 15." She explained that those were the dates she got her dividend checks from her investment account. Although she had worked as a cook in a small restaurant on the main street of Pierre her whole life and had been paid very little, she and her husband had saved and invested regularly and she now had this source of investment income. I came to learn that her generous quarterly gifts, even though she was not even a member of our congregation and never attended services with us due to her hearing loss, made her one of the largest givers to our church.

However, she also wanted to give something to me, personally, to say "thank you," she said. I assured her this was not necessary. But one day as my family was taking our turn cleaning the church building, she drove into the parking lot, again scolded me for not taking her check for myself, and presented our infant daughter, still in her car seat, a small gift-wrapped box containing a Black Hills Gold ring.

Another time, as I was leaving her home after one of my quarterly visits, I mentioned how beautiful the flowers were beside her house. She went and got a shovel, dug up the plant, and sent me home with an addition for our yard. While chatting on another visit I said my sister and her husband were coming to visit. Mrs. Anderson went to her freezer and gave me several packages of steaks from the side of beef she had there. I found it a little embarrassing, but also deeply moving—and greatly appreciated.

This generosity continued over the years, and on the last visit I made before moving from the parish, Mrs. Anderson announced that she had a going-away gift for me. The hand-knitted (by her) afghan she handed me was beautiful. Beautiful, if somewhat unique: it was about four feet wide… *and eight feet long.* "I made it for my niece who is going off to college, but it kind of got out of hand," she said. "I was embarrassed to give it to her, and thought maybe you could use it." Turns out it was perfect—later after we'd had our second child, the two little kids could lay at each end of the couch and snuggle under it with plenty of comforter to spare.

Thank you, Mrs. Anderson, not just for the afghan, but for helping me to see firsthand what joyful generosity looks like. She reminded me of Milt Hanson from our congregation—I wish they could have known each other.

May she rest in peace.

Didn't See That Coming

They were brothers, Ed and Tom. They bore a striking family resemblance. Tall, gaunt, and gray, with chiseled features, they looked to be right out of a Marlboro commercial. Born in a sod house way out on the South Dakota prairie, they were both well past retirement age when I met them.

I'd see Tom and his wife in church. He had his own business, working as a handyman. It was not unusual to see him driving his rusted old pickup around town. His presence was often announced by the sound of the empty beer bottles rolling around and clanging in the pickup bed.

I hadn't known about Ed until I had been in the parish for almost a year. He was living in a nursing home, and Tom's wife asked one day if I would be willing to stop by and pay a call on Ed—maybe bring him Communion. He had lived a difficult life. He had been a hired hand on many if not most of the ranches in the area. He had been a rodeo competitor, riding both broncs and bulls. I never knew the whole situation, but from little snippets here and there I gathered that Tom and his wife were financially supporting Ed's residency at the home, since he had no retirement income.

I located the nursing home and found Ed with no trouble. Despite all the apparent attempts by the staff and by Tom's wife to brighten up his room, it was depressing. He was a man of few words, as they say. We talked for a while, me doing most of the talking—and by talking, I mean me asking questions and Ed responding with mostly one-word (or grunt) answers. Before leaving, I asked if he would like to have Communion. The quick answer was "No."

Going back for a second visit was hard. Memory of the first visit loomed in my mind as I entered the facility and was met by "that nursing home smell." I found Ed sitting in the beat-up recliner in his room. I introduced myself again, since he gave no sign of recognition or even acknowledgement of my presence. But, "Yes," he said, "I remember." We started repeating the script from the previous visit, complete with the same one-word answers.

On the third visit, there was something new. There was a card table in his already-cramped room—a card table with a box of dominoes on it. After a little tortured conversation like the previous two times, I remarked on the table and dominoes. "Do you play dominoes?" I asked. "Yup." "You have time for a game right now?" I asked, immediately wishing I had phrased that differently. Ed didn't seem to notice or mind the irony of the question.

We opened the box, set up the game, and started to play. I was amazed. I hadn't played dominoes since I was a kid….Ed was a shark! A total dominoes shark! He pondered each move with intensity like I had only seen before among my seminary classmates as we strove to recall the declensions of Hebrew verbs for exams. He didn't just beat me, he humiliated me. At the end of the visit, I congratulated him on his crushing victory.

My next visit was a replay with one exception. Once again the dominoes were on the table. Once again I was humiliated. This time, however, when I asked if he would like Communion he said yes. I set up the elements, went through the brief liturgy, and served him Holy Communion.

This pattern continued pretty regularly for the rest of the time I served in that parish. I did actually manage to win the dominoes game a time or two, but mostly was drubbed soundly.

At the farewell party when I was leaving that parish, Tom's wife pulled me aside. She said, "Ed couldn't come today, but he wanted me to thank you for your visits and tell you that you are the best friend he ever had."

I had to step into the next room and wipe my eyes.

National Guard Chaplain

About halfway through my time in Pierre, my mentor and good friend, Pastor Ed, left the large Lutheran church across the street from the state capitol building. He asked if I would help his associate who remained in that parish to cover some of the responsibilities he had accumulated over his tenure in that large, prestigious, and highly visible congregation. One of those responsibilities was conducting a monthly worship service for the "weekend warriors" of the National Guard unit based in Pierre. "Of course!" I replied immediately, without even asking for any of the details. "Great!" he replied,

"The service is at the National Guard Armory, first Sunday of every month, 6 a.m."

There was no extra preparation involved—I had to write a sermon for my own congregation anyway—but the 6 a.m. part was a bit of a surprise. It was strange to drive the streets of Pierre with almost no traffic, to the National Guard Armory which was on the edge of town. Arriving at 5:45 I found that no one seemed to be aware of a religious service taking place there. I finally found a guy who claimed he was the "Chaplain's Assistant" and who ushered me to an isolated hallway where he told me they usually met.

He and I set up a few folding chairs in a couple of rows and he scurried off to round up the worshipers. A scragglier gaggle of "churchgoers" is impossible to imagine. Almost all hanging onto a cup of "java" (the apparent *nom du jour* among them for coffee) and with eyes smarting from the early hour, they scattered themselves around in the chairs we had assembled. Singing (acapella, of course) was frankly pitiful, bleary eyes fighting to stay open during the service, the worship time seemed like an eternity for them…longer for me.

The first Sunday of the following month seemed to arrive in an instant. At least, knowing what to expect, I had shortened things quite a bit, but it was still a very unfulfilling worship experience. After five or six of these ordeals, a new pastor arrived at the downtown church and I was finally relieved (in every sense of the word) of duty.

When my final "amen" was said there, however, the agony was not yet over. On the way from the Armory back to my church after that last Sunday's service, I picked up a tail. The officer followed me the last several blocks and right into the church parking lot. He parked right behind me and came up to the driver's side window.

I managed to quickly re-insert the white tab into my clergy collar that I had removed for the drive, so when I opened the window and he stepped up beside me, I had my "uniform" in place. His eyes grew large when he saw me "clergified." "Oh, Father, I'm so sorry," he stammered. "You were only about five over the speed limit…I guess I can let you go this time. I'm… I'm really sorry. Please forgive me…I mean… Drive safely…" And with that, he slunk back to his car and was on his way.

Remember how clergy collars can have unexpected effects?—sometimes welcome!

Thus endeth my stint as a National Guard "Chaplain."

Culture Shock on the Prairie

When Pastor Ed resigned to go take another call, another one of the "extra" community duties of his that I had agreed to take on until his replacement arrived was conducting a worship service one Sunday afternoon a month at Grace Lutheran in Hayes. Hayes was a wide spot in the road about thirty-five miles west of Pierre, and the congregation was so small that they couldn't afford their own pastor.

The first Sunday I was to conduct worship there, I loaded my robe, hymnal, and sermon notes into the car and headed west. The church is right beside the highway and has a small gravel parking lot beside it. I pulled into the lot, got out of the car, opened the back door to take out my robe which was on a hanger, and started to go into the church. Suddenly a very large rancher, dressed in a western-style suit, appeared next to me. "What the hell are you going to do with that thing, son?" he asked in a deep western drawl. I was able to quickly discern the correct answer, which was, "Uh, I guess I'm going to put it right back in the car."

Having figured out the level of informality that was expected, I was not surprised when my new friend stood up and introduced me to the congregation (all six of them) when it was time to start. I went to the center of the chancel to begin the service, but was surprised to see my mentor stand up again before I could speak, straighten his western duds, and proceed down the center aisle directly towards me. He climbed the three steps up to the level on which I was standing, walked around me to the altar, and fumbled in his pocket to produce a wooden "farmer" match. Match in hand he started looking for a place to strike it. Finding none, he pulled open the flap on the front of his fly, lit the match on the metal zipper, lit the candles, and returned to his pew. NOW I could start the service.

When it came time for the sermon, I found that the sun was shining directly through one of the windows and into my eyes. Our acolyte-turned-usher stood and said, "Do you want me to pull the window shade, Pastor?"

"Thank you, that would be great," I replied. With the shade drawn, it was a little difficult to see my notes, so I pulled the chain switch on the pulpit light—to no avail. Once again, my friend jumped to his feet and said, "That damn thing isn't plugged in. You want me to plug it in?" "Yes, please. Thank you very much."

On the way home I wondered how many hapless preachers my new

57

friend had helped, and how he might recount his experiences to his family and friends.

I also found myself reflecting on the classes on Liturgics I'd taken in seminary and thinking about worship practices in various contexts...

Pink Place

"Desire pastor to call," was the box checked on the visitor's card left in the offering plate. This was after the community Good Friday service sponsored by the Ministerial Association and hosted that year by our congregation. I called and spoke to a woman who asked if I would "come out to the ranch" to visit since her husband was homebound. The directions she gave were a little curious. After all the twists and turns she described, she concluded with, "It's the pink place. You can't miss it."

After carefully following the convoluted directions and finding myself fifteen or so miles outside of town, I rounded a bend and found, as she had said, "the pink place." It was a "ranch" (South Dakota lingo) with a largish house, a small barn, and several other assorted outbuildings, all somewhat run-down and wanting for attention. And she was right—I couldn't miss it. Every building on the place was painted pink—bright, Pepto-Bismol pink. *Everything* was pink. There was no contrasting trim color. There was no exception to the pattern. Everything was solid pink. It was, indeed "The Pink Place."

Gathering myself for what promised to be an unusual experience, I got out of the car and headed to the (did I mention pink?) house. The path was lined by bowling ball-sized rocks—each painted pink. As I got almost to the house, several chickens scattered in front of me. PINK chickens.

My knock was answered by a small woman who looked to be in her late sixties to early seventies. She invited me in and led me to an upholstered chair placed to form an "L" with a couch. Seated at the far end of the couch was her husband. He did not look up from the paper he was reading or acknowledge my presence in any way. The woman pulled up a folding chair directly *behind* me and sat down with a folded newspaper in her hand.

I surveyed the room and was immediately struck by the absence of anything pink. In fact, it looked quite normal except for the presence of a life-sized mannequin made from two-by-fours and clothed in slacks, sweatshirt, and a baseball cap placed jauntily on top of the inflated brown paper bag head.

The conversation was quite normal too, except for the fact that I had to continually be looking over my shoulder, even after swiveling as much as I could in the chair. I learned that she was a graduate of Gustavus Adolphus College in Minnesota, a Lutheran school with which I was familiar. We discussed my home state of Minnesota, the congregation I was serving, the big Lutheran church in town of which she was a member, and current events.

When she suggested that she prepare "a little lunch," I consulted my watch and realized that I really had to leave, but thank you very much. As I rose to depart, I discovered that the whole time we had been talking she had been sitting with the newspaper folded on her lap and had been underlining each line of print. She wasn't underlining key words or phrases or sentences— she was just underlining every line.

As she was getting my jacket, she said, "Pastor, let me show you something here," and opened one of the doors that led away from the main room. In that adjoining room, there were twenty to twenty-five more of the life-sized two-by-four mannequins with the paper bag heads, each dressed in different outfits. She informed me that she changed them out by whim and/or season. She also pointed out that the one on display in the living room was wearing a Gustavus Adolphus sweatshirt, in honor of my visit.

Driving back into town I decided I should stop at the church to which she belonged to report my visit and to assure them I had not known of her membership there before going to visit and that I was not out trying to "steal" members from them.

The pastor laughed and said they had experienced a number of "adventures" with this woman—the latest of which was the potluck where she brought two roasted chickens. When everyone raved about them, she explained that she had developed a new way of cleaning chickens. She did it in the toilet so that she could just flush all the feathers away.

This was one of the most unusual and memorable visitor calls I ever made.

Sticker Shock

It was a long drive to camp—six-and-a-half to seven hours long. It seemed a lot longer trapped in my '68 Chevy four-door with five pre-teens. Add in lunch/snack/potty breaks...you're talking a full eight hours.

At one of the stops, a snack of the banana variety was purchased by one of the kids.

Said banana purchaser was one of the older in the group and was seated in the back seat right behind the driver...me.

Soon after arriving at the camp, I started to see a puzzling pattern develop. I was being referred to as "Chiquita." Now, I have nothing against the name Chiquita. Although it is not inherently a part of the Northern European culture from which I descend, I do get positive vibes from the name. Visions of sweet, ripe bananas make my mouth water. Enhanced visions of bananas in a dish with a couple of scoops of ice cream topped with chocolate, maybe some whipped cream—*ahhh*...

But I digress. Quite puzzled by my new nickname, I asked one of the counselors what was going on. "Find a mirror and look at the back of your head," he said, laughing.

Yup. Right there on my bald little pate...a nice blue Chiquita banana sticker had been affixed.

A quick replay in my mind of the drive, the stops, and the placement of the passengers, sent me to visit with Bob. Trying bravely to maintain a straight face, he finally admitted that it had been he who had applied the adornment. At my (minimal, truth be told) expense, a great time had been had by all.

That boy, Bob, was my best confirmation student. Very bright, always involved in the discussions, with a blazing wit and a mischievous twinkle in his eye, he brightened many a dreary confirmation class. Bob's family was very involved with the church. It was to their home we had been invited to watch the moon landing right after we had arrived as brand-new pastor and wife and didn't yet have our TV hooked up. Another time I had been invited over to watch Bob launch a small rocket he had built.

Bob was one of those kids you just can't forget—always present, ready to help, full of life and fun; a "stinker" when a fun stinker was needed. He always added life and richness to any situation.

He is now a professor of chemistry and chair of the chemistry department at one of the premier liberal arts colleges in the US. Bob is the author of several textbooks, a glider pilot, and an inspiration to many.

But a word of advice: Don't turn your back on him if there are any produce stickers around.

A Spirit of Service

In the 1970s the Pierre Ministerial Association hosted an annual Churchmen's Legislative Seminar (pre-inclusive language days). All pastors from every denomination were invited to the state capital for a one-day event, in which there were presentations on different issues of interest by various state legislators or their staff members. Usually, the governor also would make a presentation to the assembled clergy.

As a member of the organizing committee for the seminar one year, I was charged with the responsibility of organizing and scheduling the presentations. It seemed logical to contact the governor's office first to check on his availability and to work around that.

To say that South Dakota is a Republican stronghold is an understatement. Of the thirty-four governors since the state's inception, there have been twenty-seven Republicans, five Democrats, one Populist (1897), and one "Coalition" (whatever that meant) governor (1899).

Richard Kneip served as governor during the time I was a pastor in South Dakota. He was one of the five Democrats mentioned above. At the age of thirty-seven, he was the youngest governor ever to serve in the state's history. I had met Governor Kneip when he was serving in the legislature before his election as governor and had seen and greeted him a time or two on the streets of Pierre. In a small town like Pierre, much of the formality practiced in other state capitals is disregarded.

Nonetheless, it was still somewhat daunting to meet "The Governor" in his office. I had made an appointment for our three-person committee to meet with him to try to schedule a brief presentation to the annual seminar, as was customary. At the appointed hour we were ushered into the governor's office and he, with shoes off and tie loosened, got up from his desk, shook hands with us, and invited us to have a seat in an informal sitting area across the room.

We introduced ourselves and explained why we were there. Governor Kneip said that we should make the most advantageous schedule for us and just let him know when we wanted him there. He'd adjust his schedule accordingly. He then thanked us for taking on the responsibility of organizing the event and explained that he found that kind of gathering to be immensely helpful both for himself and for the legislature as a whole.

He then went on to say, with a real weariness in his eyes, that most often when people came to see him it was because they wanted something for themselves—some exemption from a law or regulation, some tweaking that would benefit them or their business. He said, "You gentlemen come here each year asking for some of my time to help inform the pastors of this state, and through them their membership, of the many things that are going on in the government. You are not asking for something for yourselves or your business or company. You only seek to serve. I find that so immensely refreshing. Thank you for your service to your communities and to the state. Thank you!"

We then sat and just chatted, as you might with a friend you hadn't seen for a while. As we got up to leave, he thanked us again for coming "selflessly and in the spirit of service."

Though he was barely ten years older than I, the strain of the office seemed etched onto his young features. But his openness, kindness, and genuine inquisitiveness made a lasting impression.

Pastoral Care Takes Many Forms

Bob and Judy were a charming young couple in our small congregation mostly made up of charming young couples. They had been married a few years, lived in a mobile home in a nice, neat mobile home park, and were excitedly expecting their first child. One day word came that Judy had gone to the hospital. Everyone was surprised when July delivered twins—two bouncing baby boys.

The delivery was very difficult, and Judy was hospitalized for over two weeks to recover. The babies were doing great. Bob was in shock. Judy fully recovered and returned home. We didn't see them in church for quite some time.

One evening my meeting at the church was much shorter than expected, so I decided to drop by and check on the newly enlarged family. I went to the door, rang the bell, and was confronted by a very frazzled Bob, holding a screaming baby in each arm.

"Do you need some help?" I asked. "Oh, could you do that? I'd really appreciate it." I went in, took one of the "punkins" and started walking the floor along with Bob. After what seemed like an eternity, both of the little guys were quieted and fell asleep. "Where's Judy?" I asked.

"Oh, she's bowling. She's the lead on her team and hadn't been able to bowl during the last part of her pregnancy. She's feeling so much better now and her sub couldn't make it tonight, so we thought she'd give it a try," Bob said.

"Thanks so much for dropping in tonight. Don't know what I'd have done without you."

They hadn't taught baby-walking at seminary. Sometimes the simplest things can be the best pastoral care.

Who Would've Thought?

The class of student nurses was a delight. Once a week the Catholic priest and I met with them in the single classroom in the basement of the local Roman Catholic hospital. It was a teaching hospital, licensed by the State of South Dakota to train nurses, and our classes with them were to introduce the future nurses to various faith traditions they might encounter while serving in various hospitals and communities. The nursing program was two years, at the end of which these students would emerge, subject to successful completion of a state exam, as Licensed Practical Nurses (LPN).

With students coming from all across the state and beyond, the program was, of necessity, residential. The students lived in a residential hall affiliated with the hospital. Over the course of their studies and with the housing setting, the students became very close.

Four of these student nurses had formed a vocal quartet. The quartet was really good and was asked to sing at a number of functions around town from time to time. These four young women became especially close with each other. One day toward the end of their second school year, one of the quartet members approached me following class. "Do you have a minute? she asked, starting to cry softly. "Sure. What's up?" I replied.

"My fiancé and I are planning our wedding," she began, "and I would like for the quartet to sing, but my pastor will not allow it," she sobbed. "I was wondering if you would perform the wedding?" As we talked, I learned that she was a member of the Wisconsin Synod, a very conservative and strict branch of the Lutheran Church. It was, at least for her particular pastor, policy that while non-members of that denomination could *attend* a wedding performed in their facility, they most certainly could not participate in any manner. All members of the wedding party had to be members of that denomination. Organists, soloists, ushers—every participant. She was crushed that her quartet friends, who had come to mean so much to her, would not be welcome to enrich her wedding with music.

"Absolutely, I will perform your marriage ceremony," I replied.

We began planning in earnest. All the details began to take shape. She was able to re-form the wedding party to include her closest friends who had previously been excluded. The quartet started working on the music. She and her fiancé visited our sanctuary one evening to get a feel for the space.

The wedding day broke bright and sunny. Everything came together and the wedding was beautiful! Her quartet sang, a couple of the other student nurses were bridesmaids, it was grand.

After the wedding, the bride made a point to find me and thank me tearfully for working so hard to make the day "perfect beyond compare," as she put it.

I bumped into her about a month after the wedding at the local hospital. Following graduation, she had been offered a job and went to work there. We chatted some, and I invited her and her husband to come to worship some Sunday. She seemed shocked at my invitation, replying that they had no need or desire to visit, as they were regular members at…the church that had refused to perform their wedding as she had wanted it.

Stunned at her refusal, afterward I found myself reflecting on how strong a sense of belonging to a particular church community can be—come what may.

Expert Witness

"Pastor, my attorney wants to know if you'd be willing to testify in court," said the voice on the phone. Asking for clarification, the answer I got was a long story. The man's wife, in her mid-fifties, had been arrested for shoplifting, and not for the first time. In making the arrest, the police searched her car and found a wad of unpaid parking tickets, rolled up and bound neatly with a rubber band. The husband explained that he and the family had been aware of some of this, but not the extent of it. The hearing coming up was to determine her competency and some sort of consequence, whether treatment or punishment. The family's attorney was recommending they request commitment to the state mental hospital for evaluation and treatment.

The hearing was scheduled, and I appeared as requested. As the only witness, I was called to the stand immediately. The magistrate listened intently as the attorney did the questioning. All the identification questions that one might expect were asked of me: name, address, position, and how long in that position. Then came the shocker.

"Tell us about your education." "I graduated from the University of Minnesota." The attorney interrupted: "What was your major?" "I majored in psychology." "Ah," said the attorney, "as an expert in the field of psychology, do you feel that Mrs.____ would benefit from being committed to the state hospital?"

How to respond? "I'm not an 'expert'"? I had taken a lot of very basic psychology classes and observed lots of rats in mazes (the U of M faculty was a leading force in the behaviorist psychology movement), but I'm definitely not an "expert in the field of psychology." When I tried to protest, the attorney interrupted and asked the judge to instruct me to answer the question, which he did.

Question repeated: "Do you feel that Mrs. _____ would benefit from being committed to the state hospital for observation and evaluation?" "Yes, I do." "So ordered."

Following the hearing, the family gathered and thanked me profusely for my "help." I moved away from that community before her yearlong evaluation period concluded, so I have no idea what the outcome was. I can only hope that she received the help she needed and was able to return home to a more "normal" life.

The experience left me shaken, however. In this case, I did believe that everything that was done was for the benefit of everyone involved. However, I reflected on how easy it would be, under different circumstances, to misuse this system to silence someone, or punish them. Shaken, uncomfortable, unsettled, I made the long drive home.

Pickles

In the 1970s, some of the Lutheran churches in eastern South Dakota would together rent three school buses to make the trip to White Earth Lutheran Camp on the shores of White Earth Lake near Waubun, Minnesota. The buses would wind their way through the small communities picking up a few campers here and there until the bus capacity of one-hundred-twenty-five was reached. There were also, of course, several stops in the eight-hour journey for "bio breaks."

At each of these breaks, the riders would be mixed and moved around from bus to bus so that, through intentional programming on the buses, the kids would get to know each other on the way even though they were from many different small towns. This way, even though missing a day of actual programming at the camp because of the long Sunday travel, there was at least some community-building on the first day of the week-long camp experience. For this "South Dakota week," the camp staff didn't start the regular camp programming until Sunday evening, when the three buses would arrive.

One year we pulled into the camp on Sunday evening, road weary but feeling good about the success of our process of rotating and acquainting campers through the buses—and I was shocked to see two additional campers standing with the staff to greet us. It was explained that there had been a mix-up in the registration process and these two girls had been allowed to register apart from our travel group. I knew that young teens could sometimes be bad at accepting outsiders or newcomers, especially kids who are "different," and so to see that one of the girls who hadn't been with us on the bus, Susie, had Down Syndrome made my heart skip a beat with concern.

The camp staff gathered everyone in a big circle, welcomed us all, taught us a couple of quick songs, and started a tour of the cabins, dropping off eight to twelve kids at each cabin to get settled in. Janet, one of the girls from Sioux Falls, sized up the situation with Susie quickly, went over to her and the other girl, and said, "Come on, you can bunk with us," indicating several other girls from her large Sioux Falls congregation.

Janet became Susie's inseparable companion. She seemed to fall naturally into the role of protector, helper, encourager, and explainer. As the week progressed, I never saw one of those two girls without the other. Susie, supported by Janet, took part in every aspect of that camp week—but all without speaking. She swam, she canoed, she shot a bow and arrow, she ate s'mores at the campfires, she sat in the Bible study circles. Every morning I would go to the table where she was eating breakfast with Janet and say, "Good morning, Susie." She would smile, drop her eyes, but never say a word. To the best of my knowledge, she did not speak all week. Whether by shyness or embarrassment was unclear, but she wouldn't—perhaps couldn't, I wondered—speak.

The last night of camp was always Skit Night. Each cabin had to put on a skit, and every camper had to have a speaking role in that skit. All of a sudden it hit me: Susie...speaking role... I was filled with a bit of dread for Susie and her cabin. My apprehension grew as we went through all the cabins' skits.

Now, you have to understand: these skits are usually pretty bad. Picture young teens, embarrassed to be performing in front of others, but free from parental constraints, and emboldened by this being the last night. (Think: "So what are they going to do to me now if I'm inappropriate? Send me home?")

Janet and Susie's cabin was last on the program. They did a skit about a woman getting on a bus holding a box. In the skit, all the seats are taken. She asks one of the seated passengers if she can put the box on the shelf over the seated woman's head. "What's in the box?" she's asked. "Pickles," is the reply. Once the box is placed on the shelf above the seats, it starts dripping. The woman below the box moves aside so it isn't dripping on her but puts her finger in the puddle on the seat to taste what kind of pickles they are. Each of the girls as they get off the bus tells the seated one that the box is dripping on her. She smiles and replies, "It's OK—it's just pickles." The punch line is when the original box carrier retrieves the box to get off the bus and the seated passenger asks what kind of pickles they are. The passenger, now with the box cradled in her arms replies, "Oh, no, it's my new little puppy, Pickles."

Janet and Susie were the last passengers to disembark, together. I was really worried for Susie and the "rule" about speaking at that point. When they got next to the seated passenger, Janet said, "Excuse me, but that box seems to be dripping on you, isn't that right Susie?" Susie, holding tightly to Janet's hand, standing in front of the whole assembled camp—campers, staff, pastors, everyone—and squeezing Janet's hand for all she's worth said, "Yes, that's right!"

I watched Susie and Janet as they stepped off the stage area as the skit concluded, and dried my eyes as those two hugged and hugged and patted each other on the back. I wondered who had learned the most from camp that week, and decided it was me.

Out of the Ordinary Baptism

The understanding of baptism is one of the topics that divide Christians. Among all the issues involved, the most basic is: "Who is the actor in this sacrament?" One understanding is that the person being baptized is the actor. This understanding emphasizes that a person must choose to be baptized. It involves a person coming to the awareness that he/she is born separated from God as an individual and must "accept" God before being baptized.

Another branch of the church believes that baptism is God's action and that in the sacrament of baptism God is marking the baptized as God's own. Lutherans are in this camp. Hence most of the baptisms in Lutheran churches are infant baptisms and many, if not most, Lutheran Christians have never witnessed the baptism of an adult.

One young couple, newly married, had moved into town, into a house right across the street from the church. A really nice couple, they had started attending church and were present every Sunday. One weekday the wife dropped in to the church office for a chat. She had noticed that we were going to be receiving a group of new members into the congregation shortly and wanted to be included in the group. The issue was her husband. It turned out he had never been baptized. I explained that we could fix that quite easily. "Not so fast," she said. "He wants to know more about what this means." She asked if I would be willing to come to their home to talk to him about baptism. Thus began a wonderful string of weekly meetings.

Mike was a construction worker, a foreman on a road construction crew. Tall, lean, bronzed, and muscular he looked every bit the part. A man of few words, visiting with him could be difficult. As we talked, it became obvious that he was intelligent and well-read. We talked about all kinds of things, from current affairs to politics to church. We finally got around to discussing baptism and he was full of questions. Finally he said, "Pastor, do you have any books on baptism that I could look at?" "Sure," I replied. "I'll drop off a book tomorrow and when you've read it, give me a call and we'll go over it."

The next day I dropped off the book, a primer on baptism, in their mailbox. Late that evening I got a call from Mike. "I'm done with that book," he said. "It was really interesting, got anything else—maybe something on the history of baptism in the church?" I went to my bookshelf and dropped another book off at their house. This second book was a little more detailed and dealt with church history as a whole with a special chapter on the history of baptismal practices. It was several days before I got the call from Mike that he was done with that book, too. I went to Mike's house that evening and we had a great discussion on the book with a number of very insightful questions from Mike.

"You know, pastor, I have some other questions about church and all, do you suppose we could meet and talk over some of them?" Who could turn down a request like that? And so, we started a weekly routine of Mike reading something and then he and I, and usually his wife as well, sitting and discussing it together. He was bright and perceptive and seemed to thoroughly enjoy these sessions. One month stretched into two, and then more. Finally, one evening when we were done with another interesting discussion, Mike said, "I think I'm ready. I would like to be baptized." "Great," I said, "When would you like to do it?" "Next Sunday," he replied. And so the arrangements were made.

During the service that following Sunday, I announced that it was time for the baptism. I had never performed an adult baptism, so didn't really know what to expect. Mike and his wife got up and came forward. Mike was a big man and his footsteps echoed through the small building as he strode purposefully toward the altar and baptismal font. He was wearing a western-cut sports coat and clean new jeans. He came down the aisle of the church, his footsteps heavy and determined. His size was accentuated by the tininess of his wife beside him. She was radiantly beaming at this culmination of the long process. There was a hushed silence, since most of those present had never witnessed an adult baptism either. I removed the cover from the font and set it aside. All of a sudden I realized that, as big a man as he was, I was going to have a hard time—perhaps a messy hard time—to get any amount of water on his head. Sensing that problem, he said in his booming voice, "How about I kneel?"

Why hadn't I thought of that? "That would be great, Mike."

"Mike _____, I baptize you in the name of the Father (splash), and of the Son (splash), and of the Holy Spirit (splash)." There was a hushed silence in the church as Mike remained kneeling, head bowed, for what seemed like a long time. Finally he rose, and pulling a handkerchief from his back pocket wiped the tears from his eyes. In a voice softer than I had ever heard him use he said, "Thank you, Pastor. Thank you for your patience, for all those wonderful Wednesday nights—all your time—and thank you for caring about me."

Of all the baptisms over the years—all the darling babies, all the screaming babies, all the smiles and laughter and pictures, and all the "Here, pastor, you hold her/him for the next shot" moments—Mike's baptism stands out in my heart.

REDEEMER/BLACK RIVER—THIEF RIVER FALLS, MINNESOTA

First Impressions

After serving for three years in my first parish, I accepted the call to the Redeemer/ Black River Lutheran two-point parish in Thief River Falls, Minnesota.

The movers had done their thing. Our family had gone first to Minneapolis to see parents/grandparents for a few days, and now we were off to the new setting. The drive from Minneapolis to Thief River Falls takes about six hours. With a two-and-a-half-year-old and a six-month-old, a six-hour drive is a challenge. Add to the sheer grind of driving that far with young children the nervousness of moving into a new setting with all new people, and all the unknowns of a new parish assignment…it's no wonder that frazzled-me wasn't paying attention to the speedometer.

About twenty miles from TRF we rounded a curve and saw a highway patrolman ahead parked on a side road, checking the speed of passing traffic. Looking down, I realized I was one of the folks he was looking for. We passed the road where he was sitting as I was trying desperately to slow down while not looking like I was slowing down, if you know what I mean. Continuing on our way I watched in the rear-view mirror as the officer sat unmoving in his vehicle. Around the next curve I breathed a smug sigh of relief as it appeared we were going to be safe. Not much farther, I could see his lights flashing as he overtook us.

The ticket read: "Speeding—76 mph in a 55-mph zone." Ouch!

What we would later learn is that all traffic offenses in that district were reported in the local newspaper: Name of criminal, date, offense, and fine. So, my first ink in the local paper: "Keith Prekker; (Date); Speeding—76 mph in a 55-mph zone; $100 fine."

Double ouch: The paper came out the Friday before my first Sunday in church! Also before my first Sunday, I thought I should go out to the country church to get familiar with its setting; at my interview, I had only visited the town church of the two-congregation parish. Located seventeen miles outside the town of Thief River Falls, Black River Lutheran Church is a classic "Nebraska Gothic" white country church surrounded by farm fields and widely scattered farmsteads. Nestled beside the church is the cemetery.

I pulled into the "parking lot," a row of dirt parking places in front of the church, and headed inside—up the outdoor steps, through a small narthex, and into the sanctuary. A Swedish Lutheran church, the interior was painted white with white chancel furnishings trimmed in gold. I saw there was an addition that housed several classrooms and an office space. The church basement had a kitchen and a large gathering room.

Having finished looking around, I headed back to my car. When I came out of the building I found one of the congregation members waiting by my car. He had been plowing in his field which abutted the church property, had seen me drive up and wanted to introduce himself and say hello. He looked to be in his late sixties and was one of the "old timers" there, he informed me. We chatted, with him giving me much of the history of the area and the congregation. At the end of our conversation he said, "Yup, I've lived here all my life except when I went away to college. I've been a member of this congregation all that time and I've seen a lot of regimes come and go," referring to my pastoral predecessors.

It kind of caught me up short. I had never thought of myself as a regime before.

Having Words

"Oh, and by the way," the church secretary said on my very first day in the new parish, "there is a 65th wedding anniversary celebration scheduled in the Fellowship Hall on Saturday, and they have asked you to say a few words."

Let's see…just five days away…65th anniversary…I had never met these people…the year I was born they had already been married for thirty-seven years… They want me to say a few words? Okay, put it on the calendar.

So, in addition to getting settled into a new house in a new community, getting settled into a new office with all that that entails, learning all the new realities of a new parish (where are the bathrooms, etc.), writing a "First Sunday" sermon, finding the country church part of the two-point parish, struggling with starting to learn nine hundred or so new names…I wrestled with how to deal with the 65th wedding anniversary celebration and saying "a few words."

First step: schedule a visit to the farm to meet the folks. As a city kid, this was in itself a project. Quick phone call, Wednesday afternoon appointment was set. Before GPS, of course, I got the best directions I could, with lots of approximate distances and local landmarks. I was ready.

Arriving at the farm I got out of the car, fended off the friendly dog and headed up the sidewalk to the house, noticing the well-worn path to the outhouse. On being welcomed at the door by the wife I was ushered into the kitchen, where I had my first encounter with "a little lunch." That had been the phrase she used when I called to make the appointment, and the phrase used in the welcome at the door: "Hi, Pastor! You're just in time for a little lunch!" In grand rural Midwestern style, the table was heavily laden with many different kinds of sandwiches, chips, Jell-O, assorted salads, breads, cake, etc. "A little lunch" was a feast!

Edna was a tall, large woman with a big smile, outgoing manner, and a happy approach to life. Elmer was short, slender, and kind of dour. We chatted about the farm, their history together, their family, and their long involvement with the congregation.

Finally, looking for some kind of a nugget to use in my "few words," I said, "So tell me, Elmer, after sixty-five years of marriage, do you two still fight once in a while?" Elmer fell silent, grew increasingly red in the face, and finally semi-exploded. "You bet we do!!" he exclaimed. Taken more than a little aback I asked the next obvious question, "Well, what do you fight about?" "The same…damn…things…we fought about the first day!!" he practically bellowed.

Okay. Let's try a different approach…

I went to the library the next day to consult an almanac, searching out how long they had already been married when the telephone was invented, when the Wright brothers made Kitty Hawk famous, and other historical milestones, so that I could manage a "few words." I'd let someone else delve into the more personal stuff—if they dared.

Meeting the Kids

In the process of getting going in my new two-point parish, it came time to go out to the country church for a youth group meeting. The youth group there was large and lively. The twenty-five or so members of the group were mostly related to each other in some way.

As I drove up to the church, I saw most of the kids already assembled on the front steps of the church, chatting and horsing around. I got out of my car and headed up the sidewalk.

Having been bald, at this point, for a number of years, I had become inured to bald jokes at my expense, and pretty much knew them all. However, I wasn't prepared for this one.

"We want to know how you make your head shine so brightly," one of the kids said.

Another one chimed in with, "Do you use Mop and Glow?" Another student offered, "No, he uses Johnson and Johnson" (I would later learn he came from a well-known family in the community bearing the Johnson moniker).

The quickest wit in the bunch quickly proclaimed, "Come on, guys. He's a pastor—he uses Pledge!"

After a lifetime of ministry, nine hundred miles away and a half-century later, I performed the funeral for that girl since become a woman. Bittersweet…I remember that marvelous sense of humor, recall fond memories, and cherish the friendship formed that was enduring.

Rest in peace, Roseann.

Johnny

Not long after starting in Thief River Falls, I met Johnny. Johnny was a twenty-five-year-old man with Down Syndrome, living at home with his parents. His father was retired, and his mother was a homemaker and care provider for Johnny. These three were in church every Sunday and very active in the life of the congregation. Everyone knew Johnny and loved him for his sunny personality and his outgoing manner.

Early on, Johnny and I developed a pattern which I suspected his mother had coached him some on. Each Sunday morning, as he and his family came through the door at the end of the service, Johnny would shake my hand and say, "Good morning, Prekker." I would reply, "Good morning, Johnny."

He would follow that with, "I loved the hymns today." My response was always, "Oh good, I'm glad. I liked them, too." He would then smile the most infectious ear-to-ear grin you can imagine, turn to his mother for her approval, give me a hug, and be on his way.

One Sunday I noticed Johnny's family hanging back, letting the line pass on out the door before them. When everyone else had left, he and his parents came through the doorway. Johnny and I performed our regular ritual and then his dad said, "Johnny has something to ask you." Turning to Johnny I had no chance to ask what it was before he almost exploded with, "I want to take the offering." Johnny's dad explained that he loved to watch the ushers move down the aisle taking the offering plate from the end of one pew and starting it down the next one. The ushers then brought the plates up to the front of the sanctuary and handed them to the pastor to be placed on the altar.

I told them I was certain that could be arranged.

When I was leaving the church that morning, I approached one of the ushers and told him Johnny's request. Instantly he assured me that would be fine. We decided that the ushers would work with Johnny to explain things to him, and then follow him along as he performed his part in the service.

The next Sunday, Johnny almost exploded as he and his parents came through the door. "Richie wants to usher, too!" he exclaimed. Richie was Johnny's best friend in the world. He was about the same age as Johnny, and also had Down Syndrome. He, too, attended church with his parents, although not every single Sunday like Johnny. I assured Johnny that I would try to make that happen.

The next week after church I saw the head usher working with Johnny and Richie both, showing them how to hold the plates, how to pass them to the first person in the pew, how Johnny's plate would go down the first pew, while Richie's would start from the other end, down the second. Since the sanctuary was fairly large, four ushers would split up with two on each side of the center aisle, each team of two following the same pattern. The rehearsals for Johnny and Richie continued for several Sundays.

Finally, the big day arrived. Both newly-minted ushers arrived early, brimming with excitement. Their first task was to stand at the main door to greet attendees and hand them a bulletin as they entered the sanctuary. Never were bulletins distributed with more purpose, concentration, and enthusiasm. That having been accomplished, everyone seated and settled, the service began.

It was hard for me to keep from constantly looking out into the narthex and smiling at the ushers—usually kind of wandering around and quietly chatting during the service, but this Sunday sitting and participating in the service along with Johnny and Richie.

Finally the big moment was at hand—the collection of the offering. Usually, the four ushers would walk down the center aisle to each receive an offering plate and then proceed to pass them down the pews. This Sunday, six ushers appeared: two regulars, followed by Johnnie and Richie in their best suits and ties, and the final two regulars, to help as needed.

I passed out the four plates, one each to the first two regulars and one each to Johnnie and Richie. The first two experienced ushers went to one side of the congregation while Johnnie and Richie went to the other side accompanied by the other two regulars. Johnnie went to one end of the first pew and Richie went to the other, each with their helper at the ready. Johnnie started his plate down the front pew while Richie sent his down the second, each of them retrieving the plate that had been passed toward them and then sending it down the appropriate next row, just as they'd practiced. So it went, until all sixteen rows had passed the plates.

The ushers all then assembled at the back of the center aisle to bring the offering plates forward and present them to the pastor, who would turn and place the plates on the altar. The pride on the faces of the new ushers added several lumens to the brightness of the sanctuary that day.

After the service, Johnnie was beaming as many congregants thanked and congratulated him and Richie for the great job.

The very next Sunday as Johnny and his parents came out the door following church, Johnny's dad said to me, "He has something to tell you." Johnnie, beaming from ear to ear said, "Now I want to give the announcements!"

We had Johnny stick to taking the offering.

The Black River Singers

Seventeen miles outside of Thief River Falls, Black River Lutheran Church had an outstanding group of teens that formed their youth group when I arrived as the pastor. Many were related to each other—they were a cohesive bunch of neighbors, cousins, brothers, sisters, and a few others. They were mostly junior high age with a couple older and a couple younger. The group numbered about twenty.

A couple of the moms were gifted musicians and leaders. The kids loved to be together, loved to sing together and have fun. Thus was born the group called The Black River Singers.

Arriving as the new pastor, I found this group already formed and often singing for worship at the little country church. One day after church, the mother who was the director of the group and the de facto coordinator wanted to chat. She said the group was thinking of making a record. We talked a little and decided to proceed.

Several companies that specialized in such recordings were contacted and one was selected. Rehearsals ramped up, excitement mounted, and on the appointed day the group arrived at the local community college whose auditorium had been chosen to serve as the "studio" for the recording session.

Amid much excitement, nervousness, and expectation, the recording tapes were made (with remarkably few "re-dos" required). And then the waiting began. Every Sunday upon arrival at the country church for worship, I'd ask the big question: "Any word from the recording company?" The answer was always the same and in the negative. Until finally one Sunday the answer was, "Two weeks."

Finally, the long-awaited LP record albums arrived, to the delight of the whole congregation.

What happened next was amazing. Somehow, a relative of a neighbor of a cousin (or something like that) played the record for their pastor, who shared it with someone else, who played it for the Synod President (equivalent to a bishop in our polity of the time). Then, an invitation was received for The Black River Singers to sing at the next annual Synod Assembly! Several hundred representatives from congregations in a three-state area would gather—We had hit the big time!

It was a wonderful experience for the kids. Then after all the excitement of singing at the Assembly, we went home…and life was back to normal. Nashville never called. No contacts from Hollywood, or New York, or anywhere else.

But there were memories—good, rich, lasting memories. And that's definitely not nothing.

It's Complicated

Now that I'm older, I see this from a different perspective.

At the time, I was in my late twenties; she was in her mid-sixties. She had been serving in the role of church secretary (today we'd likely say office manager or parish administrator) for many years—I had been a pastor for three. Here I was—ostensibly to be her boss. It was a rather awkward situation.

We were both trying to make the best of it. I really needed her experience and her long-term knowledge of the congregation and community. She really needed… Hmm, I guess I don't know what she really needed from me.

She very graciously taught me about the congregation: the building, the people, the traditions. I tried to bring her help in terms of upgrading and making current some of the technology in the office.

For my part, I found the existing system of two phones on her desk to be cumbersome. One line rang in her office with an extension in my office. The other also rang in her office with an extension in the kitchen. If there was a call for me, it rang on the first phone. She would answer, put the person on hold, and press a button on her desk that rang a buzzer in my office. I would then pick up my phone and be directly connected to the caller. If she had some information about the caller or the call, instead of pushing the buzzer, she would come down the hall to my door and give me the scoop.

I suggested keeping the two lines, but putting them on one phone on her desk with push buttons so she could put the caller on hold, talk to me on the intercom with any background or information I might need, and then transfer the incoming call to my phone. She was opposed at first, but we did make the upgrade and after she had a little time to adjust, she loved it.

For her part, she proved invaluable in helping me sort through the family connections among the members, understand longstanding conflicts/slights, and navigate the minefields of old feuds and hurts that are found in any group of people, churches not exempted.

We seemed to have come to a comfortable working relationship. Until one surprisingly tumultuous day.

We had started using a dictating machine—basically a small hand-held tape recorder. I could dictate correspondence while driving in my car to home visits on the isolated country roads. She could later type the recorded contents at her convenience. It sped things up considerably.

On the fateful day in question, I had to send a letter to the bishop. I had dictated it and brought the tape to her office as usual. I said, "This letter needs to go out right away." Maybe it was the tone of voice I used. Maybe it was a bad day for one or both of us. Maybe it was the culmination of the numerous "updates" and "changes" we had been making. But whatever it was, it rubbed her the wrong way. In as aggrieved and dismissive a tone as she could muster, she replied, "Just put it on the stack. I'll get to it when I have time."

Her "huffy" response rubbed me in the same wrong way that my request had apparently rubbed her. In an equally huffy tone I grabbed the tape back and said, "Never mind, I'll type it myself." I went back to my office and started to type the letter. About halfway through the typing, she appeared at my door and said, "I can type that letter now." I replied in as self-righteous a tone as *I* could muster, "No, that's okay, I'm almost done."

Sadly, I think that marked the beginning of the end of our working relationship.

Due to congregational growth and the subsequent increased demands on office support, we soon needed to expand her job from part-time to full-time. She chose not to stay on in the position, citing the longer hours. I suspect the prospect of starting to computerize office functions may have also played a role.

But down deep, I've always carried a bit of guilt about that letter to "headquarters." I can't even remember what it was about.

A Tough Call

Hans was a true craftsman. He was technically a carpenter, but as one of those rare individuals with multiple skills, incisive intellect, and the ability to "get things done," he had become an invaluable manager in the firm that had built our church building. Short, slight, and somewhat stooped from all his years in construction, he was not a commanding figure; but with a razor-sharp mind, incredible skill set, and years of experience, he was one of the main reasons his company had been selected for the job.

Even though he had retired right after completion of our building, he was still the one who would get the call with the question of where some switch was located, or how some setting on some control could be adjusted; that probably felt natural because he was also a member of the congregation. He was always happy to be consulted and to have the excuse to come over to the church and solve the problem.

When I arrived in Thief River Falls the congregation's new building was not quite a year old. Hans came over to visit and took me into the kitchen to explain how the vast array of cabinets had been built. It turns out that the subcontracted firm that was to have supplied this critical part of a church had gone out of business. "Crunch time" came and the absence of cabinets was holding things up.

Hans and his brother Peder had taken on the task. They went into the nearly completed kitchen, took exact measurements, went to Hans' garage, and built the cabinets by hand. It was a large commercial-sized kitchen, and the task was no small matter. When the cabinets were completed, they had been transported to the new church kitchen and installed with nary an adjustment required. Hans was really proud of that.

Hans knew every square inch of that building. He could (and often did) explain in detail the depth of the footings required for each exterior wall section. The front sanctuary wall was sixty feet tall, solid concrete block with a brick veneer. Hans could explain how much concrete had to be used and how deep the footings had to go to support that size of a wall!

But there was a problem. The flat roof over the narthex leaked.

My first rainy Sunday at that nearly brand-new church building found the narthex filled with wastebaskets, buckets, and containers of all kinds—catching the water dripping from the ceiling. The building was less than a year old, and I asked how long that had been going on. "From day one," was the answer.

We set about finding a solution. A member of the congregation who was an attorney began digging into the situation. He found that the architect claimed his design was fine; the problem was with the contractor (Hans' firm). The contractor deferred blame to the roofing subcontractor. The roofing subcontractor claimed he had installed the roof exactly according to plan, and therefore the blame belonged elsewhere. No one admitted to having responsibility for it, no one was accountable.

Meanwhile, every time it rained there was the hunt for more containers, cautions to not trip over all the wastebaskets arrayed on the floor where everyone had to walk to get to/from the sanctuary, and the growing frustration and consternation of congregation members and leadership. Ultimately it seemed the only solution was to sue all parties involved and let a judge sort out who was to blame. The suit was filed.

The next day Hans was in my office. He sat silently for a time and then started to cry softly. "Pastor," he said, "I was so proud of how hard I worked on this building. I put in so many extra hours in overseeing everything. The building is beautiful, and functional. And now my own church is suing me…" He cried silently for a long time. I tried to explain that this was no reflection on him personally, but was the only way to try to get some accountability from someone in order to stop the roof leakage.

"My own church is suing me…" his soft voice trailed off. I didn't know what to say. After a painfully long silence, he stood and left.

It hurt.

A lot.

The legal issues were eventually resolved. The roof was repaired. The buckets and pots disappeared.

The anguish, however, so palpable in that room, is burned into my memory.

Christmas Gifts

Several days before my first Christmas in Thief River Falls I got a call from a member of the congregation. Her daughter was in the hospital, soon to become a mother. She was unmarried, had not wanted her mother present for the delivery, had driven herself there—the mother asked me to call on her in the hospital.

Pre-HIPAA (Health Insurance Portability and Accountability Act of 1996), I was able to go to the front desk, look in the card register, and get the room number I needed. Being still rather new in town and having never been on the maternity ward previously, I got turned around and unwittingly entered the wrong room—I was surprised to find the mom-to-be in there had a young man sitting in a chair beside her. I introduced myself, and they realized my mistake and explained that the woman I wanted to see was across the hall. Embarrassed, I apologized profusely and left as quickly as I could. Going across the hall and entering the correct room, I had a good visit with our church member.

The next day I returned to the hospital for a follow-up, got to hold one of the cutest little boys in the world, and had a chance to visit a bit with the tired, but very proud new mom. As I was taking my leave, she said, "Pastor, remember the couple you met here yesterday?" More than a little chagrined, I confessed to remembering and asked how she knew about my mistake. It turned out that both women had given birth after I left and had been roommates for a while after the births. In their conversations, the young couple talked a bit about the hapless pastor who had stumbled into their labor room the day before, and they had all shared a good laugh.

The new mom got real serious and said, "Pastor, I'm really worried about them. He's a student at the community college. They're from out of town and have no one here to help them. They're renting one of the tarpaper shacks just outside of town in 'shantytown.' I don't think they have many supplies for the baby at all. Is there anything we can do to help?"

On the way out of the hospital I stopped and checked the admissions book again. The couple was still listed and I made a note of their address. The next day I paid a visit to their rental. It was one very small room. There was a wood-burning stove. The baby was asleep in a cardboard box next to the stove, and the wind was blowing through the tarpaper-covered, poorly insulated walls. I learned that the dad was indeed a student and would be graduating in the spring, and they were making do with very little for themselves or the baby.

The next day was Christmas Eve, and at the two services I told the story of these visitors in our community and their situation. Being very new in the congregation, and in fact still fairly new to professional ministry itself, I didn't know what resources there might be to help these struggling kids. I just told the story.

As people were leaving the church and I was shaking hands at the door, my hand came back from handshakes many times with money in it. The chair of the Women's Group was waiting for me when everyone had left, and she explained that their group had been assembling layettes to go overseas. She took me into their storage room, got a big box and filled it with blankets and diapers and powder and lotion and rattles and any and everything else that a baby might need. I counted the money that had "mysteriously" appeared in my hand after the handshakes and found over $500 (roughly $3,600 in today's dollars).

Christmas Day, I made another call on the young family at the edge of town. I brought the box of supplies and had the thrill of watching them go through the items. I can't imagine happier people on a Christmas Day anywhere. I then gave them a card with the money I had received for them— but only half of it. Tears of thankfulness and joy flowed freely. I've not had a more genuinely thankful and happy Christmas before or since.

Yes, I had put only half of the money given me into their Christmas card, by design—it gave me a good excuse to visit them again a week later, in their now much cozier abode. They had used some of the blankets for wall coverings to help with the lack of insulation. They had fashioned a better crib and a small changing table. Their shack had become a home—humble to be sure, but a home. I gave them another card with the rest of the money in it, and witnessed their joy and gratitude spill over again.

As I was leaving, they told me that they had named their son and asked if I wanted to know the name. "Of course," was my reply. They proudly told me that instead of a name they had given him two initials.

He was legally named "TR." In response to my bewildered look, they explained that TR stood for Thief River, since the people of Thief River Falls had been so kind to them in their time of need.

What a Christmas that was!

Sink or Swim

Basically overnight, I had gone from a congregation in South Dakota with average weekly attendance of just around fifty, to a two-point parish in Minnesota with both a rural and a town church: two congregations, three Sunday morning services, and an average weekly attendance of around five hundred. The shock was instant and overwhelming. Among other things, in the three years I had served in my first congregation I had experienced three funerals, total; moving to the second parish, there were three funerals *a week* for the first three weeks I was there.

And two of everything! Two church council meetings each month, two women's groups, two youth groups, and on and on it went. Very quickly it became apparent that this new assignment was more than one person could adequately handle. It was also clear that the cost of an additional pastor would be more than the combined budgets of the two congregations could handle at that point. What to do?

A more cost-effective solution occurred to us: a seminary intern. At that time seminary was a four-year program; there were two years of classroom instruction, one year of internship in a congregation setting, and a final year of classroom instruction followed (upon successful completion) by ordination. The internship congregation had to supply housing for the student and family, travel costs to and from the site, a minimal stipend for the intern, and a fee to the seminary for its support of the program—all adding up to significantly less than what a second fulltime pastor's salary plus housing and benefits would be.

The decision was made. The application was submitted and accepted. We became a part of the internship program of Northwestern Lutheran Theological Seminary.

Our parish ended up being served by five interns consecutively. Each brought a unique array of gifts and strengths. The congregations absolutely loved having these young enthusiastic men (still all men in those years) as a part of their congregational lives. Each of the five guys expressed gratitude for the opportunity to "spread their wings" a little. And I was thrilled to have the extra help.

The problem with the program was that for the first few months each of these green rookies needed time to adjust and come to an understanding of their roles and how to perform them. Just like it had taken me some time—to assess the situation in the new parish, learn the customs and expectations, find out where the "tricky" places were, who the "helpful" and who the "difficult" people might be, etc.—so too each of these men in turn had to do the same. It seemed about three months—a full quarter of their time with us—were required for settling in and learning the routine. But the rest of the year they became increasingly helpful as they grew in skills and understanding of their role.

One other downside was with the youth group. Each year the kids in the parish would grow close to the intern only to have him pack up and leave. Each fall, with the arrival of the new intern I could expect a visit from an informal "committee," (oddly enough, usually made up mostly of tenth-grade girls for some reason) to drop into my office and, often tearfully, tell me how much they had appreciated the former intern and how the new one just wasn't anywhere near as good as the former. (And this script would play out again the following year, and the next…)

Both churches continued to grow, the town church quite rapidly, and the operating budget grew accordingly. At the end of the fifth year of the internship program, the decision was made to discontinue it and call a second full-time pastor instead. With the continuity of not having a new face every year, plus the considerable gifts of the associate pastor who was called, the remarkable growth we were experiencing only accelerated!

In retrospect, it is instructive to reflect on not just the specific gifts of the various personalities and skills that each of those interns brought to that parish setting, but also on how much the gift of a co-worker meant for me personally and professionally, and how important that example of teamwork was for the congregation.

In life, it seems, a solution to one problem often creates another. That was the case here: stabilizing the staffing situation meant we then grew so fast that we needed more space.

So, a building committee was formed. But more on that later…

Tradition, Tradition

The Lucia Festival is a favorite tradition at Christmastime in Swedish Lutheran churches. Saint Lucia was a fourth-century Christian martyr in Rome. She brought food to the Christians hiding in the catacombs. To aid her mission she wore a candle on her head to light her way so that her hands were freed up to carry more food and supplies. To commemorate this saint, whose crucifixion date is marked on December 13, Saint Lucia is usually pictured in a white robe with a red sash symbolizing her blood as a martyr, and with a wreath of candles on her head, reflecting her service in the dark catacombs.

My first December in TRF I had been unaware that the Swedish Lutheran church I was serving had a particular Saint Lucia tradition: The high school girl in the senior class who had been most active in the church was chosen by the Women's Group for the honor of dressing as Saint Lucia, and processing down the aisle at the beginning of the service on the Sunday closest to December 13. She would sit on a large red chair up front during the entire service and recess out with the pastor at the end, to then serve cookies to worshipers in the narthex.

Not being Swedish myself and having previously only read about Saint Lucia—and not having been informed by my new congregation about this practice of theirs, ahem—I was a little surprised on that first Sunday nearest December 13 when Lucia suddenly appeared. I was also surprised to see the huge red upholstered "throne" which had appeared mysteriously and was placed directly in front of the altar. I proceeded with the service as best I could.

I reflected on the experience afterward. It had looked to me, for all the world, as though we were worshiping this blond girl with candles on her head instead of the creator God in Christ Jesus. I made a mental note to try to fix that the next year.

The next year as plans were being formed for the Christmas season, I entered the fray. Explaining my concerns to a skeptical worship committee, I suggested an alternative: How about if Lucia came in like always, but instead of sitting right in front of the altar, her big red chair would be off to the side? She would still recess with the pastor at the end of the service and serve the goodies, but just wouldn't be the center of attention throughout worship, blocking the altar.

"Oh, Pastor, we couldn't do that. WE'VE NEVER DONE IT THAT WAY!!"

Being young (and foolish), I responded, "Well, either we do it that way or we don't do it at all."

We did do it "that way"…and the building remained standing, despite my brashness.

A few years later there was another big to-do around their tradition of Saint Lucia Day, which also always included a big Swedish Family Festival in the afternoon, featuring a huge spread of beloved Swedish Christmas delicacies—*lefse, krumkake, sandbakkels, rumagrut,* and more (all of which happen to also be beloved Christmas goodies from my own *Norwegian* heritage, happily).

Part of the congregation's tradition was that the whole town was invited to the festival. But sadly, seemingly also part of the tradition was that very few non-Swedish people from the town ever attended. The third part of the tradition was the meeting of the women's planning committee to evaluate the festivities, at which meeting there was always real disappointment and consternation at the poor community turnout.

After living in that small town for a few years, I had come to realize that it was composed mostly of people of Norwegian descent. Those of Swedish descent, like at our church, were somewhat in the minority. What you need to know is that there is a semi-joking, semi-serious antipathy between these Scandinavian cousins.

(In my first year in the parish, we had had a pancake breakfast fundraiser for the youth after church. As we were sitting around chatting at the conclusion of the breakfast, one of the old Swedes asked me what part of Sweden my family had come from. I explained that my family was from a "suburb" of Sweden called Norway. *Yumpin yiminy,* I thought the roof would come off the church. After everyone settled down, it was informally decided that since I was already there I probably ought to just stay on. They were only partially kidding. I was the first non-Swedish-descent pastor they had ever had.)

With all this in mind, it was with some trepidation that I approached the committee that was meeting to evaluate the most recent Swedish Family Festival. Once again, the disappointment with the lack of community turnout was real and disheartening. The congregation itself always turned out in droves for the traditional goodies—but the wider community not at all. I made a stunning suggestion: Why not change the name of the event to the *Scandinavian* Family Festival so as not to be seeming to exclude the Norwegian "cousins" (who had the very same delicious traditional goodies)?

"Oh, Pastor, we've never done it that way."

But we tried it. There were overflow crowds. We ran out of every last food item. A great time was had by all.

Another year, there was yet one more "dust-up" around the Lucia Festival tradition...

The responsibility for selecting our Lucia each year belonged to the Women's Group, which was made up of several separate "circles"—subgroups that each had their own focus, membership, schedule, and meetings in between the larger meetings of all of them together. Each of the circles would hold their own votes in their separate meetings regarding which high school girl they deemed to have been most active in the church that year. Those results were submitted to the general Women's Group organizers, compiled, and the resulting "winner" was notified, as were all the women at their next general meeting.

One year the girl who was selected through this process was a brown-haired girl with a German-sounding last name. She had been very active in congregational life and was clearly the standout choice. However, in the discussions in the parking lot and on the phone lines and in the supermarket after the general meeting, there was a feeling expressed among the women that she wasn't blonde and blue-eyed and "Swedish enough." There was a call for a re-vote and suddenly a new Lucia was chosen who checked all the boxes for appearance as Lucia. The first girl was then notified that there had been an "error" and that after further review, she would not be serving in the honored role after all. She was crushed.

Not being part of or privy to the whole process as it was happening, I didn't learn about this shameful situation till after Christmas was long past. At that point it was too late for corrective action, but I went and apologized to the girl and her family profusely. When the next Christmas was approaching, I met with the Women's Group before their various circles met to make the selection of that year's Lucia. Instead of the lambasting I frankly wanted to give, I proposed a change: "What if we eliminated Lucia from the worship service itself, and then had all of the senior girls" (unspoken but clearly implied: "no matter their looks or heritage") "dress as Lucia and be present in the narthex following the service to serve goodies to everyone?"

"Oh, Pastor, we can't do that. We've never done it that way." "Well, let me put it to you this way, either we do it that way, or we don't do it at all."

It was really nice to see all the senior girls dressed festively as "Lucias"—and, there seemed to be more cookies!! A win for all, it turned out!

Ah, Those Swedes

Alfred was a retired farmer who lived on the family farm on the edge of town, with his two elderly sisters and a brother. He was the oldest and the only one of the four who was still a member of our congregation. Though they were a family of staunch and proud Swedes, his younger siblings had decided to switch to the (Norwegian) Lutheran Free Church down the street—it was a more conservative church that was more to their liking.

One Monday morning, the volunteers who were counting the offering from the previous day's service came into my study, with a check from Alfred. There was an error on the check. In the blank for the numerical entry Alfred had written "$200," but on the blank for the written-out amount he had entered "Two thousand dollars." The counter was kind of clucking his tongue and saying, "Poor Alfred—he's really getting up there in years." I volunteered to contact Alfred and get it straightened out. The counters left the check with me and made that day's deposit without it.

I called Alfred and explained the situation and he said he would come right into town to fix it. He came into my study, sat down and chatted a bit, took the faulty check, ripped it up, and wrote a corrected version for the $2,000 he had originally intended. We chatted a little more, I thanked him for solving the problem and for the very generous donation, and he left. (That $2,000 donation would be worth over $10,000 today.)

I had recently learned of Alfred's situation. His family farm was the first farm you saw when leaving town going east. He and his siblings had sold a large portion of the land to the state for a community college to be built. Rumor had it that the price was very high—perhaps not for the community college system, but certainly so for the economy of this small community. Alfred and his siblings had suddenly become wealthy.

As Alfred was leaving the building, he went through the secretary's office. She was assembling the monthly newsletter and was in the process of stapling the several pages together for each one. He watched her for a time while they chatted, and then said to her, "You know they make electric staplers now that would make your chore a lot easier." She said she knew, but it wasn't in the budget. Alfred replied, "You tell that pastor to go downtown and buy one of those staplers and send me the bill!"

I went that afternoon and did as instructed. The stapler was great, and greatly appreciated. The next Sunday after church, I invited Alfred into the church office to show it to him. I demonstrated it on a sheet of paper. He smiled and said, "Can I try it?" I slid it over to him and he inserted the paper to trigger the mechanism. He smiled at me. He triggered it again. Another smile. Then he repeatedly and rapidly inserted and removed the paper resulting in a row of staples all along the edge of the sheet of paper. He turned to look at me and with a big smile said, "Us Swedes love gadgets!" and left.

A few months after that Alfred's brother died suddenly and unexpectedly. The funeral was at the above-mentioned Lutheran Free Church. A few days after the funeral, Alfred came into our church office.

He explained that he and his sisters felt that any memorial money donated by members of our congregation should come to our congregation. He said he knew that we had a fund established for two new pieces of office equipment—a paper-folding machine and an addressograph. He asked how much money we had accumulated toward each.

I explained that instead of collecting for both at the same time, we were designating all donations that had come into the folding machine, to purchase it first. He asked how much we had collected. I told him. He said that the memorials from his brother's funeral from members of our congregation totaled twenty dollars and he'd like to dedicate that amount to the other machine that had no balance in the fund. Mustering my patience, I explained that if we divided the gifts up, it would take longer to get both machines, but if the gifts all went to one, we could purchase it sooner and then collect funds for the other while enjoying the benefits of the first. Alfred still insisted that the money from his brother's memorial go to the second machine.

More than a little exasperated, I gave in. He then asked what the total cost of the second machine, the addressograph, was. He took out his checkbook and wrote a check for the amount needed to buy it as well—in memory of his brother.

Those Swedes love gadgets. Those Swedes love family. Those Swedes love the church.

Fifteen minutes after leaving the church, Alfred returned. "Pastor, I feel terrible." "Why, Alfred, what's the matter?" "I didn't include enough for the sales tax on that machine." I replied, "Alfred, churches are exempt from sales tax in this state." "Oh yeah. Thanks. I feel much better." He left, at peace.

Cemetery Fence

Like so many others, the little white country church stood out in the landscape, surrounded by acres and acres of scattered family farmsteads. Looking somewhat lonely from a distance, as one approached it took on a warmly cozy feel, with large trees on two sides of the cemetery adjacent to the church building. The faint outline of a ballfield was distinguishable in the ground where games were played right next to the cemetery. The occasional moose would come to munch on some of the bushes, sometimes catching a nap on the church lawn.

At a council meeting one evening, one of the members expressed a concern. The cemetery was filling up. With the congregation approaching its 125th anniversary, it was perhaps not surprising that this situation might arise. This problem then became a topic of discussion over several subsequent monthly meetings. Perhaps in part due to having grown up as a "city kid," I often found the pace of decision-making terribly slow and I could become frustrated at this aspect of church life in a rural community. My own approach usually was, "Bring up a problem—find a solution—execute the plan—problem solved."

After the fifth or sixth monthly discussion of this particular problem, I suggested a solution that seemed obvious to me: "Why don't we just move the fence out to enlarge the cemetery?" After all, there were many acres of land available to the church that had been donated at its founding. Somewhat aghast, but trying to be patient with the foreigner from the city, the council members explained: "Well, Pastor, we can't do that because of the graves outside the fence."

I was caught up short. "What graves outside the fence?" I asked.

"Well, over the course of our history there have been three suicides," they explained. "Because suicide is a sin, the pastors wouldn't allow the perpetrators to be buried in the church cemetery."

I was vaguely aware that in times past suicide had often been called "the sin against the Holy Spirit," and was considered "unforgivable." The previous pastors they spoke of apparently adhered to that line of thinking—but by the time I was there, that reasoning was definitely outdated, and diminishing in belief and teaching, thankfully.

"Are the three graves marked?" I asked. "No, no markings were allowed," was the response. "Do you know where the graves are?" "Sure, everyone knows where they are."

I tried to explain, as best I could, the theology of sin as the separation from God: that we are all separated from God, that there are not gradations of sin, that Christ came to forgive sin (i.e., all sin)—and that there could be no justification for pastors or church councils or anyone else to determine who was or wasn't "qualified" to be buried in a church cemetery. I ended my "sermon" (tirade?) by suggesting that we get some flashlights and shovels and go out to the cemetery right then and move the fence!

The fence moving occurred—not that night, but a few weeks later after the necessary materials could be assembled. It was done with no fuss or ceremony. The unmarked graves were properly marked with no special attention drawn to them. Congregational life went on.

Years later, when my time in that parish eventually came to an end and I was making arrangements to move, I received visits from each of the three families involved. They expressed gratitude for the change in policy, enabling their loved ones to be included in the community.

Eye-Opening

The first intern we hosted in Thief River Falls was just about done with his year with us. It had been a rousing success. People loved the enthusiasm and youthfulness he brought to the congregation's life, and there was a palpable sense of loss as we pondered his departure. We opted to continue the intern program and applied to host another.

The internship program was a year of practical experience between the second and third years of classroom instruction, giving the students a chance to try to apply their theoretical knowledge in a real parish setting under the supervision of an experienced pastor. I was barely qualified for the role of supervisor, since I had had only four years of parish experience myself before we began the program. However, since the first year had gone well, we were hoping to embark on year two.

The student we were assigned as our second intern made a trip to TRF to interview and see if the fit was good for both parties. When the candidate arrived at the parsonage, he got out of his car, came over to me, and said, "We're the same age." I was a bit taken aback by this being nearly the first thing out of his mouth, though I had seen in his paperwork that ministry was going to be a second career for him; and yes, I had read that we were right about the same age. A bit startled by the strangely blunt introduction, I did remark that I was older by a bit (two months or so).

But the second and more shocking-to-me news from his mouth was "I'm divorced and remarried, but I think that will help me relate to other people who have experienced divorce."

That really caught me off guard. Back then in the early 1970s, there were very few divorced and remarried clergy. I wasn't so sure that he would be as readily accepted as he was predicting.

But, he was right, I was wrong. It turned out he completed a successful internship with us and went on to have a long and successful career in parish ministry, serving well in several challenging parishes.

I was some years out from seminary, and I was learning that my education was likely to continue indefinitely, out here "in the real world" of ministry.

Lesson Learned

A chill ran down my spine. A chill of realization of how naïve and foolish I had been. I had never even given this a thought before. But now it hit me like a bucket of ice-cold water.

It was a busy "Church Night"—almost all non-Sunday church activities were scheduled for Wednesday nights. That was by design, as many of the congregation's families were farm families and they tried to make as few trips to town as possible. So, we picked one night on which to do everything. There was choir, youth choir, and a Bible study—all on the same night.

At the end of the night, one of the members of the choir asked if she could talk to me a little. "Sure. Come on into my office," I replied.

Her son was in confirmation. She was a single mom; her divorce had happened before I had started serving that parish. Other than being aware that she sang in the choir, she was one of the congregation members I didn't know well, and we hadn't had much interaction. We sat down and she started to talk. Halting at first, then the words seemed to come out in a rapid flow. Life was hard. She didn't make much money at her job. Her son was a "good kid," but had started acting out a bit more as a teenager. Her ex was being difficult. Her list of concerns and frustrations grew longer. The whole recounting was washed in quiet tears.

She talked, I listened—for quite a while. Finally, she slowed down and eventually stopped. We prayed, and then sat a moment in the silence. She apologized for taking so much of my time, then stood and turned to the couch where she had been sitting to pick up her coat. As she bent over the couch, she stopped still and said, "Do you want to have an affair?"

I was stunned. What words do you actually say to that?

"No!"-? "No thanks!"-? "Never in a million years!"-?

I stammered something like, "I don't think that would be good for either of us," and went to the office door. As I opened the door and waited for her to put on her coat and gather her things, I realized that we were the only two people still in the building.

That bucket of ice-cold water hit me as I recognized just how vulnerable a situation this was. If it turned out she wanted to cause trouble, she could easily make any false claim she wanted and it would be her word against mine. However a dispute like that might play out, I would then be under suspicion and have to live with the uncomfortable uncertainty that suspicion would always bring.

Thankfully, none of that came to pass. But the experience of that realization burned itself into my memory.

From that moment on, I made a very conscious decision to never be completely alone with anyone in a counseling situation again—male or female. I would only see someone if there was someone else in the building. And the closer to my office the better.

Chopped Alfalfa

One day Gladys appeared in the office. "Pastor, have you got a minute?"

We went to my study. Gladys was a farm wife who had married into a long-time family in the congregation. Most of her kids were grown; the youngest was still at home, a sophomore in high school.

"I'm really worried about Jimmy," she said matter-of-factly.

"Oh yeah? What's the concern?" I replied.

"Well, I was 'straightening up' his room yesterday, and I found a plastic bag—kind of a stiff plastic in the shape of a book. It was filled with what looked like a finely chopped-up green plant material like chopped leaves, or something. I asked him about it, and he told me it was 'chopped alfalfa.' I told him I thought it might be marijuana, but he insisted it was chopped alfalfa."

I asked what he might be doing with chopped alfalfa in a bag, and she had no idea to offer. "Why don't you bring it in to the church and I'll take it to the sheriff. I'm sure they can test it to see if it's marijuana or not," I suggested.

The next morning Gladys came in to the church with the plastic bag. I took it from her and put it on my desk to take to the sheriff when I went uptown to the hospital later in the day. That afternoon I grabbed the bag and headed off. I threw it on the front seat of the car next to me, turned on the radio, and started uptown.

After a couple of blocks, it dawned on me what I was doing. I had not called ahead to give the police department any heads-up about what I was doing. Before cell phones, I had no way to do that from the car. Here I was, driving with a bag of possible marijuana on my front seat for anyone to see. An accident, a traffic stop, a casual visit with a passing cop—I could have a lot of explaining to do… (Remember, this was decades before medical—not to mention recreational—marijuana became acceptable or legal anywhere in the US.)

I slowed to a crawl, drove with both hands on the wheel, looked extra-carefully both ways at every single intersection, and finally pulled into the parking lot at the police station, never so glad to be anywhere in my life.

I brought the bag in to the sheriff and explained the situation. He assured me they could send the bag to the lab and let me know what they found.

The next day the sheriff called with the results: the bag contained chopped up alfalfa hay.

After I expressed great relief, the sheriff said, "Not so fast. This kid could be in deep trouble. If he's selling this chopped hay to kids at the school as marijuana, the repercussions when the truth comes out could be worse for him than what he would face in a court of law if it were really marijuana."

Gladys and I had a long conversation. I left it to her to deal with her son, and I never heard another word about the situation.

A Real Dutchman

"Pastor, Dad's in the hospital. He went in yesterday. He's doing fine. They found a couple of issues, gave him a blood transfusion. They'll send him home tomorrow or the next day. But he's become withdrawn. He won't talk to anyone. We were hoping you'd go up to see him."

"Dad" was an eighty-something retired farmer, who had sold his farm and moved onto roughly ten acres just outside of town. He had bought a largish garden tractor and kept his hands in the soil by planting, tending, and harvesting a garden that covered most of the ten acres. His last name reflected his Dutch background—rather unusual in northern Minnesota where most folks were of Scandinavian descent—which he proudly proclaimed every chance he got. He and his wife were in church every Sunday, sitting in the same pew each week and taking part in all of the special events that took place in the church community. His hearty speech carried a strong trace of his Dutch heritage, and his resounding laugh broadcast how much joy he had experienced throughout the years.

Entering his hospital room, I found him sitting quietly in a dark corner, no lights, window shades mostly drawn. His normally cheery, over-loud greeting was instead a muffled, "Hi, Pastor." The barely half-eaten lunch on the tray looked like the nursing staff had left it in case he felt hungrier later on.

"Hi, Ed," I responded. "What's going on?"

In a voice that I hardly recognized as his he started to explain. "Feeling tired...no energy...not a kid anymore...hard to 'keep up'... thinking of selling the tractor...need to cut back." We talked about all of that for a time. Then, with tears in his eyes, he spoke his real concern.

He told me he had received a blood transfusion; in fact, two of them. After a long pause, it came out: "Pastor, with all of the Norwegians in this town, I'm afraid I'm too Norwegian now and not full-blooded Dutch anymore."

The deep, pained concern on his face expressed the real despair he felt—and helped me to desperately stifle the sudden laughter that nearly burst out of me. I managed to swallow it, composed my face, and tried to patiently explain that the term "full-blooded" was not a literal or scientific term. I assured him he was still the same staunch Dutchman he had always been.

Ed returned home. He did sell the tractor and did "cut back some." A year or two later his wife of many years died. It was really hard on him. The funeral was huge—most small-town funerals are. We didn't see Ed in church the next Sunday—or the Sunday after that, or after that. I stopped in to check on him from time to time and we had good, if subdued, conversations. Finally, he came into the church office one day. He said, "Pastor, I've been attending a different church on Sundays. I just can't stand the thought of coming to our church and sitting in the pew where we always sat together, without her being there. I'm sorry, but I just can't do it." I told him I understood. The important thing was that he find a community that would care for and support him. We parted with a prayer and a warm hug.

The church he transferred to was...the Norwegian Lutheran Church.

Thanks But No Thanks

They were a nice middle-aged couple, new in town, who had visited our church and several others, and had decided they would like to join ours. Sitting in my office one afternoon, they went on to explain that there was one condition. They would like to start a Bible study which they would lead. Being more than overloaded with many parish responsibilities, this was an appealing idea to me, to say the least (especially the part about someone other than me taking it on!).

As the conversation progressed, however, my enthusiasm cooled as they went on to explain that they were "blessed with the 'gift of tongues.'"

In the mid-seventies, there was a new/old development in the church in the US. Dubbed the "Charismatic Movement," it featured an emphasis on the "gifts of the Spirit." While the New Testament speaks of several spiritual gifts in a number of places, this mid-seventies movement often focused primarily on the "gift of tongues."

On the Jewish festival of Pentecost, the New Testament tells us, the disciples were filled with the Holy Spirit and were able to speak in other languages. This enabled them to preach to the many visitors from different lands who were in Jerusalem to observe the religious festival. Note that they spoke in known languages to people who understood those languages.

Somehow, over time, this has morphed in some traditions to "speaking in tongues," which to most people sounds like a nonsense garble of sounds and syllables, which only someone who has the "gift of interpretation" can translate. It is a belief and a practice not commonly accepted in mainline Christian denominations, and not by me, either.

Perhaps you can grasp my discomfort with the prospect of a husband receiving a "special message from God" which he speaks in a language that no one can understand except his wife, who then interprets/translates its meaning into English for the group's benefit (or vice-versa, as to which spouse does the speaking and translating).

Wow! A direct message from God! Who can argue with God? Wow! Who needs scripture? Who needs two thousand years of accumulated wisdom and experience in living the faith?

Does that sound fishy to you?

Well, it certainly did to me.

I thanked these good folks as sincerely and calmly as I could manage and suggested they might want to look a little further for a church that could use their "amazing" gifts.

Rising (just like my blood pressure had), I showed them to the door.

Without a Trace

Her life story was incredible. I'll call her Ingrid. Growing up in East Germany, the earliest years she remembered included a harsh life under communism, the long and difficult walk to the West, and climbing under the barbed wire to freedom. After graduating as an occupational therapist, she went to a country in Africa as a medical missionary. I'm not sure if this is when the sounds and voices started, but this is where they picked up in the story she was telling me.

Now living in our town, she had been a regular worshiper in the congregation. We would sometimes wave and/or chat a little when I'd see her while calling at the local hospital where she worked.

The first I learned of her background was one dark and rainy afternoon when I called at her apartment at her request. The apartment was above a local business in the downtown area of our small town. As we sat and visited, I got introduced to her hard life. The details of life under totalitarianism, the grim realities of escape to the West, the disillusionment of a difficult albeit "free" life in post-WWII Germany, adaptation to life in a small African village—it was overwhelming.

It wasn't clear to me when the voices began. She began detailing them as she described the hut in which she lived overseas. It was a single room with a thatched roof, with some sort of an attic. She would sometimes hear a rustling up there. Eventually, she started making out voices in the sounds from above. Finally, she was able to hear her name being called softly: *"Ingrid…Ingrid."* Then the messages started—mean messages, hurtful messages, threatening messages. Always, these messages included the instructions for her to return to East Germany.

She reported this to her superiors. Her hut was searched to no avail. When this process repeated itself, she was sent back home to Germany.

It also was not clear to me how, when, or why she came to the US, but here she was. And the reason I had been summoned to her apartment was because the voices had begun again. As we were visiting, it started to grow dark and the light rain outside increased slightly. Not sure just how to proceed, I asked for some clarity on the voices. Male or female? "Can't tell." Loud or soft? "Very soft."

Suddenly she stiffened. "There—there. Did you hear that one?" A pickup truck had started up, somewhat loudly, following the traffic light change at the intersection outside her window. "It called my name. *Ingrid... Ingrid... You must go home...I-n-g-r-i-d...I-n-g-r-i-d'...*"

She turned toward me, and asked conspiratorially, in a slow, strained whisper, "Didn't... you... *hear*... that?"

A chill ran down my spine. I wasn't sure at all what I was doing—I think the term is "over my head"—so I tried to extricate myself. I told her that I knew one of the doctors at the hospital (thinking of the head of the psychiatric unit who had come to be a good friend). She knew immediately to whom I was referring and why, and rejected the suggestion out of hand. "You think I'm crazy. That's what the others said. I'm not crazy. I won't see that doctor!"

I found I had a nagging suspicion that her aversion might be because of the psychologist's obviously Jewish name, not just his profession. In any case, looking at my watch, I said I had to leave and asked if we could continue the conversation at another time—perhaps in my office.

That suggested continuation never happened, at least not in the way I had envisioned or intended.

Instead, one Sunday a couple of weeks later, Ingrid asked to visit for a moment in my study after the service. I was surprised when she immediately asked if I knew the chief of police. I said yes, and she wondered if I could arrange for her to meet the chief to discuss her situation.

It seems she had "traced" (in her mind) the voices she was hearing to either her clothes dryer or an electric clock on the wall near the dryer. She thought the police chief should come over to her apartment and inspect these items for signs of tampering. Perhaps the East German police had traced her to our little town and were trying to get her returned for punishment for her escape to the West.

I was now certain that "over my head" was not nearly a strong-enough phrase to describe my situation, and so consulted with the hospital psychologist. He and I met with the police chief, and they decided that the thing to do was for the chief and me to visit Ingrid's apartment and the chief to do the requested inspection. Supposedly finding something suspicious in the clock, the chief would remove it to be "sent in to the lab" in Washington. The hope, on the part of the doctor, was that removing the clock would give Ingrid some relief and at least allow her to get some sleep.

The ruse was conducted. The hoped-for relief came, but lasted no more than a week. Ingrid made more and more frequent calls to the police department to get the results of the FBI investigation. It seemed that ultimately our ploy only increased her suspicions.

Then she quietly disappeared. I have thought about and prayed for her regularly.

She just disappeared. Without a word.

Without a trace.

I Misunderestimated*

The war in Vietnam had ended. The aftermath was becoming clear: people fleeing for fear of reprisals, refugees being housed in totally inadequate conditions, and suffering on a massive scale. The Lutheran Church, through a service arm called Lutheran Refugee Service, put out a call for congregations willing to host a refugee family or families. Hosting involved welcoming them to your community and helping them to get settled, find schooling or a job, and start the process of building a new life in a strange land. This was not something new for the Lutheran Church; following World War II, the Lutheran Church was instrumental in resettling thousands of refugees, and got pretty good at it.

But there were some differences this time. The new refugees didn't have relatives in the US already, like many of the WWII refugees had had. They were Asians and not Europeans—they didn't "look like us." They weren't "fellow Christians," but often Buddhists. There was widespread suspicion and distrust.

Nonetheless, the need was overwhelming. It was "all hands on deck" time. I called a special meeting of the Church Council to consider the possibility of our sponsoring a family for resettlement. Expecting opposition, I marshaled all the arguments, checked into what the possibilities might be in our town of 10,000 people regarding housing, education, employment, etc., and moved forward with some fear and trepidation.

The meeting began with prayer. I then explained the situation, drew the council's attention to some of the displays I had assembled, and asked them what they thought.

One of the members, a local businessman, raised his hand. "Isn't this what we're supposed to do as Christians?" he asked. "Yes," I responded. "Well then, I move that we sponsor a family right here in our town." The vote was unanimous.

Just like that.

Committees were formed. Plans were made. A family from a neighboring church called to offer help. Housing was secured. The local school district was notified and they began planning an English as a Second Language program. Volunteers were enlisted to assemble supplies. It seemed as if everyone was pitching in. All was ready and the waiting began.

Finally the day arrived. We organized a caravan to drive the seventy-five miles to the nearest large airport. Disembarking from the plane—disheveled, bewildered, overwhelmed—was a family of four. Small, frail-looking, and frightened, it was hard to imagine what these Vietnamese refugees had been through and our hearts went out to them. We loaded them and their few things into the cars and headed "home."

It was summer when our new neighbors arrived. They kind of settled in and got started on learning English and a whole new way of life. Summer turned to fall and the temperature started to drop. One day there was a knock at my office door. When I opened it, there was Tran. He had on a big parka, hood up, with a scarf around his neck. He proudly explained that he was learning to cope with the cold.

It was 55 degrees and sunny…

Winter's arrival in Northern Minnesota was brutal that year. On visits to their home, I found the windows fogged up and dripping water. They tried to maintain an eighty-five-degree temperature inside the house, while it was not unusual for the temperature outside to be twenty below zero. The family was beset with sniffles and colds. When spring arrived these folks announced they had made contact with relatives who had been previously resettled in California with a group of other Vietnamese refugees. The California group had gathered funds to buy bus tickets for them, and our new friends set off to a warmer new life in the Golden State.

There was genuine disappointment within our congregation and community. After a little discussion, the decision was made to sponsor another family. The second attempt resulted in a family from Laos coming into our midst. These folks were Hmong, some of the mountain tribespeople who had aided American forces and, as a result, were suffering horrible persecution and retaliation from their government after the US left.

More planning and arranging was undertaken. Once again, the seemingly interminable waiting was endured. Another "big day" came. Another caravan to the airport took place. Once again, a group of very bedraggled people got off the plane. This time there were nine folks—though we had been told there would be seven. (After several months had passed and some trust had been established, they confessed that two were not their children, but cousins whose family had been waiting in miserable conditions in a refugee camp for five years. The parents had decided to send their children for a chance at a new life in America with relatives rather than let them languish in the hopelessness of the camp.)

Once back from the airport and with several days of rest and re-orientation under their belts, we began the process of getting their new lives underway. With the help of an interpreter we started gathering information, hoping to minimize their disruption as much as possible. We asked the father in the group what his work had been in Laos. He proudly stood a little taller and informed us he had been the village chief. Since that job title of course didn't appear on any of the forms we were dealing with, after some discussion he agreed to be enrolled in a welding program at the local technical school.

Again, the harsh northern Minnesota winter proved extremely difficult, and in the spring the family moved south—to St. Paul. There was a burgeoning Hmong community already established there and arrangements had been made by relatives for them to resettle within that group.

While the final results in both of these situations were not what had been hoped for or envisioned by our congregation members, there was a sense that we had been able to help some fellow human beings caught up in the messiness of life in the 20th century.

Sincere thanks to former President George W. Bush for the perfect terminology for the title!

Picture Perfect

There is an old tradition in some places that there should be no weddings during Lent, the six-and-a-half-week period preceding Easter. Lent is traditionally regarded as a rather somber time of penitence, fasting, self-sacrifice, and preparation for the Easter feast and celebration. Traditions of all kinds can (and sometimes should) crumble, and this ban on weddings in Lent has largely disappeared, but in the late seventies in northern Minnesota, that was still the general custom.

They were a nice young couple. I can't remember the particulars—it may have been something about the groom being soon shipped overseas by the military—but it was decided that the Lenten ban on weddings could be overlooked in their specific instance.

They went through all the usual preparation steps, counseling sessions, wedding service planning procedures, everything.

The wedding was small. After the service the photographer took over, as they are wont to do: what seemed like a million different poses would be struck and photographed. In addition to the various group photos, there would be his hand on top of her hand with rings showing; her hand on top of his hand with rings showing; hands next to each other, rings showing—on and on. Knowing the drill, I asked the photographer if she could take any photos that would include me in them first, so that I could then be excused.

When I had completed my obligations to the photographic process there in the front of the sanctuary, I left to go change out of my clerical robe. The photographer continued taking pictures up front, and when I got to the back of the church and through the doors to the narthex, I encountered my associate pastor. He was laughing his head off. "What's so funny?" I queried. "Turn around and look at the front of the sanctuary," he replied.

From the rear of the church and now being able to see the whole sanctuary interior, I immediately got his laughter. Above the chancel at the front of the church was hanging our traditional Lenten banner.

These good folks had gotten married under Jesus' words: "Father, forgive them, for they know not what they do."

I hoped all the pictures were close-ups instead of wide pans.

Generous Heart

Carl and Mollie were an older married couple in the congregation. He was a slight, reserved man with thick, "coke-bottle-bottom" spectacles; she was a tall, heavyset woman with an engaging yet somewhat halting smile.

Retired, they were faithful in worship, never missing a Sunday. They owned a Nash Rambler American—a subcompact before there were subcompacts. Carl always drove the car, and even when he was sitting bolt upright he could not see over the steering wheel, but rather peered through it, with his coke-bottle glasses distorting his eyes. Their car was battered and bent, showing evidence of many run-ins with (hopefully) stationary objects. When that car pulled into the parking lot on Sunday mornings, everyone scattered.

I got a call from a tearful Mollie one day, informing me that Carl had died. I went over to the house and she and I visited for quite a while. She told me of their relationship, their history, and their love for each other. They were childless, and so just she and I made some preliminary plans for the funeral and she asked if, after the funeral, I would be willing to go to their hometown some forty miles to the north, to preside at the committal service in the cemetery beside the church there. Of course I would.

After Carl's funeral, I established the pattern of visiting Mollie once a month to bring her Communion. Since she didn't drive, she couldn't get to church. Plus, as is often the case with survivors, Mollie found that when she did accept offers of a ride to church, she found it too painful to sit alone during the service and remember, so she stopped attending. Some of the members of the congregation would pick her up for outings and shopping, etc., to stay in touch with her, but she couldn't bring herself to come back to church and the wonderful, now turned painful, memories there.

One day, one of the church members who counted the offering on Monday mornings came to see me. She said she was concerned that Mollie was giving too much money to the church; each month Mollie would send a sizeable check. This church member was also a volunteer who would take Mollie to get groceries, and told me that Mollie had stopped shopping at the supermarket and was going only to the food bank and thrift store.

On my next Communion visit, I broached the subject with Mollie. Upon entering her very modest home that day, I noticed several different items that hadn't been there before—small and large crosses, models of church buildings, posters and printed materials from various televangelists. Apparently, in addition to supporting our congregation, she was also contributing to several TV evangelists. I told her that people at the church were concerned that she was giving too much money to the church to the detriment of her own health and well-being.

Mollie started to cry softly. We sat in silence for a time.

Finally, through her tears, she said to me, "Pastor, would you take away from me the last joy I have in life?"

I arranged to visit again, bringing along another member of the congregation who was a financial planner to help her get a sustainable budget together. But I was also deeply moved by her well-intentioned generosity and commitment to the church.

Recorder Quartet

It was the big Scandinavian Family Festival in the mostly-Scandinavian small town. The church was decorated with all the Christmas trimmings. The whole community had been invited for a Carol Sing, to be followed by a feast with all the traditional Scandinavian holiday goodies. The sanctuary was packed—three hundred-plus in attendance.

In addition to the singing of carols, there were some specially-prepared musical numbers on the program. One of the special items was a recorder quartet made up of four music teachers from the local schools.

At the appointed time the teachers moved to the front of the sanctuary, set up their music stands, and began to play their selection. They were right in front of the very front pew—where my wife and two young children were seated. My daughter, Karen, four years old and dressed in all her Christmas finery, knew what was coming after the caroling. She was waiting for the after-singing lefse and cookies with all the patience she could muster as the musical numbers piled up.

The recorder is generally an accessible instrument, but there are of course varying levels of competence and artistry. The quartet was trying hard, but they were not "delivering a stellar performance," shall we say. Everyone in the sanctuary was uncomfortable and there was quite a lot of shifting in the seats.

Right in the middle of their playing, my daughter stood up on the front pew directly in front of the performers, turned to face the whole congregation, and with both hands gave a gigantic, exaggerated "thumbs down" sign.

I can't remember what followed.

They say mortification dulls the memory.

Christmas Surprise

Christmas brought gaily decorated stores, carols playing endlessly on the radio, images of Santa all over the place, and preparations for the Sunday School Christmas Program.

The congregation was fairly large and young; the Sunday School had over one hundred students. The decision was made to do something special for the program this year—there was a young couple who were expecting a baby early in December, and they were approached about having their newborn as the "star" of the show. They agreed.

An elevated platform was borrowed from the local school for the stage. Costumes were assembled. Several rehearsals were held. The star of the show was born healthy and happy. The day of the production arrived.

The little girl playing Mary was proud and very poised. "Joseph" was a little embarrassed to be playing that part. The pageant went pretty much according to plan with the appropriate carols being sung in the appropriate places. The newborn baby actor was doing great. He was actually "asleep on the hay," much to everyone's delight (and relief).

The angels had appeared and delivered their message in song to the shepherds, who wended their way to the stable. Upon the shepherds' arrival, the one glitch in all the planning and practicing became apparent. Either no one had informed them that the doll they had used in rehearsal would be replaced by a live child, or, more likely, the shepherds had been messing around and hadn't gotten the message.

When the large band of ragged-looking shepherds arrived, climbed the stairs to the stage and approached the manger, they looked in it and their mouths fell open. One of the shepherds rushed to the edge of the stage closest to the audience and with eyes wide, wide open, shouted out: "HEY MOM!! THEY'RE USING A *REAL* BABY!!!"

It was one of the more memorable Christmas pageants in congregational history.

A Listening Ear...Enough?

She was lovely. That's the best word I can think of.

Not beautiful. Not gorgeous. She was lovely.

She knocked on my door out of the blue. To my knowledge, I had never seen her before. She sat down and began her story. Her husband was in the service. Marines, I think. He was an MP. They were both far from home. Home was "down South."

They had been away from home for some months, and were living off base in a small apartment.

It had started a couple of months before. Her husband came home one day, put on a pair of white gloves, and announced an "inspection." He went through the house with the white gloves, looking for dirt. When his gloved hand came back from the top of a door frame, there it was. Dirt! He slapped her and stomped off to the bedroom.

A short time later he came out of the bedroom. He had been crying. He apologized. They hugged. They had dinner.

A couple of weeks later it happened again. "Inspection." White gloves. Dirt. This time the punishment was more than just a slap. Once again, he headed for the bedroom. Once again, the red-eyed apology.

This pattern was repeating itself more and more frequently. The punishments becoming more and more severe.

She insisted he wasn't "bad," just "mixed up" or "confused" or "frightened"—or something.

I started trying to explore with her the various options there might be through the military, or the community, or the church.

She had begun to cry softly. Jumping up she headed for the door. Opening the door, she stopped and looked back at me, "I just had to tell somebody. Thanks for listening." And she was gone. I followed her to the parking lot, but just as quickly as she had arrived, she drove away.

I didn't sleep well for a couple of weeks.

She was lovely. I felt I had failed her. I never saw her again.

Plant Doctors

The church sat kitty-corner across the street from the junior high school. Two of the junior high girls, who were also confirmation students in the congregation, lived on the other side of the church from the school, so they walked through the church parking lot to get home every day. Once in a while the two girls would stop in to the church just to chat.

I had developed a reputation in the congregation as the "plant killer." Several women had decided that I really needed a plant or two in my office. They would graciously provide a plant with complete instructions on how to care for it, but no matter what I would do, the plants would die. Even the cactus died.

My reputation was well deserved.

One day Myrtle had called with another offer of a plant for my office. I reminded her of my reputation and she said there was little chance that I could kill her dieffenbachia. She had it in the basement, but it was getting too big for the room. It was four feet tall and doing well. When she brought it into the office I had to agree that it was a nice addition to the room.

The plant flourished in my office, soon becoming as tall as I. It kept growing until it started to scrape the eight-foot office ceiling. One day I opened my office door to find the plant lying down on the floor. Feeling absolutely horrible, I called Myrtle and explained the situation. "Oh, that's no problem," she said cheerily. "Just get a knife, cut the stem into one-foot segments, stick each segment into a pot of dirt, water from time to time, and you'll have eight new plants. Keep one for yourself and give the rest away!"

Not much of a gardener, I did feel obligated to follow Myrtle's instructions—it was, after all, her plant. I made the cuts, gave seven away, and put the now one-foot-tall stick that I had chosen to keep on a shelf in my study and pretty much forgot about it.

A few days later, the two junior high students stopped in to chat, and they asked about the forlorn-looking stick in the pot on the shelf. I explained the whole situation and they were astounded. One of them walked over to the shelf, grabbed the foot-long stick, pulled it out of the dirt and after exploring the base said, "Nope. No roots yet!" We laughed as she replaced the stick in the pot.

The visits from the girls continued almost weekly. Each visit was the occasion for another inspection of the plant/stick. The girls started calling themselves the "plant doctors," and we continued laughing at the hapless stick that made no progress.

One day, taking a break from whatever project was on my desk, I glanced over at the dieffenbachia—still a one-inch-in-diameter, one-foot-tall green stick in a pot—and noticed what looked like a small bump on the side of it. Going over a little closer, sure enough there it was. I went and got some water and moved the plant a little more into the sunlight. That afternoon, when the plant doctors made their visit, I jumped up to defend the plant from being pulled out of the dirt for the weekly examination. Though the bump was barely discernable, the docs agreed it was definitely there.

The plant doctors and I thoroughly enjoyed watching that dieffenbachia grow and flourish, just as Myrtle had assured, throughout the rest of their junior high careers.

A few years later I was the speaker at their high school Baccalaureate Service. I brought the dieffenbachia, by that time a full five feet tall, told the story of the plant doctors, and tied it to Psalm 1—"Like a tree that's planted by the water..." I encouraged the students to find some water wherever they got planted after graduation (find a congregation, a presence of the "living water"), and put down roots.

A few years ago, one of the plant docs called me out of the blue. She's been a social worker in a hospital for many years. After we got caught up a little, she said, "Do you remember that dieffenbachia?"

We shared a good laugh.

"I'm the church council president in my congregation here in my new town," she told me.

She'd put down roots, and she remembered the psalmist's lesson.

Vision in the Mirror

Jarred into consciousness by the incessant ringing of the doorbell. I tried to focus on the clock. 5:30 a.m.

I quickly and clumsily pulled on a robe and rushed to the door hoping that my three- and five-year-olds, sleeping soundly, wouldn't be disturbed. On the doorstep was Mark, a young adult member of our congregation. He was married and the father of a preschooler. The family was marginally active in the congregation but I knew them best because of the big hug I always got from their little daughter whenever they came out the door after church.

Mark was a little hard to recognize this particular morning, because he was standing rigidly, arms raised slightly, face stiff and distorted. He said nothing—just stood there, panting slowly, evenly, heavily. Quite disconcerted, I stepped out onto the landing with him, staying between him and the door out of some concern for my family inside. "What's the matter?" I asked. In a loud, gravelly voice that I wouldn't have recognized as his, he replied slowly, between panting breaths, "I'm...possessed." Quite taken aback, I asked, "What do you mean?"

Slowly, almost painfully, and between his continued deep pants he said, "I was (pant) shaving (pant). As I (pant) looked in the (pant) mirror (pant) my face (pant) changed (pant)." He continued in this disjointed manner to explain that his face appeared to him to be half his normal face but with red stripes running up and down through it while the other half was the face of the devil. The wild look in his eyes as he described this while still panting loudly was deeply disturbing.

Because of my family inside, I did not want to invite him into the house, so I told him to wait in his car while I dressed and we could go over to the church to talk. He agreed and I rushed inside, making sure to lock the door behind me. Pulling on clothes as fast as I could, and with a hurried explanation to my spouse, I went on out to find Mark leaning on his car and appearing somewhat more "normal."

He followed my car in his to the church, and by the time we got there his breathing was more regular and he seemed to have calmed down. We went to the church kitchen and I put some coffee on. By now, Mark was much more relaxed and acting like himself. We were able to talk about the incident somewhat matter-of-factly, but it was clear that he was extremely upset and agitated, and he was convinced of the reality of what had happened and what he had seen in the mirror. He insisted it was no dream or delusion—it was very real and very frightening. After several cups of coffee and a couple episodes of him ranting and crying, I suggested that it might be good for Mark to meet my good friend, Steve, who worked at the hospital; he was the psychologist who headed the psych unit.

It really took some coaxing, a lot of reassurance, and some attempt at humor and connection by recounting to him my recent fishing trip with Steve during which he'd managed to hook me in the face while attempting to cast his lure into the lake, to get Mark to agree to go. I called Steve at home to ask him to come to the hospital early, and he met us there. He was able to establish a good relationship with Mark right away, and I left the two of them talking intently.

I never saw Mark again. He was admitted to the locked psych ward of the hospital and later transferred to a state-run facility. His wife and kids moved to be closer to her folks. She didn't want to talk to me. There was no further information available on his condition or progress. I wonder to this day whatever happened to him and his family.

Misunderstanding Put to Rest

Most Lutheran churches that I know of follow the practice of having an annual meeting, usually in January when the new year is just beginning. This is, logically, the time to review what has happened in the congregation the year before, and make plans for the coming year. While the function is universal, the form of this meeting can vary greatly depending on the circumstances of the congregation.

For the country church I was serving, Black River Lutheran, the annual meeting was a festive event. Usually preceded by a potluck, the meeting was informal though comprehensive in nature. The reports from the various committees were heard, elections were held, and the budget for the next year was discussed and approved.

And then the final event: a list of four or five worthy recipients would be presented by the pastor, such as Lutheran Social Services, the church camp, a nearby children's home, Lutheran World Relief, maybe a local family in dire straits, or some other known need. When the choice of one or two was made, a motion was then made to give them virtually everything that was left in the treasury, keeping just $1.00 in the account.

Mind you—one of the regular budget items was always the standard "Benevolence" item, a category which itself includes support of the regional and national church structures and organizations like Lutheran Social Services, Lutheran World Relief, Lutheran Disaster Services, etc. Even so, each year they disbursed any remaining funds and started the New Year with just one dollar in the bank! The generosity of these folks was inspiring.

And so that's why I was caught off guard one year when, at the very end of the meeting before adjournment, but after everything else had been covered, one of the members stood and said, "There's one more thing. Pastor, several of us have been talking and we think you are way overpaid." He went on to explain, "Last year, with your salary and benefits you made much more than I did—and I farm over a thousand acres. We think that's wrong!"

I was stunned. Stunned and hurt. Fighting hard to be calm and measured, I said, "You know that's not right, Darwin. You are comparing your total *profit*—what you have left *after* your new tractor" (which a friend who was an implement dealer had previously explained to me cost more than my house), "new pickup, your summer vacation which you take annually after planting, your winter vacation" (which always included a trip to the Super Bowl before they went overseas), "and all your other bills are paid. You are comparing your profit amount to my salary, from which I have to make my house payments, car payments, and feed and clothe my family. That comparison just isn't fair."

Someone quickly made a motion to adjourn the meeting and everyone hurried home.

The next morning my first office visitor was Darwin. "Pastor, you were right last night," he said. "I'm sorry for the totally wrong comparison. Period. But," he continued, "there is a part of my life you don't understand either. Every year I go to the bank and borrow $25,000" (roughly $125,000 in today's dollars). "I use it to buy seed and I go out and plant that seed in the ground.

Yup. Bury it. I have no guarantee that anything will come of it. It could rain and flood and I'd be washed out. There could be drought conditions and the seed would all dry up and die. No guarantee whatsoever. It's a huge gamble— I'm a gambler. Some years I win. And there are years when I lose—lose big."

I acknowledged that all that information was new to me, and I appreciated learning it from him.

We looked at each other in silence for a long time. Though we looked at each other over a huge chasm, a chasm between our lived experiences so wide and deep that I don't think either of us could ever fully understand the situation of the other, still I think we each realized in each other a common concern for people, for the physical needs as well as the emotional and spiritual needs of others.

Darwin stood to go. He paused at the door, turned, and said, "Thanks. You're doing a good job, keep it up." He left.

A few seconds later the door opened again. "I'm really sorry."

Then he was off to the Super Bowl. And Egypt.

Long-Distance Pastoral Care

Darlene was our kids' favorite babysitter. Always smiling, kind, and thoughtful, she was also our favorite as parents. She graduated from high school and decided to pursue a course of study that would take her to another state—her first venture out "on her own." Her family was very close and it was hard for them to see her go. Her new school was in a distant state in a mid-sized city. I got reports that she had settled in and was doing well.

It was surprising to get a phone call from her one evening—surprising and upsetting to hear her quiet sobs. "Would you be willing to go out to the farm to be with my folks tomorrow when I call? I have some news for them that will be very upsetting." (Long pause.) "…I'm pregnant." There followed a flood of tears.

After I had agreed to go to be with her parents, and her tears had subsided, I heard her story. Lonely and frightened, she was befriended by a "nice guy." One thing led to another and she became pregnant. Mr. Nice Guy took off and now she was alone with no idea of where to go or what to do. I got her phone number and location and when we hung up I went to our denomination's yearbook. Each of the six thousand-plus congregations in our denomination was listed in this resource and I tried to find the one closest to her location. There were four congregations in her city and (before

Google Maps) the one that seemed to be closest to her was one of the smaller ones. I called the pastor and introduced myself. Explaining the situation, I learned that this pastor was, indeed, close to her location, was aware of several resources in the community that could be helpful to her, and, if she wished, was willing to get involved to help her.

The drive to the family farm the next day was not that far, but the dread in my heart made it seem like forever. When I arrived the parents were already upset from the unusual arrangement of my visit coupled with the mysterious call that had been set up by their daughter, and had figured out pretty much what the situation was. The tears were flowing by the time I got there, and when the phone rang they flooded. Mom was all supportive and wanted to head out right away. Dad wanted to be stern and gruff, but he ended up crying harder than his wife. Darlene resisted her parents' entreaties to "come home right this minute," and informed them that she planned to stay where she was and continue her education. When I reported on my finding a resource in Darlene's community, the parents relented.

Her parents and I stayed in close touch with each other as the weeks and months went on. The pastor in Darlene's town was absolutely phenomenal. He got her into a community prenatal clinic. The community food bank, located in his church, got good nutritional food to her (some of it in the form of hot meals prepared by his parishioners and delivered with loving care). The knowledge of the loving concern and care she was getting buoyed both her worried parents and me.

Finally, the call we anticipated the most came. It was a girl! Now there was no holding her parents back. In spite of her protestations that she and the baby were just fine, the grandparents were on their way to visit, support, and help.

I never had a chance to see the mother and child before I moved on to another parish, but I truly felt that a better example of the church at work is hard to imagine.

Heavy Burden

Dave was a farmer, a single guy in his early forties. We didn't see him much in church, but he was part of a family that went way back with the congregation. He dropped in one day and asked if I had a minute. We sat down and started to chat. He was not involved in Alcoholics Anonymous, he told me, but "had been looking at some of their stuff." He wondered if some of their ideas were good. I said yes, I thought some of their ideas were really good.

He was intrigued with the fifth step of the twelve-step program, where the person admits to themselves, to God, and to another person that they are powerless over alcohol and the exact nature of wrongs they may have committed. We talked some more and finally he blurted out, "I'd like to take that fifth step right now."

In AA that fifth step is often taken with a pastor or other spiritual advisor. I had never formally "heard" someone's fifth step admission myself, but since Dave wasn't actually in an AA program, and I had done quite a bit of work on AA in seminary, I felt that I could do that for him and said, "Okay."

When Dave began, it was obvious he had been thinking about this a lot. He started his narrative back in grade school. There were fights and bullying and cheating on schoolwork and on and on. We worked our way through junior and senior high school. These memories were of specific people he had hurt, situations he had caused or been involved with, and sometimes feelings he felt were wrong or "shameful"—a word he used quite often.

At about the one-hour mark, I asked if he'd like a cup of coffee. We took a break while I brewed a pot. Settling back into our chairs, we picked up where we had left off. After another hour I thought he may have run out of things to get off his chest. By now we were down to some really petty things—things anyone would have felt were questionable as to their seriousness.

Then Dave fell quiet. He paused a long time, and then started weeping softly. Finally, he said, "There's one more thing, Pastor. I've never told this to anyone. One night, years ago, my friend and I, he was my drinking buddy, got drunk. He was in real trouble financially with his farm. It was so bad the bank was threatening foreclosure. He couldn't see a way out. Our 'stinkin' thinkin'' from the booze hatched a plot. We could burn down his barn, collect the insurance money, pay off the debt, and he'd be home free. We went and got some cans of gasoline, doused the barn real well, and threw in a match. Then we went up the hill to watch it burn.

"We sat down under a tree and watched the flames grow and spread, telling ourselves how clever we were. All of a sudden, we could hear the horses. We were so drunk we'd forgotten to turn the horses out of the barn! The horses, six of 'em, were trapped. They were crying out, desperate, kicking the walls, trying to escape..."

With tears now streaming down his face, he managed to choke out, "They were all killed—burned to death." The emotion which he had been trying so mightily to contain poured out with his flood of tears. He wept bitterly and loudly for a long time. When finally there were no more tears, he slumped back into his chair and stared off into some inner world.

After a bit, composure somewhat regained, he seemed to sort of wake up and sat up straight. "I'm sorry," he croaked in a rough whisper. "I'm so, so sorry. Can I ever make it up? Can I ever look myself in the mirror again?"

I explained that the AA program talks about "making amends." Even though he was not involved in the actual program, it was clear that he was very familiar with its tenets and teachings. He said he had been wrestling with that concept for some time and was starting to formulate some ideas.

We sat in silence for a long time. Finally, tears starting to run down his cheeks again, he whispered hoarsely, "Could I have Communion, Pastor?"

We went into the sanctuary. He knelt at the altar rail while I went into the sacristy to get the elements. After receiving the sacrament, Dave got up slowly, and with the assurance of God's love and forgiveness fresh in his mind causing the flow of tears to start up again, hugged me so hard that it hurt, turned, and went out of the church.

I never saw Dave again. I tried to follow up with him, to no avail. As time passed I was called to another parish, and moved without ever being successful in making more contact with him.

Danny and the Guinea Pig

The last day of Sunday School for the year was always marked by recognitions and thank-yous during church, followed by a pancake brunch. One year after the brunch, a few of us continued sitting around and visiting while the kids were playing and enjoying the beautiful late spring weather.

My son Danny and his classmate, both four years old, were down in the end of the other wing of the building. There was a daycare group that used that part of the building during the week, and the children from the church, even though they weren't supposed to, liked to go and see the various displays and toys there for the daycare's use.

Settling in with my second cup of coffee, I was suddenly interrupted by one of the older kids running into the fellowship hall shouting, "Pastor, Pastor! You better come quick! Danny just drowned the guinea pig!"

The daycare center had a pet guinea pig that had been a bone of real contention for some time. Though they tried to keep it clean, it would constantly throw the sawdust, along with what was on the sawdust, out of its cage. It smelled up that whole end of the building. Instead of just eating its food, it would throw pieces of its food out of the cage, which then attracted mice. I confess I hated this little monster, and everyone in the congregation knew it, and loved to tease me about it.

When I ran into the daycare room, I found a group of children standing in a circle watching a thoroughly drenched guinea pig lying on the floor hiccupping its last. The other kids scattered and I was left alone with my son. "What happened?" I asked. Danny answered, "Jon and I were playing with the guinea pig. We were being funny fellows and we put him in different containers—his food dish, the waste basket, the desk drawer..."

The last place they put him was the aquarium. Turns out guinea pigs don't swim well. They fished him out, and put him on the floor.

Now came the dilemma. What the boys had done was wrong and they needed to know that. But I didn't want death associated with punishment. I felt I was walking a tightrope.

Someone took care of the little deceased animal, and I told Danny we were going home and we would talk about what had happened when we got there. Taking him by the hand, we walked down the hallway to the parking lot to go home. Along the length of the hall were people who all knew how much I hated the guinea pig, graciously trying hard to keep from laughing, and being totally unsuccessful.

When we got home, he and I had a long talk about boundaries and why it was wrong for him to have been in the daycare center in the first place. I explained that there would have to be some kind of punishment for him violating the prohibition on being in the daycare center rooms—but trying not to associate the punishment with the death of the guinea pig. He seemed to understand and accept the verdict.

Then...a couple days after the incident, with things pretty much back to normal at home, Danny came to me and said, "Dad, can I ask you something?" "Sure," I said. "Did the guinea pig die?" "Yes, the guinea pig died." That was it—he ran off.

A few days later he came and asked, "Dad, do people die?" "Yes, people die." Again, that was it.

Another few days passed. Then he came and said, "Dad, do dads die?" "Yes, Danny, dads die too."

And that was it.

It seemed that was enough.

Powerful memory.

Full Disclosure

The town church, Redeemer, was growing rapidly and the need for additional space, especially for our large Sunday School, was apparent. Plans had been drawn for a building addition. Application for a loan from the national church body had been submitted and approved. One of the conditions of the loan approval was that a Capital Fund Appeal must be conducted using a fundraising group from the national church. Theirs was a uniform, "cookie cutter" approach, designed and implemented by a group of dedicated laymen from the East Coast.

Now, there is a world of difference between the East Coast and our little Midwestern farming community, but that didn't seem to register; or if it registered, it didn't seem to matter to our assigned campaign director. Clarence was a retired money manager who was now working for a group that had been organized to help Lutheran churches in the area of fundraising, primarily for building additions. He arrived in town, rented a room, and started working furiously.

He worked down his checklist. Committee enlisted—check. Committee chair selected—check. Campaign title and slogan—check. Campaign brochure printed—check.

One day he came into my office and said, "Pastor, we need to talk about the stewardship sermon you need to preach to kick off this campaign." I was nonplussed. Each year in the fall, when the congregation was starting to work on a budget for the next year, I would try to touch—though (very) gently—upon the topic of stewardship. Our congregation's budget had been growing modestly, but mostly because of the growth in numbers in the congregation.

Now Clarence, this "foreigner" from the East Coast, was in my office telling me not only *what* I had to preach about, but *how* to do it. You see, he presented me with an outline of sorts. I read it over. Without going into the details, it was not at all like something I might ever normally preach. I pointed out to him where I disagreed with what he had presented and how his heavy-handedness would be a total turn-off to the "nice" people of the Upper Midwest. The discussion got really heated, but we both hung in there. I conceded that he and his organization had many more years of experience and much more success in terms of fundraising than did I. And he agreed that his "big city, East Coast" understanding of the world and of people's mindsets might not fit rural northwestern Minnesota.

We went back and forth, back and forth, and finally came to an approach we both could live with—with one major exception. His organization had found it to be absolutely essential that for a campaign to be successful, the pastor must disclose, in a sermon, the specific amount that he and his family (this was still before the ordination of women in our denomination) were pledging to the campaign. I was firmly opposed to doing that; I felt the amount was a private matter. We ended the heated discussion and he left, with no resolution on that one big sticking point.

One sleepless night followed another as I wrestled with this issue. I thought back and I remembered Milt Hanson back in Pierre who had had such a powerful impact on my life with his witness to his giving pattern. I also remembered the jarring impact back in seminary, when we learned that one of our seminary professors didn't just tithe (donate ten percent), but rather donated forty percent of his income back to the various branches of the church. (For clarity, it should be noted that he was retired and drawing a pension, as well as Social Security and his salary as a full professor—but still...)

I decided to give in. I preached the sermon he wanted me to. I told about the Capital Fund Appeal, how important it was to the life of the congregation, how desperately we needed the space for the large and growing number of kids in our Sunday School. I concluded by stating that my family had made a pledge to the Fund already, and what the amount of that pledge was—all according to Clarence's script.

First thing Monday morning the phone rang. I had hardly settled into my chair when I found myself getting lambasted by the voice on the other end. What did I think I was doing? Didn't I know how unfair it was? Of all things!! "For you, the pastor of the church, to brag about giving to this building campaign when everyone knows that pastors don't donate anything to the church because the church pays them!" She went on and on and on. I waited until she ran out of gas.

Marilyn was one of the less active members of the congregation; her husband had a job that often took him away from town on weekends and she often was left at home with their young family. I barely knew her but was certainly getting to know her now. I waited patiently, listening as calmly as possible as she blew off steam.

Once she was out of breath, I started trying to correct her misconceptions;

I was very frank with her. 1) I told her our family did indeed contribute to the congregation just like (hopefully) every other congregational member. 2) I chose to tell her the exact amount of our family's weekly contribution (which, I had been told by the financial secretary in an unguarded moment, made us the second largest giving unit in the congregation—I did not include that point in my conversation with Marilyn). And 3) I asked her not to repeat these numbers to anyone, in order to respect my right to confidentiality.

There was a long, long silence at the other end of the line. Then, I heard crying. "Oh, Pastor, I'm so embarrassed," she stammered. "I had no idea..." She sobbed for a couple of minutes on the other end of the line and then said, "You need to tell this to the whole congregation. People *need* to know this. You have to promise me that you will tell everyone about this phone call. Please don't use my name, but please, promise me!"

"Let me think about that," I replied.

There followed a few more sleepless nights as I wrestled with both Marilyn's request and Clarence's ongoing demands. I finally agreed in my mind and set out to write the second sermon. It started with a recounting of my phone conversation with Marilyn. I did not use her name or anything else that would enable anyone to identify her, but I did give all the numbers, both my family's pledge to the general church budget fund and, again, our pledge to the new building fund. It was very quiet in the church. I tried to be matter-of-fact and informative. I strove to not trigger guilt, but rather to encourage generosity.

Clarence was ecstatic, aside from the several suggestions he made about how "it could have been more forceful," or something to that effect. We completed the other steps he'd laid out in the lead-up to receiving the pledges.

When the pledges came in, we had met our goal, and then some.

A small side note: I got a visit from the financial secretary at the end of the year. She reported that, as she'd mentioned before, up until that year our family had been the second-largest giving unit in the congregation. This in a congregation that included several professional people, a couple of successful business leaders in the community, and a few really big farmers. But that year, my family became the tenth-largest giving unit in the congregation—and our giving had not decreased. You do the math...!

Oh, and the building fund campaign? Very successful.

Score one for Clarence.

Explosive

It was the final session of the four-part series of pre-marriage counseling meetings that I typically had with couples before each wedding. They had previously completed a written inventory of attitudes and concerns about the upcoming wedding. We had gone over each of the issues raised. I thought it had gone well—nothing out of the ordinary. We had planned the service, which was now about two weeks away. The invitations had gone out, caterer had been contracted, and arrangements were mostly completed.

They came into my study in silence. They sat at opposite ends of the six-foot couch, looking as if they wished it were longer. The silence was deafening. After a bit she broke down weeping, while he sat seething in apparent anger.

After a long period of tense silence, she blurted out through copious tears, "I don't think I can go through with it! But all the invitations have been sent, and RSVPs have already come back. My parents have spent a ton of money already. Everything is in place. They'll kill me if I cancel now." I assured her that her parents wanted, above all, for her to be happy. I knew they would much rather be out a little money than to have her go on into an unhappy marriage. I offered to go with her to see her parents and help explain the situation if she thought that would help.

With the tears becoming a torrent, she thanked me profusely, sank back into the couch and sobbed.

Meanwhile, I could see the silent would-be groom becoming more and more enraged. The bulging veins in his face and neck pretty much told the story. He leaped to his feet, his face distorted in fury. He began by cursing, first at his now ex-bride-to-be and then at me. The cursing done, he approached me, stuck his nose into my face, and informed me that he had been an Army Ranger demolitions expert and that whenever I started my car from then on, I should think about that.

I explained the dim view I took of threats like that and suggested he remove himself at that point before I called the police.

The ex-bride-to-be called home, said that she and I were coming out to the farm with some bad news, and then went completely to pieces.

When we got to the farm, the bride's parents had already figured out the reason for our visit. Her mom enfolded her in a giant bear hug, her dad nearby. When the hugging and crying died down a little, we began to walk through what had happened. Her parents were as supportive as they could possibly be. The plans for notifying the former expected guests began, and I took my leave. As I got out to the car, the father caught up to me and thanked me deeply. Both he and his wife had been uncomfortable with the proposed marriage, and were greatly relieved to see this end.

Several years later, I did perform a wedding for this young woman and her new fiancé. No drama, no change of heart, and no histrionics; smiles and joy and laughter prevailed.

There never was a bomb. But I have to admit I did look over my shoulder and hold my breath when I started my car for quite a spell after that.

All Things Made New

Stan was a colorful guy. He was a near-legend around town. A local boy, he had built a very successful construction company from the ground up (so to speak). In a highly competitive field, his firm had been a standout. With that success, in addition to financial reward came incredible stress. There were always deadlines to be met, bids to be completed, employees to be hired and managed, new projects to take on. It was a lot.

In everything he did, when he did it, he did it big! Unfortunately, that included his drinking. I imagine it started small—maybe a "relaxer," or a "celebration." But it grew—boy, did it grow. Once he told me, with that alcoholic's strange sense of pride/shame, that he had been famous around town for bringing his dog to the bars with him and ordering drinks for the dog. His other claim to fame—again the pride/shame conflation—was that he would light cigarettes for himself and others with fifty-dollar bills.

His fame grew until he lost everything. It all came crashing down, and Stan was admitted for treatment.

After a long and complicated rehab process, he was back in town and rebuilding his business. But he had lost so much—not just the actual business, but his home, his wife, and his kids, and also the trust of many in the town.

So, when his was the best proposal for our building project—in terms of cost, appearance, timeline, and every other metric we could think of—a tough decision had to be made. Do we actually believe in redemption? Do we believe in new beginnings? Do we believe that "all things are being made new"?

We made the plunge. And Stan turned out to be a total gift. His rehab complete, he had immersed himself in AA, and that powerful program had helped him to re-establish himself in his field and in our community. He knew construction from front to back. He knew people who knew people. And because of help from the church in his rehab process, he was committed to the church and the Lord of the Church.

Long story short, we signed a contract with Stan. He took our preliminary drawings, made a few suggestions, got a structural engineer to draw up plans, and came up with a marvelous addition to the church building that has served well for many years.

Thank you, Stan. Thank you, Alcoholics Anonymous. Thank you, God.

Saint Peter, the VW, and the Cop

It was Lent. Both the town and the country congregations were doing mid-week Lenten services on Wednesday evenings. The services were preceded each week by a simple soup supper in keeping with the Lenten tradition of self-denial. Our theme that year was "People Around the Cross," and my creative associate pastor had written monologues for congregation members to portray different biblical characters each week, dramatizing their parts in the Lenten story. There was a woman in the congregation who made/assembled costumes for each of the characters.

This particular week the character was Saint Peter, and he was being portrayed by my associate himself. He had memorized the script, worked on the dramatic presentation of it, and performed it first at that evening's service in the town church. The drive to get out to the country church was at least seventeen minutes. To be on the safe side, we had scheduled the two churches' Wednesday Lenten services to allow for thirty. What could possibly go wrong?

Well, we went a little overtime at the first service. And then it proved more difficult, and time-consuming, to load a fully-costumed Saint Peter into my Volkswagen Beetle than to get someone in street clothes into it. The one traffic light on our way out of town seemed to stay red forever. But with a little extra courage and the wind at our back, we figured we still had a chance to be on time.

Out on the open road, I decided to bend the speed limit a little, to make sure we'd make our service time at the country church. The VW was responding quite well, when, what to my wondering eyes should appear?

But a red light…though, no, not the nose of a reindeer.

The officer—obviously not familiar with midweek Lenten services, and just as obviously not amused at the theatrically-costumed, bearded, and grinning pastor in the passenger's seat accompanied by a liturgically-robed and clerical-collared racecar driver behind the wheel—took a long while to get his head around the situation. He took my driver's license and returned to his car to call it in.

I later learned that the man working the dispatcher's desk that night was a friend of mine, who was Catholic and so was familiar with Lenten services. Jim had immediately figured out what the whole situation was and later told me he'd tried to encourage the officer to speed things up. Instead, all the background checks and driver's license check, etc., seemed to be intentionally "slow-walked" by the cop. When he sauntered back to my car window to return my license, insurance card, and registration, there was no hint of amusement. In fact, he seemed to relish handing me my ticket for speeding (seventy-five dollars, please).

The people at Black River Church, however, laughed heartily when we arrived twenty minutes late, and related the story. They laughed even harder when I tried to explain that I would be leaving the ticket with the church treasurer since it was earned "in the line of duty," after all.

Nope, they wouldn't let me get away with that—darn!

Camp Buddy

The kid was a problem. No matter what the camp activity was—meal time, study sessions, recreation, discussion time, quiet/rest time, swimming, lights out—the kid was a problem. Even among the generally rowdy, fun-loving pre-teens, he was a problem.

Finally, his cabin counselor asked if I would step in and help. The counselors were college kids recruited to work at the camp during their summer break. As a pastor volunteering a week at our church camp, I was largely present to help with questions that might come up in discussion sessions, and to relate to the kids in informal settings, or if they wanted to talk about something in particular.

There were about a hundred kids each week, from congregations in small towns all across the Dakotas and Northwestern Minnesota, each with a different background and with a different expectation of what "Church Camp" or "Bible Camp" might be like.

Robbie was a smallish kid, and a loner. He didn't seem to be friends with any of the kids from his home community. And he was a troublemaker in every sense of the word.

I attached myself to Robbie. His schedule became my schedule. When he was in a study session, I was in that session (sitting in close proximity). When he acted up during recreation activities, I was there. When he disrupted a serious discussion, I moved to sit right next to him. When he decided to display his remarkable collection of vulgarity, I took his arm and escorted him away.

We developed a special relationship that week, and a pattern seemed to develop. He would disrupt some activity—meal, discussion, sport competition, even swimming—and then he and I would move away from the group to "talk."

And did we talk. We talked about him—his home, his life, his family. He was nervous about going home from camp because his dad would be there when he got home. He hadn't seen his dad for a couple of years—since before he got sent to prison. And, Robbie's mom would be gone when he got home. She was starting *her* sentence. He thought he might be going to live with his aunt and uncle. He wasn't sure.

Life had been hard for Robbie. Home was uncertain. Meals were sketchy. Supervision for him and his siblings was almost non-existent. He really seemed to need someone to talk to—some adult who would listen to him, encourage him, hear him out…care about him. At camp, I became that someone.

I finally just accepted that role of caring adult, and there was no longer need for him to act up to get my attention. He and I became "buds."

Then, the week was over. It was the final campfire. I knew the drill. It went like this: Start with every rowdy, goofy song that the kids knew. Slowly, as the sun set, the songs became a little more mellow and serious, the tempo slowed, the mood shifted to some more serious discussion. As the fire went down and the mood changed, there would be some talk of returning home the next day, and to home congregations, and how to bring the warm loving community of camp back into the real world. There were often tears as camp friends realized that they would be separated by miles and miles and possibly never see each other again. Finally, after a long period of silence, everyone around the circle was invited to hold hands and pray together the Lord's Prayer.

Earlier in the evening I had noticed Robbie across the circle around the fire—had waved across at him. Suddenly, as we began the Lord's Prayer, my grip on my neighbor's hand was broken and Robbie insinuated himself between me and the person I was standing next to. Instead of holding my hand, Robbie put his arm around my waist; mine went around his shoulder. At the conclusion of the prayer, he gave me a hard hug, and was gone.

The next morning at breakfast I looked for him. He was gone. Someone had come and picked him up before the meal. I never saw or heard from him again, but he has lived in the recesses of my mind all these years.

I remember him well and pray for him still.

Take a Message

Milt Hanson, formerly of my previous parish in Pierre, South Dakota, had moved to Colorado and was hired as State Supervisor of Child Welfare. He lived in Littleton, a suburb of Denver, and had joined a church there. When his daughter was to be married, their congregation was between pastors. I got a call from Milt asking if I would be willing to come out to Denver to officiate at the wedding, as I had been the bride's confirmation pastor and had been close to the family when we'd all lived in Pierre. (See previous story in the Pierre section, "One of My Best Teachers Never Attended Seminary.")

The wedding was to take place at the Hanson home. A nice house, the main floor was "open concept" with a freestanding wall separating the kitchen from the rest. There was a curved stairway up to the second floor where the bedrooms were located.

The bride was to come down the dramatic stairway accompanied by guitar music, and process to the "altar" area which had been arranged right in front of the free-standing eight-foot wall dividing the kitchen from the rest of the main floor. The guests were seated on folding chairs, some in the large foyer and others in the living room. It was lovely.

As the bride appeared at the top of the staircase, the guitarist modulated into the song chosen for the processional. The guests rose from their chairs for the bridal entrance.

Suddenly the kitchen phone rang out (back before everyone had cellphones). No one had thought of this eventuality. The bride's brother dashed around the wall to the kitchen, and the open design of the house allowed all to clearly hear him answer fumblingly, "Hello… Yes, she's here, but she can't come to the phone right now… No, she's uh…she's uh…she's getting married…"

The eruption of laughter was spontaneous, tension-relieving, and prolonged.

The bride, gamely, retreated up the two steps she had traversed. The guitarist started over. And the wedding proceeded (with the phone taken off the hook and safely tucked into a kitchen cabinet drawer).

The wedding was unique, relaxed, lovely, and definitely memorable!

What's in a Name?

In the days before the HIPAA (Health Insurance Portability and Accountability Act) regulations went into effect, information on individual hospital patients was not closely guarded. One hospital I visited had a registry book that listed each patient's name, address, date of birth, religious preference, doctor's name, and room number.

This was a lot of information, and it was frankly very helpful to pastors who were visiting. The pastor could look up specific members of his/her congregation that he or she knew to be hospitalized, but could also browse for other members of his/her denomination who might be from out of town and who might appreciate a visit from a clergyperson. (While helpful in this way, making that much information on individuals available to the public was also problematic. HIPAA has been a good corrective for protecting privacy.)

One day I had just finished perusing the register and was preparing to head out on some visits when my good friend, the Assemblies of God pastor, came in to also make some calls on his hospitalized members. I handed him the register and he began looking through it. Suddenly he exploded—"I hate these abbreviations!" he shouted into the silence of the reception area. Startled at his outburst, I asked what he meant and moved over to look at the register with him.

In the book, the spaces for recording all the information were quite small—everything had to be abbreviated. In the religion column, Lutheran became "Luth," Catholic became "Cath," Methodist became "Meth," and, unfortunately, Assemblies of God became, "Ass of God."

It didn't help the situation when I suggested that the Bible tells us we are all parts of the same body.

On my next visit I noted that Pastor Jim's wild-eyed rantings had borne fruit. His congregational members were now referred to in the registry as belonging to the "A of God" denomination.

Words matter. Abbreviations matter, too.

Christmas Story

There is an ongoing struggle that is waged within the hearts and minds of many pastors. The church, having long been seen as a source of comfort and assistance—and rightly so—has unfortunately also long been seen as a "mark" by those who would cheat and steal. Speaking for myself, I came to receive requests for assistance with a certain amount of skepticism over the years.

A helping hand to the needy—absolutely. A rip-off by a greedy scammer—no thanks.

It was Christmas Eve. The church was packed and the service was about to begin. Outdoors, the scene was a picture postcard, fresh snow sparkling in the moonlight. We had completed the first service—standing room only, lights dimmed, everyone holding a candle and singing Silent Night…it had nearly brought me to tears. I knew my wife and two very young children would soon be arriving to attend the second service. The kids were too young to appreciate the fullness of the Christmas message, but old enough to respond to the lights and music and joyful "hubbub."

As I was about to leave my office and walk down the hall to the sanctuary, there was a knock at the door. Standing in the hallway was a young man—probably mid-twenties, unshaven, disheveled, in a dirty white T-shirt. T-shirt!—it was well below zero outside. He started to tell me about his need. He had a wife and two very young kids in Minneapolis (a six-hour drive away). They were separated, but she had agreed to let him come visit with gifts for the kids. He had managed to get some money for a couple of gifts for each child, and he even had bought a Christmas tree that was strapped to the roof of his car out in the parking lot, but he didn't have money left for gas. Could I help him out? Even now as I write this I am moved deeply by the memory of the emotions of his story. I looked in my wallet. All I had was a twenty-dollar bill. I gave it to him and told him to drive safely, feeling warmth in my heart thinking of him reuniting with his family.

Fast forward to the next Christmas: The scene was the same. The carols were the same. It was a little colder with a little more snow coming down. I'm just ready to leave my office to head toward the overflowing sanctuary when there's a knock on the door. Lo and behold there stands the same guy. I swear he's even got on the same dirty T-shirt—same hang-dog look, and I hear the same story almost word for word. I stood stunned for a moment. Finally I said, "How did it go last year when you went to Minneapolis?" Now he was the stunned one. I said, "You were here last year on Christmas Eve with the exact same story. Maybe you need to get a better memory, or a better story." Eyes wide open, he ran full speed down the hall and out the door. He didn't return the next Christmas for a third try.

It's both infuriatingly disgusting and heartbreakingly cruel. Not only because of the callousness of the fabricated story and scamming, but because repeatedly experiencing such scams can cause the scammed person (pastor…) to develop their own degree of callousness, creating the danger of dismissing out of hand someone who really does need help.

The solution? I guess, take one case at a time. Listen carefully, try to do the wheat/chaff sorting thing. Deal with each situation itself. Know these are real people—God's own people. Know you will make mistakes. Pray for forgiveness when needed, and do the best you can.

Not a Typical Call

It was late afternoon when the call came to the church office from the police department. "Pastor, we have a prisoner here who is asking to talk to you. Could you come on down to the jail? And please hurry."

I headed out trying to remember if there had been some crime report in the paper, or if I had heard any scuttlebutt. Nothing came to mind.

Arriving at the jail, I was ushered into a small room where I was met by two deputies. They took my keys and wallet and everything else that I had loose on my person. Once I was "clean" they explained the situation: He was a young man who had been picked up on suspicion of robbery. He had been found loitering around a convenience store near where a robbery had taken place. He "kind of" matched a rather sketchy description they had gotten from the victim.

Once transported to the jail, he had become violently non-cooperative. It took three deputies to get him into a suicide watch cell for his own protection. Once in this cell, a bare room with padded walls and an observation camera— nothing else—he had seemed to quiet down. Some time later in making a regular check of the camera monitor, they saw him lying in a pool of blood. He had managed to unscrew a light bulb through the metal cage that protected it, break it, and use the jagged glass to try to cut his wrists.

The staff had rushed in, cleaned up and bandaged the cuts, and put him in restraints. Once he was strapped into a chair and had calmed down enough to talk to them, he asked to see me, by name.

It turned out that he was from a town about a hundred miles away, was a member of the Lutheran church in that town, and had once been to church camp during a week when I happened to be serving as a staff pastor. He had remembered my name and asked for me.

With all kinds of dire warnings, they informed me that they had put him in a special interrogation room for our visit—a room fitted not only with cameras but also a large one-way observation mirror. They would be watching our conversation for my protection. They assured me they could enter the room at the slightest sign of danger.

With that, I was led to a door, it was opened, and I entered a totally bare room with a large mirror on one wall and a large wooden armchair in the middle. Strapped into the chair was one of the smallest, most frightened-looking boys I had ever seen. His clothing, neck, and arms were smeared with blood and he had a couple of nasty-looking bruises visible, along with heavily bandaged wrists and forearms. He looked to me like he was five-foot-five or -six at the outside.

In a very small voice, he thanked me for coming, gave a pretty matter-of-fact explanation of his arrest and transfer to the jail, and then asked if I would contact the pastor from his church. He talked a little about his camp experience, how much that had meant to him, and then started to cry and asked me to leave.

Back at the church, I called his pastor and relayed the information. The pastor thanked me and assured me he would step in. I never heard another word about the boy or the situation. The pastor said he was sworn to confidentiality. The police chief said the same.

I've often wondered what became of him.

Trial Witness

It was the biggest news in our small town in a long time.

Young couple, newly married, settled into their trailer in the local mobile home park. Before long, the bride falls for the neighbor guy across the street. She moves in with him. After a week or so, the husband calls across the street on the phone at 3:00 a.m. He goes across the street "to talk"…with a shotgun. He forces his bride to watch as he makes the neighbor lie on the floor and shoots and kills him. He makes her continue to watch as he puts the muzzle of the gun under his chin and prepares to kill himself. (He knows that's what her father had done when he had committed suicide during her childhood.) She lunges at him and deflects the barrel of the gun so that when it fires he gets some superficial scrapes and burns on the side of his face. He flees with the shotgun. Shattered and frenzied, she calls the police for help.

The young woman was a distant relative of a member of our church, and so knew of me and asked the police to call me, to come to the hospital where they had taken her for sedation. I honestly didn't know who she was, but when I got to the hospital I was directed to the area where she was in protective custody. When she saw me approaching wearing my clergy collar, she got up, totally disheveled, and with tears streaming down her face came running over to thank me for coming. However, before she said another word, the police came and rushed her away to an undisclosed location, because they had spotted her husband's car in the vicinity of the hospital.

The town was ablaze with this story and with news of the manhunt that ensued. After a very long week, the killer was apprehended in a neighboring state and returned to our town to await trial in jail. The trial was finally scheduled for many months later, and life returned to somewhat normal.

As the attorneys were preparing for the trial, I received two phone calls— one from the prosecutor and one from the defense counsel. Each was the same: "Did you go to the hospital to meet with this woman early on the morning of the shooting?" "Yes." "Did she tell you anything about the shooting?" "No." I thought that was it.

The town began buzzing again. For weeks the local paper was full of stories about the trial and everything leading up to it. The day of the trial the sheriff called me and said, "They've issued a subpoena for you to come and testify. You can either come on down to the courthouse, or I can come and get you." I told him I'd be right there. On the way, I stopped in the office of a young congregation member who was an attorney and asked for his advice. He suggested I get a signed document from the woman giving me permission to share what she had told me. When I explained that she had told me nothing, he said I should get her to sign "some kind of release" in any case. But I never had the chance.

I got to the courthouse and was immediately ushered into the courtroom by the sheriff. As I came in, the bailiff hurried off to notify the judge that I had arrived. The room was packed, but I saw one empty seat over by the wall. I clambered over a whole row of people's laps to get to that seat, and sat down just as the judge entered the courtroom and was seated. No sooner had I sat than the bailiff called my name, and directed me to come forward and be sworn in.

Not wanting to immediately again disrupt all the people I'd just clambered over, I attempted to instead step back over my seat to the aisle that was right behind our row. I got over the seat with my lead leg, but managed to get my trailing foot caught between the seat and the radiator along the wall, making a loud clatter and causing a resounding round of laughter in the courtroom.

I had been given no instructions as to what to do. After dislodging my foot, in front of the packed courtroom I went down the main aisle, went through the railing gate, approached a woman behind a desk, and raised my hand to be sworn in. The woman eyed me coldly, said she was the court reporter, and pointed across the courtroom to another woman seated behind another desk—the bailiff. More laughter. I crossed over to the second station, raised my hand again, swore to tell the whole truth, and was finally told to go sit in the witness stand.

The witness stand was a raised platform attached to the judge's higher platform, with a railing in front and a wooden chair mounted on a single pole affixed to the floor. I sat down on the chair and immediately it tipped back far enough that my feet lifted off the ground at least three feet. By this time the courtroom was awash with laughter, and I was completely mortified. But, as they say, the best was yet to come.

The prosecutor approached, asked all the questions about name, education, profession, etc. He then asked if I had been called to the hospital on the morning of the shooting. "Yes."

The next question was, "Did the victim give you any information regarding the shooting?" "No."

"No further questions."

When the defense attorney informed the judge that he had no questions for me, I was dismissed.

About a month later I got a check from the county for eight dollars—witness fee. The verdict was "Guilty." It was the last I ever heard of the matter.

I thought comedians made better money than eight dollars per show.

Sweet Dreams

Karl was a Swedish bachelor farmer.

Norwegian bachelor farmers have been made somewhat famous by Garrison Keillor on his longtime radio show, "A Prairie Home Companion." I learned that Swedish bachelor farmers are quite different from Norwegian bachelor farmers: They are Swedish.

Karl farmed land adjacent to the farmstead where he had grown up. He was in his eighties, quiet and reserved, but with a disarming sense of humor that would often catch you off guard. The twinkle in his eye, though sometimes barely discernable, would give him away. Short, extremely shy, a little overweight from those long hours on a tractor, a person probably wouldn't notice him in a crowd.

I had developed a good relationship with Karl. Though I usually had to work a little to draw him out, we seemed to have quietly bonded. It was with a certain amount of alarm that I received the news that he was going into the hospital the next week for gallbladder surgery.

Early on the morning of the surgery we visited, he was quite nervous and me nervous for him. It was his first visit ever to a hospital as a patient and all of the pre-op procedures and medical machines were overwhelming to him. I stayed a little longer than usual with him, shared a prayer, and watched as he was wheeled down the hall to the operating room.

Later after a full day of parish activities, I stopped back at the hospital to check up on Karl and see how it had all gone. I found him out of recovery and back in his room. Seated next to him and holding his hand was one of the student nurses who had been assigned to accompany and observe him during his post-operative experience. I learned that he had experienced some difficulty following the surgery but now, quite a bit later than normal, he had just gotten back to his room. He had those eyes that looked at you yet you could see were unfocused and that rolled back into his head from time to time. He "kind of" looked at me and was able to smile wanly and say, "Hi, Pastor."

After a few moments of one-sided conversation—me talking and Karl smiling—the student nurse saw her opportunity and said, "Well, Karl, I'm going to leave you now. I have to get back to my supervisor." No response from Karl. "Okay, Karl, it was nice to spend some time with you. I hope you are feeling better soon." No response. "Karl, you'll have to let go of my hand now." Karl, eyelids half opened and eyeballs rolling every which way in their sockets said, "Honey, I've waited all my life for you and I'm not lettin' go of you now!"

Karl was still a Swedish bachelor farmer…but for a moment there—at least in his drug-addled brain(!)—he had almost changed that.

A couple of months after the surgery, one Sunday morning while shaking hands at the church door, I couldn't resist asking Karl if he had any memory of my visit at the hospital following his surgery. He said no, he didn't. I asked if he remembered the student nurse who sat with him in his room. The light in his eyes and the smile at the corners of his mouth gave me the answer. He didn't remember my visit—not because of the drugs, not because of me—but because his memory was filled by more wonderful visions.

Peaches

Being basically bald since my early twenties, I have embraced the "bald is beautiful" concept. I've had to. I've learned that it can be disarming, apparently even endearing, but in my opinion necessary, to openly embrace my "shininess."

During the heyday of the CB (citizen's band radios) craze, I decided to purchase one of those amazing devices. As I was serving in a fairly remote corner of Minnesota and often had to make one-hundred-fifty to three-hundred-mile drives in sub-zero (think twenty to thirty degrees below zero) conditions, it was not hard to justify, in my mind at least, this acquisition.

Seeing this as an opportunity for some light-hearted wordplay and a way to liven things up in the parish, our staff, with my full cooperation, sponsored a "Suggest a 'Handle' for Pastor Keith" contest in the church newsletter. The contest was a smash success, with many, many people choosing to submit ideas. Predictably, quite a number focused on the obvious: my shiny dome. "Chrome Dome" was popular, as was "Shiny Top." "No Cheap Furniture" (as in "they don't put marble tops on cheap furniture") was a dark horse candidate.

People seemed to be having fun with this whole project—that is, people except my early grade school-aged son. One evening he sat me down and, very seriously, told me how much it bothered him that people were making fun of his dad this way. "It's not right!" he said. He went on to explain that he had a better idea and that he wanted to submit a suggestion, but didn't know if it would be okay. I asked what his suggestion would be.

He went on to repeat a family story that I didn't even know he was aware of, but that he had heard and it had stuck in his mind. It had happened before he was born, while I was on my internship in Europe. At the end of my time there, my parents and sister had come to visit us and to travel a bit. My parents headed up to Norway, and my wife and I, with my sister and brother (who had separately just spent his summer working for the YMCA in Germany), drove south to Italy. Well into Italy, but still on our first day, we stopped for a meal at a small local restaurant. Knowing neither the Italian language nor anything of Italian dining customs, we ordered antipasto for our meal. Gesturing with hands and feet, as one does in these situations, we did finally get a full meal.

For dessert, everyone made a different menu choice. I chose a dish of peaches covered in whipped cream. The waitress approached our table with a tray of luscious goodies. She couldn't remember who had selected what and looked at us with a bewildered expression. Trying to be helpful and to keep things simple, I raised my hand and said, "I'm peaches."

Now, I will tell you that even today and after years of extended ridicule by my siblings, that response still makes perfect sense to me. Simple. Direct. To the point. Clarifying. Helpful.

To the rest of our group that day, however, it was hilarious. It might have been a comic release of the tension surrounding novice travelers in a strange circumstance. It might have been the end of a long day of stressful driving trying to navigate a foreign land and tongue. It might have just been sheer joy in being together after a long separation. But whatever the case, "I'm peaches" has been repeated time and time again within our family, partly to tease me and partly to relive and enjoy that time together.

My son Dan had heard and remembered the story, and liked the idea of poking just a little fun at Dad, while finding the cranial references of (many) congregational members and other newsletter readers offensive and definitely not to his liking.

Knowing all this, the judges chose his submission, "Peaches," as the winner of the contest, and it has been my CB handle—and sometime nickname—to this day (though I don't have a CB anymore).

Thanks, Dan!

True Communion

The Regional Youth Gathering for all the congregations in our denomination's Central Region was to be held in Denver over the Christmas break from school. A three-day event, it took place every three years with the idea being that each student could attend once during their high school career. The location moved from city to city to provide variety and so that the same planners weren't called upon every time. The Denver location meant a long ride on a school bus from northern Minnesota. Several congregations went together to rent three buses which picked up high schoolers from many congregations and drove in a "convoy" to Denver. We made arrangements to sleep on the floors of two churches along the way.

The trip was long and grueling for us adults, but we were buoyed by the ebullience of the high schoolers we were chaperoning. The conference was great. There is just something about having several thousand enthusiastic high schoolers together, studying and celebrating and singing and enjoying each other.

Then the conference was over. Everyone was worn out from all the fun and study and singing and horseplay that you expect on such an outing. We exhaustedly boarded the buses for the long homeward journey and hit the road. Some hours into the journey we noticed a shift in the weather. As the clouds built and the temperature dropped and the snow started to fall, we tried to pick up radio stations as best we could (this was long before smartphones).

What we could gather was that we were driving into a fairly major snowstorm. We stopped at a town along the interstate when it got too bad. There was a congregation from our denomination in that town and they graciously allowed us to sleep on the floor of their fellowship hall overnight. The next morning dawned; we climbed aboard our buses, headed off, and drove right back into the storm.

That second day, however, included a complicating factor. One of the girls in the back of our bus started crying and complaining of a pain in her stomach. One thing led to another and she became nauseated. We found a garbage bag for her to use (which she did). As she became sicker, the weather became worse. Finally we came to a spot where the interstate was closed. I got off the bus and explained our predicament to the highway patrolman who was handling the closure. He radioed for help and soon a large highway snowplow appeared to lead our buses into the closest town and right to the hospital. Our sick girl was so exhausted from her ordeal that I had to carry her into the hospital's emergency room.

The plow then plowed the road to the local church, which had agreed to let us spend the night there. By this time our joyful group had become quite serious and there were lots of tears and concern. It was Saturday night, and the one condition our impromptu church hosts had presented us was that we had to be out well before the service the next morning, so everyone bedded down and tried to sleep. I wasn't able to at all, and so got up very early. The snow had stopped falling. I trudged the several blocks through knee-deep snow to the hospital. Thankfully, the girl's condition had improved greatly overnight. It was the flu and she was going to be all right, but was too weak to be discharged to leave with us on a bus. Her parents had been notified and were on their way to pick her up the next day.

I returned to the church to find the kids gathering up their stuff and packing up. The group gathered around me for my report from the hospital and a big cheer went up from the good news. As we were climbing aboard the buses, one of the girls came up to me and said, "You know, Pastor. We've been through so much together, and some of us will never see each other again after we all get home. I was thinking it would be wonderful if we could have Communion together before we get home and split up."

Duh! Why hadn't I thought of that?

That bright girl and I scoured the church looking for bread and wine. Surely the church would have some bread and wine sitting around, right?

Everything in the place was under lock and key. The cabinets were locked. The drawers were locked. I kid you not: the refrigerator had a lock on it.

The only thing we could find was one stale donut and a can of cream soda. Gathering the group together in the snow outside the buses we prayed for our friend who we were leaving there in the hospital, we prayed for safety on the rest of our journey, we spoke the words of a much-abbreviated Eucharistic liturgy as best we could together remember them, and we communed with the crumbs of a stale donut and sips from a can of warm diet cream soda.

Unusual? Yes. Unforgettable? Absolutely!

Some years later I was at a meeting in Fargo, North Dakota, at our Synod Office. At lunchtime we went out to eat to a little local restaurant. They had arranged a large table for us—we were about nine or ten, both pastors and lay people. The waitress came to take our orders. As she went around the table, she came to me last. She said, "And you, Pastor Keith, what will you have?" I was stunned. "How did you know my name?"

She replied, "I was on the trip to Denver for the youth gathering. Do you remember the Communion with the cream soda and donut in the parking lot? I'll never forget that as long as I live. That was the most moving Communion service I've ever been a part of!" She teared up recalling the memory.

It's one of my favorite memories, too.

A Saturday Phone Call

One Saturday morning I stopped in to the church office to quick pick up some resources to help with some last-minute sermon preparation for the next day. As I was leaving the building, the phone rang. I hesitated, but decided I better pick it up. There are always emergencies in parish ministry.

The caller identified himself as the chairman of a call committee of a church in suburban Denver, Colorado, and wondered if I had a couple of minutes to talk.

I had been serving the two-congregation parish in Thief River Falls, Minnesota for ten years at that point. During that time, I had been contacted and interviewed about possible moves several times—moves to other parishes, to administrative positions, seminary assignments, and even a nomination for bishop. I had also gone through an experimental program of the national church to help pastors assess their interest in and potential fit for a move out of the church and into the business world. None of those various possibilities had seemed the right choice for me, if even an option. So, this out-of-the-blue contact that Saturday morning was startling, but not unappreciated.

Among pastors, there are different schools of thought as to how long one should stay in a given parish. After ten years in Thief River Falls, this question was growing in the back of my mind.

The "couple of minutes" turned into a phone conversation in excess of an hour, and before I knew it, my wife and I were on a plane headed to Denver for a visit and an interview. The interview went well, we were invited back to meet the congregation, the vote was positive...and our family was soon on our way to the Mile High City.

KING OF GLORY— ARVADA, COLORADO

Transitions

Saying goodbye to dear friends and tearing up ten years'-worth of roots was extremely hard. My first call in South Dakota had lasted three years and that goodbye had been emotional, but the experience of leaving Thief River Falls, Minnesota, was excruciating, especially for the kids. To move, not just to a new community, but to a new state and climate and time zone, is challenging for anyone, but for a fifth grader and a seventh grader, it is brutal.

But with prayer and preparation, we managed the transition for the whole family, in order for me to take this new call in Colorado.

The new parish was quite a different situation from the one I'd left: one congregation, in a suburban setting, with fewer members than the combined membership of the two congregations I had served in Minnesota. It was more cohesive in that there was only one monthly council meeting, one youth group, and two Sunday services instead of three in two different places.

But the schedule was frenetic. In addition to myself as Senior Pastor, there was the staff of an Associate Pastor, a full-time Christian Education Director, a Secretary, and a part-time Youth Director—all driving a jam-packed schedule of meetings and classes and meetings and community involvements and meetings and meetings and more meetings.

I had to transition, too.

Our Lady of Kmart

As it was located next to a large Kmart store with our parking lots adjacent to each other and often serving overlapping clientele, it was not surprising to learn that people often jokingly referred to King of Glory Lutheran Church in Arvada, Colorado, as "Our Lady of Kmart."

The fact that the assistant manager at Kmart was a member of KOG and was willing to loan the famous flashing "Blue Light" cart to the church for its special events (which were often called, none too creatively, "Blue Light Specials," just like the then-famous Kmart lingo) made it obvious that the church should be dubbed as it was. That moniker was lightheartedly used by members of the congregation, by clergy in the area, and neighbors near and far.

The church had a fairly large brick sign at the entrance to the parking lot. The local police found it to be an ideal spot to conceal a cruiser, inside of which an officer sat perched with a radar gun. This didn't sit very well with the congregation. Polite requests from the church, followed by urgent pleas, and culminating in a firm demand, finally brought an end to this practice.

The building itself was quite unique. It consisted of a pyramid-shaped sanctuary connected by a long outdoor colonnade to a one-story office/classroom/fellowship hall wing. The one-story portion of the building was the "first unit," with its original sanctuary having been remodeled into a fellowship hall.

The building served well, with one notable exception: the fellowship hall was at the far extreme end of the building from the new sanctuary. That meant that for events with lots of visitors unfamiliar with the building, like weddings and funerals, somewhat long and complicated directions had to be given after the service in the sanctuary to get visitors to the fellowship hall for whatever kind of reception might be following.

We almost felt like we needed to provide a handout: *"Our Lady of Kmart—Please refer to the attached map to get to the reception."*

Herb and Eileen

I was just the third pastor in the church's history, following a long-serving and deeply-loved guy. When any congregation is newly formed there are cobbled-together measures to "git it done" on the fly. Once the congregation is established these temporary measures can, and usually should, be re-arranged to make things more permanent and workable for the long run.

One of the arrangements that had developed in the early days at King of Glory had been the placement of the copy machine (actually, a mimeograph, since this was before today's photocopiers) in the home of a couple who had been charter members of the congregation, and were now older and retired. It was in their basement, and the duplicating process involved the church secretary typing a stencil master which would then be taken over to the home of this couple, placed on the mimeograph machine, and the copies run and then taken back to the church.

Needless to say, this was extremely inefficient—both cumbersome and time-consuming. After a week or two of observing this procedure, I asked what in the world was going on. "Well, no one wants to hurt their feelings," was the answer I got. "We've tried to get them to relinquish the machine and the responsibility, but they won't hear of it."

Despite being very new in the congregation, I was acquainted with this dear couple pretty well already. They were the folks who were always there, always helping—finding their identity and purpose in the ongoing life of this vibrant congregation. But this crazy process had to be fixed and I saw it as my role to fix it.

I made an appointment to visit their home. As I entered, I was greeted by a tiny white chihuahua with little brightly colored ribbons affixed to the base of its ears. The pooch was barking ferociously and flashed bared teeth at me when I tried to pet it.

Looking to ingratiate myself with the folks I said, "How cute! What's her name?"

"*HIS* name is Oscar," I was told—somewhat scoldingly.

Lesson learned: Don't assume the gender of a dog, no matter how it looks.

We did get the machine back in the office where it belonged. Herb and Eileen remained active and happy members of the congregation. But Oscar and I—well, that's a different story.

Team Building Under Stress

It's not clear if the surrounding drainage had shifted as the City of Arvada built up around the church, if the original landscaping plan was flawed, or if the ground had sunk a bit, but whatever the reason there existed a flaw in the way water did or didn't drain away from the church building when there was a heavy rain.

I wasn't yet aware of this, being brand new in the congregation and just starting to get my feet wet (so to speak). I was meeting with my associate pastor trying to get acquainted with schedules, routines, plans already in the works, and plans just being formed. We were sitting in the fellowship hall, which had been the original sanctuary before the building expansion took place. Deep in the process of getting me up to speed and getting to know each other, we hadn't been paying much attention as the gentle rain outside began to intensify.

All of a sudden, my new ministry partner jumped to her feet and screamed, "Oh, NO!! It's happening again!!"

The rainwater running down the hill on which the church was situated had run over the curb, down the embankment, and was running under the door and onto the carpeted floor of the room in which we were meeting.

Apparently having had some previous experience with this, she immediately notified the staff, ran to the boiler room, retrieved a batch of shovels, and put us all to work out in the rain trying to dig channels to divert the water away from the building.

After twenty minutes or so of frantic labor we were victorious. We stood proudly under an overhang of the building, soaked to the skin, bedraggled and chilled, but triumphant!

Surveying the ruined hairdos of my soaked and shivering female co-workers, I couldn't help but point out one of the advantages of my male-pattern baldness.

It was team building in an unplanned but very effective form.

Sometimes You Just "Click"

It took a while to get to know her. In fact, it took a while to get to even meet her. She was the Youth Director in my new parish setting.

Except for the organist, the other staff members were all full-time. But Ann was part-time, and a student at the University of Colorado as well, so she was usually not available for our staff meetings. I knew, of course, that she was working hard—the youth group was going very well. The kids were excited about all the fun happenings. The parents were happy that the kids were excited. I didn't need to worry about the youth program. It was almost entirely in her very capable hands.

As the school year came to an end, Ann became a more regular presence among the staff. Short and energetic with a winning smile and a very sharp sense of humor, she was fun to have in staff meetings, and quick with a witty comment or retort. And finally with the opportunity to do so, she and I bonded pretty quickly. We were a good team, a great fit.

Her excellent work as youth director became even more apparent when she graduated from the university…and left to go to off to seminary. Her departure left a big hole in the staff that took a long time to fill.

From time to time, we would get reports on her progress at seminary. When she came home on vacation she would usually touch base with us at the church. Each time she would visit I realized again what a big part of the staff she had been and how much I missed her quick wit and sharp humor.

Later on I kind of lost track of Ann after I left King of Glory and moved to California. The grapevine reported that she had graduated from seminary and had taken a call to a church in Iowa. At some point after I moved back to Colorado I heard that she had accepted a call as an associate pastor in a church in Casper, Wyoming.

A couple of years later at a regional pastors' gathering, the Wyoming Conference was in charge of the worship services and Ann was slated to be the preacher at an evening service. "How nice," I thought. "How good that she will get the experience of preaching to a room full of pastors," I thought. "She'll probably be scared to death," I thought. Then…

"WOW!"

Her sermon that evening was the highlight of the conference. Pastors with many years of preaching experience were blown away by her presence, her confidence, her content, delivery, and power. Cute little Ann was a powerhouse preacher.

I made up my mind that if I were ever in a position to work with another pastor in a staff relationship, I would try like everything to have that pastor be Pastor Ann—for the congregation's sake, and for my own.

Can You Do That?

They were an older couple. They seemed pleasant. They always hung around after the end of events to chat once everyone else had left. That was okay. A little pushy and a bit off-putting at times, but okay. I had the feeling that they wanted to be somewhat special. She especially wanted to be my buddy, it seemed. There are people like that, and that's okay.

But then it started—slowly at first, but with a rapidly increasing tempo. A dig here. A "gotcha" there. All directed at my associate pastor. She was a little older than I, but with fewer years of ministry experience. She had gotten her kids well into school before going to seminary. This was her first parish and she had been here for five years. This was when it was still something new in our denomination to have a woman pastor, since the ordination of women had begun only a few years previously.

At any rate, the hints from this female parishioner had become quite blatant, along with suggestions of how to deal with "the situation." After I confronted her and her husband about all of this on a Sunday morning, telling them in so many words to knock it off, we made an appointment for me to visit them in their home. I had no sooner made it in the door when the torrent of complaints, innuendo, and misinformation began, all of it directed at my ministry partner. I listened for a brief time and then said, "You should be saying all of this to her and not to me. I'm going back to the church, picking her up, and bringing her back here so that you can talk to her face to face." And I did.

My associate was hesitant to go with me to confront this couple, to say the least, and I can't blame her. But I insisted we had to do this. As we were going out the door of the office, I grabbed a Letter of Transfer form. This is the standard form that is used when a person or family transfers from one Lutheran congregation to another. It has all the wording printed out with blanks to insert the names of people transferring, and the congregation to which they are going.

We got to their home and things immediately went off the rails. The couple had had enough time to realize what was happening and get their courage up and their "attack" planned. They started in immediately: Her preaching was no good; she was snooty and had ignored the wife one time, walked right past her without acknowledging her; her father, a widely-known church official, would be disappointed in her because of her many failings— and on and on and on. My ministry partner held up pretty well under the onslaught, but finally broke down in tears.

I said, "That's enough. You've said your piece. It's clear you are not at all happy at this church." Reaching into my coat pocket I pulled out the transfer form. I explained what it was and where they should enter their names and the name of the church to which they were transferring. There was a tear-off slip at the bottom of the form that their new church could return to us so we'd have a record of where they had gone. I wished them well in their new congregation, whatever and wherever that might be, signed the form on the required line, set it on their table, and escorted my still-teary associate past the stunned couple and out the door.

Once in the car, my associate sat in disbelief. "Can you do that?" she asked. "I don't know, but I just did."

Twenty-some years later I got a phone call from the husband. He explained that his wife had recently died and was wondering if he and I could get together for coffee sometime. I replied, "Sure."

I never heard more from him.

Organ Snafu

One of the things I had learned at my first church council meeting at King of Glory was that they had ordered a brand-new pipe organ to be installed in the sanctuary. This was to be made to order for the uniquely shaped sanctuary, by a small independent organ builder in a small town in southern Colorado. This craftsman had been building organs in the area for many years and his workmanship and integrity were beyond reproach. The organ was to be installed by Easter of the next year.

With the flurry of things involved with the move from Minnesota to Colorado—meeting new congregational members and learning names and stories, getting settled in a new house with new routines, new schools for the kids, learning a whole new metro area, hospital locations, synod office location and staff, etc.—the issue of the new organ kind of fell through the cracks for me.

Easter had come and gone, and at the following council meeting someone said, "What about the new organ?" The property committee chair said he had been in touch with the organ builder and there had been a few problems, but we'd definitely have it by Christmas. At the first council meeting after Christmas, the question was again raised, "What's happened with the organ?" Communications with the builder seemed to have fallen off. "Well, he's more of an artist than a businessman," we were told, along with assurances that he could be trusted.

The council determined that an emissary should be dispatched immediately to see what was going on. A group of church council members made the several-hour journey south into the little mountain town in which the workshop was located. The team reported at the next council meeting that some very big personal problems had beset the builder and the construction had to be halted. He had many of the parts he needed in his shop, but had run out of money. Financial problems, personal problems, family problems—all had piled up on him.

We arranged that we would pay him X number of dollars per month to be used for parts for our organ only (he was simultaneously working on a couple of others as well). We would make a monthly visit and if we could see identifiable progress, we would forward another check to him, subject to council approval. Two such monthly visits were completed with progress noted.

On the morning following the third council meeting I got a frantic phone call: the organ maker had died. We had actually previously discussed taking out a life insurance policy on the builder, but had decided that was too uncomfortable. The next phone call, about an hour later, was from the council president, who was an attorney. "Get your traveling clothes on. A group of us from the council is going to the organ builder's workshop. We've rented a U-Haul. We are going to pick up any and every piece of our organ that we can identify before it gets tied up in probate!"

Our convoy consisted of said U-Haul and several cars. Our group was made up of the council president, a retired FBI agent (also an attorney), two or three strong young church members, and me. The plan was for us to pull into the farmstead that housed the workshop and while the council president/attorney made his case to the organ maker's son who was now in charge, the rest of us would go through the workshop loading everything labeled with our church's name on it into the U-Haul.

Thankfully, things were very clearly marked. The organ console got loaded first. The mechanical workings, all clearly labeled, went next. Pipes were labeled with our congregation's name—in they went. As we were loading furiously, the debate in the office between our attorney/president and the organ maker's son and his attorney moved into the workshop from which we were loading. At some point the county sheriff arrived. We kept loading parts.

Finally the council president said, "Let's go!" We piled into the vehicles with the instructions from our attorney/president: "Everything we have done is legal. Don't stop for anything but gas. We need to get these pieces of our organ into the church building right away. We can sort it all out later."

There were no flashing lights on our journey home, whew. We had called ahead and there was a team of workers waiting for us at the church. They had emptied out a storage room into which all the organ parts were placed and locked up.

So-o-o… We didn't quite have an organ. We had been making monthly payments on the parts. We had also been advancing payments as any expensive piece needed to be purchased. As near as we could figure we had paid enough of the contract price that all these parts were ours. But, what do you do with a roomful of organ parts?

It turned out that our organ builder had worked for a number of years with another fellow. After they parted ways, the other guy had moved to Denver. We were able to track him down and he agreed to come over and take a look. After a thorough inspection, he averred that we had most of the parts that we would need. He didn't want to take on the task of assembling, but agreed to oversee the work of an army of volunteers to assemble the organ. Slowly, slowly, ever so slowly, it began to take shape.

It took so long, that before it was completed I ended up taking another ministry call and left the congregation, but I heard reports of it coming together. Occasionally someone would send me a picture of the progress.

The last time I was in the area I had a chance to see it completed. It's beautiful. The sound is gorgeous.

Sometimes things just work out. Not as planned, mind you, but they do work out.

Blizzard of '82

The Christmas Eve blizzard of 1982 is legendary in Denver. Seemingly without warning, it started snowing on the morning of Christmas Eve. And it snowed and snowed and snowed some more. Pretty soon it was clear that this was going to be a doozy. The announcements started coming in on radio and TV. Such-and-such a business was closing early. This road was closed. Traffic was backed up. Et cetera.

Little by little the list of churches that were cancelling services grew. At first, I tried to pooh-pooh the idea of canceling church. It was Christmas Eve! However, the phone calls from parishioners and staff, the worsening reports and pictures on the TV, started adding up to the point where we really had no choice but to cancel.

I grew up in snow country, Minneapolis to be exact, but I couldn't recall having ever seen that much snow in one event. On the one hand, it was beautiful. But the thought of being trapped somewhere with drifts of that magnitude was truly frightening.

At church, the altar guild had come in early in the day, long before the storm had gotten so severe, and had set up for Communion. They had pre-filled Communion glasses in serving trays—enough to serve sixteen hundred expected Christmas Eve worshipers. Unfortunately, no one could get to the church to do anything with those glasses filled with wine, so there they sat.

When it was over there were more than two feet of snow on the ground, every church in Denver and its environs had canceled services, and people who had not been able to get to family gatherings started to get together with neighbors instead, creating instant pot-lucks throughout the city. To this day, many people who experienced this weird weather phenomenon even recall it with warm fondness: "The Blizzard of '82."

Christmas Day broke bright and clear. It was gorgeous. The two-foot-thick blanket of snow laid heavily upon everything. Nothing was moving. By 6:00 a.m. there were ambient sounds of snow plows and four-wheel-drive SUVs and trucks plowing and playing. I decided to cross-country ski over to the church, since driving was a dubious proposition. Footprints in the snow showed some people had actually come to the door, even though we had no Christmas Day services scheduled. Someone had shoveled a narrow path to the door.

I called the local radio station and asked them to announce we would have a 10:00 a.m. Christmas Day service for anyone who could make it. Our previously-prepared Christmas Eve Communion supplies for sixteen hundred were easily able to accommodate the sixteen people who showed up. Several of those folks had arrived via four-wheel-drive vehicles. One of them gave me a lift home.

Our family had been planning to drive to Minnesota for a week of vacation between Christmas and New Year's. As the enormity of the snow totals through the previous day and night became apparent, we had given up that plan as unrealistic. But the four-wheel-drive crew at church that morning said, "Go for it!"

With several four-wheelers in a convoy, they took me home, waited patiently while we re-assembled our travel supplies, and escorted us safely to the newly plowed interstate! What an adventure!

I'm among those with fond memories of that Blizzard of '82.

Remember You Are Dust

The move had been huge. The physical distance was about a thousand miles; the cultural change was profound. Small town versus big city. The "pietism" of the small-town Upper Midwest gave way to the more relaxed openness of the West. (One telling example: Back in Minnesota, some of the pastors from even smaller and more conservative nearby communities would periodically ask me, from the "big town" of Thief River Falls, to buy a case of beer for them so that they wouldn't be seen going into a liquor store by their congregation or community members. In the metro Denver area, not an issue.)

And it wasn't just cultural norms that were different in Colorado. I found that the theological conservatism of the Upper Midwest gave way to the more open and liberal theological understandings emanating not only from the West Coast, but from the larger ecclesiastical milieu beyond insular communities. Such understandings included seeing value in, and at times drawing from, other traditions.

One particular example sticks with me. Advent and Christmas had passed. We were into the Epiphany season and doing planning for Lent. In the first planning session, someone mentioned the need to procure ashes for Ash Wednesday.

"WHAT??!!" was my response. "Oh yes," I was calmly informed, "We do ashes."

The practice of "the imposition of ashes" is marking the sign of the cross on a worshiper's forehead with ashes (ideally, from the burned palms of the previous year's Palm Sunday service). This is an ancient and, to many, very meaningful reminder of one's mortality, the sorrow they should feel for their sin, and the necessity of changing their lives. This practice has been used by the Church since earliest times.

However, during the Protestant Reformation, the imposition of ashes was tossed out in many places, along with many more "ritualistic" practices that the reformers discarded, having been deemed "too Catholic." Now, after "only" five hundred years, some of the old rituals are being re-examined and re-evaluated and, as in the case of the imposition of ashes, re-embraced by many Protestant churches.

In that moment, though, without the benefit of some thoughtful reflection on my part, but with the righteous indignation of my pietistic, anti-Catholic Norwegian ancestors, I blurted out, "I won't do it! That's not my tradition! That's Catholic!"

To their credit, the rest of the staff calmly replied, "That's okay. We'll do it without you."

I stewed and stewed about this awkward situation. I was the senior pastor, but I was also the "new kid." Who was I to change what was an established practice in this faith community I had been with for less than a year? It's not like they were sacrificing babies to the Canaanite deity Moloch or something. It was probably easier to change one person (me) than to change twelve hundred congregation members. So I "caved." At the next staff meeting, I informed them that I was willing to participate with the ashes, but reserved the right to opt out the next year if it didn't go well. Thankfully, the staff expressed understanding and support.

Ash Wednesday arrived. The church was full. Having been instructed on the proper method of applying ashes to the foreheads of worshipers, I was ready. Extremely nervous, and with misgivings barely under the surface, but ready. My associate took charge of that part of the service and, since it was a once-a-year occurrence, reviewed for everyone the procedure for people to follow: come forward to the altar rail, kneel, push aside any hair on the forehead, receive the ashes in the sign of the cross, stand and return to the pew. As the cross is marked on the worshiper's forehead, the pastor says, "Remember you are dust, and to dust you shall return." I had memorized the phrase, saying it over and over so as not to mess it up.

As the worshipers were invited to the rail and the first group knelt, I took my container of ashes and nervously proceeded to the altar rail to begin. As I got to the rail I realized that the first three people kneeling there were my wife and two children. Slowly, one by one, I looked into their eyes, dipped my finger into the ashes, and made the sign of the cross on each of their foreheads, saying to wife, daughter, and son, "Remember you are dust, and to dust you shall return."

My knees almost buckled; my hands trembled. I was sweating profusely as I continued along the altar rail, saying that powerful sentence to each person in turn. It felt like a gut punch each time I repeated it, to be sure. But the most intense, the one I can't forget to this day, was the very first time I placed the ashes on my own family—indeed, my own dearly loved children—and reminded them, jarringly, simply, yet oh-so-profoundly, of this reality of life.

Remember.

Yes, indeed. Remember.

Does Not Compute

It was the mid-eighties and computers were becoming "the thing." There had been talk of trying to introduce a computer into the church office for a while. No one knew much about this new technology.

The computers that were starting to be available were little boxes that looked like small TVs with small screens (either green or orange). They were relatively expensive, almost exotic, and viewed with real skepticism.

Into the church office one day, strode a member who owned an insurance agency. He asked if the church wanted a computer. "It's the thing of the future," he asserted. His company had bought one but now regretted the decision and wanted to get rid of it. He had tried to sell it to no avail. "I'll *give* it to you!" he said. "You can sell it if you don't want it and use the money for whatever you want."

Without waiting for a response, he went out to his car and started hauling in boxes—boxes after boxes—some with wires and cables dangling from the sides.

In between multiple trips to his car to get more boxes he explained that he had bought the thing without knowing anything about it, at the encouragement of a friend who was a computer professional. It was state of the art for the time—and very large. Come to find out, a maintenance contract was required, but not included in the price. Come to find out, the maintenance contract cost more than the machine. Come to find out, this was much more machine than his small insurance agency needed or could afford.

The solution? A tried-and-true one: donate it to the church.

It was much more machine than the church could use. But we could sell it and from the proceeds buy a computer more suited to the church's needs, he explained.

That's exactly what happened. A large law firm was interested in the machine and glad to get it at the reduced price we were asking for it. From the proceeds the church was able to buy two small IBM desktop machines.

Everyone was happy.

Cake and Crime

Typically, on New Member Sunday there would be a brief welcoming time for the new folks in each of the two morning services, during which new members were acknowledged, introduced, and welcomed, in whichever service they chose to attend. To accommodate various schedules and in an attempt to familiarize people with other members, old and new, we would have a special outdoor coffee reception between the two services on the church lawn, weather permitting.

This particular morning the reception between services was going well.

There was a small group of new folks, and many of the long-time members had shown up to welcome them and to share a beautiful summer morning, good coffee, wonderful cake, and great fellowship on the church lawn. As the reception started to wind down, I slipped away to get ready for the second service.

As I walked through the sanctuary toward the sacristy up front behind the altar, I was filled with the glow of things going well. When I entered the sacristy, that glow rapidly dissolved, first into a blur of confusion, then into a red-hot rage. During the reception out on the lawn, someone had gone into the sacristy, taken the amplifier used to power the sound system in the sanctuary, and left via the side door from the sacristy to the outside. My rage was compounded by the further discovery that, presumably to cover the amp as they made off with it, they had stolen my suit coat. Thoughtfully, the miscreant had removed my car keys from the coat pocket and left them for me on the counter. NICE.

We went ahead with the second service, asking people to move to the front, and speaking as loudly as possible so that people could (sort of) hear.

Only later did I realize that, while thoughtfully leaving the keys to my car, house, church, everything, the thief apparently hadn't discovered or cared that I had my appointment book in the inside coat pocket. I realized the enormity of that loss on Monday morning, when, arriving at the office, I had no idea who I was scheduled to see or when, going forward. What a sinking feeling!

The first phone call of the day was from a woman who lived a few blocks from the church. She described a small red appointment book that had mysteriously shown up in her yard, apparently tossed over her fence by a passerby. Looking through it, she recognized it for what it was, found my name and number, and called to see if it was missing! THANK YOU LORD! AND THANK YOU NEIGHBOR!!

I retrieved the book, thanked the neighbor profusely, and tried to get on with as normal a schedule as possible. Later that week the insurance people showed up. Thankfully, they could fast-track the replacement of the amplifier so we would have it before the next Sunday services.

There was one infuriating glitch, however. Since it was only the coat portion of my suit that was stolen, they couldn't (wouldn't) pay to replace the suit, only the jacket. I was free to go ahead and purchase a sports coat, but definitely not a replacement suit! It's called adding insult to injury.

Life did return to normal. About six months later, the secretary informed me there was a man to see me. I opened the door to see a young man with an object in a black trash bag cradled to his chest. He came into my office, set the bag on my desk, opened it up and revealed our amplifier. He explained that "his cousin" had stolen it from the church and now felt so guilty that he was returning it. That being said, he turned and ran out through the secretary's office never to be seen again.

There was no suit coat in the bag, however.

Sorry, Not Sorry

Returning to the church from a hospital call, I found our young secretary pale, shaking, and crying at her desk.

"What's wrong?" I asked. She told me a panhandler had come into the office and asked for money. When she had explained that we kept no cash on the premises, he demanded to see the pastor. Learning that the pastor wasn't in, he surmised that she was alone in the office. He became verbally abusive and threatening. When she tried to get him to leave, he came around her desk and began to threaten her. She finally was able to direct him to the kitchen where there were some cans of soup available. She told him to help himself and told him where the pots and utensils were.

After spending a little time with her, trying to calm and reassure her, I headed down the hall to the kitchen to confront this guy. Church office staff and pastors deal with a lot of requests for assistance. Sometimes the requests are legitimate, difficult, even heartbreaking. However, sometimes the requests are scams—hollow, fabricated attempts to scam the well-intentioned would-be helpers. In most cases, the legitimate ones are handled fairly, efficiently, and to the best of the staff's ability and knowledge of resources available. But this visitor had been rude, aggressive, and threatening, to the point of upsetting our normally unflappable young secretary to tears. I wasn't mad, I was furious.

Entering the kitchen, I found him stirring the can of soup he had found. He was smirking at me, and asked, facetiously, if I was hungry too. "There's plenty here," he slurred, and added, mockingly, "Unlike some people, I'm willing to share."

I lost it. Having grown up in a time and milieu in which other people, especially women, were to be respected, his total disregard for our secretary and for our church kitchen (which he had ransacked looking for the soup), his arrogance and "attitude," his dirt, his odor, his slurred speech, it all overwhelmed me.

I dumped his pot of soup down the drain. I grabbed his arm and told him to gather up his things, he was "outta here." With a look of total shock and disbelief he gathered up his things. I took his arm and hustled him to the door, all the while, loudly, trying to explain how far out of line he was and how lucky he was that I wasn't calling the police, etc., etc.

Once out the door, his shock seemed to wear off and he gathered himself, as much as his inebriation would allow. He placed his feet firmly, called me a few nasty names, and aimed a roundhouse punch at my head. Easily ducking the punch, I grabbed his arm, twisted it behind his back, and propelled him out to the street. Dumping him on the curb, I went back and got his stuff and returned to him, depositing it at his feet.

In as measured a tone as I could muster, I explained why it was in his best interest to be on his way and to never, ever return to our place again.

Thinking back over that encounter, I wish I had handled it differently. He triggered enough trip-wires in my background and makeup that I totally lost control. I'm sorry. But also, not too…

We installed a lock and buzzer system on the church door.

Disaster Pastor

Nicknames happen. And are sometimes hard to figure out, if you don't know the history or context. I'll tell you the two events that led to my nickname in this congregation—you'll understand.

One of the coldest winters on record in Colorado was upon us. Temperatures had hovered at minus twenty degrees for over a week. The "engineers" in the congregation had been forced to install rigged-up heaters for the mid-December living nativity scene on the church lawn; long underwear and insulated pajamas secreted under the robes of the actors weren't enough.

But now the outdoor living nativity had concluded, the costumes had been cleaned and stored for another year, the hustle and bustle were behind us—it was Christmas Eve. The first worship service of the evening had been beautiful; the tree was stunning, the choir was well rehearsed, even the children's nativity play inside came off without a hitch. As the congregation was filing out of the sanctuary in that special hushed aura that seems to surround Christmas Eve, the softness of the evening was interrupted by one of the ushers running into the narthex shouting, "Help, help! Come quick! A pipe has burst in the kitchen!"

The kitchen was across the covered colonnade and down a long hallway from the sanctuary. Part of the original building, it was built with the plumbing running through the ceiling. The frozen pipe had burst up there in the ceiling, spraying water into the attic, soaking all the insulation above the kitchen, compromising the sheetrock in the ceiling—which had collapsed onto the serving island and floor. It was a huge mess.

And the water was still gushing from the broken pipe, causing more and more of the ceiling to be soaked and collapse. No one knew where the shut-off valve was—everyone seemed to be shouting orders to no one in particular. Men dressed for Christmas Eve worship in their good suits were crawling around up in the attic in the soaked blown-in fiberglass insulation, frantically looking for a shut-off valve—or something, anything to stop the water from doing further damage.

Did I mention it was twenty below zero? And with the kitchen insulation now on the floor instead of in the ceiling, it was getting really cold in that end of the building.

Somehow it was eventually brought under control. Someone finally located the water shut-off. Make-shift repairs were quickly made. We managed to have the second Christmas Eve service, although the "Christmasy spell" was certainly broken. In time, full repairs were completed.

Event Number Two happened on a summer afternoon. I had been at the hospital making a couple of calls. On the way back to the church I heard on the radio that there was a severe weather warning in effect. The center of the affected area was right near where our church building was located. As I got closer to the church site, I could see flashing lights, emergency vehicles, water running in the street, and what looked like snow on the ground. Snow. In the summer. It didn't compute.

Finally it dawned on me. Hail! Sure enough, the small shopping center right next to our church was the epicenter of a freakish hail storm. I could only get close to the church by arguing with some cops in the security perimeter around the scene. The damage was unbelievable.

The church was shaped somewhat like a pyramid with a high, pointed roofline topped by a cross. Instead of shingles, the surface of the roof was concrete tile. At first glance, as I approached, it looked as if every one of the concrete tiles had been shattered by the hail, not to mention the high windows in the peak of the pyramid. There were still hailstones on the ground. Many were literally the size of softballs. My son had been in the sanctuary working on a confirmation service project with another boy. They had seen the peak windows shatter, and were able to seek cover. There were shards of glass from the broken windows embedded in the pews.

Each of the classrooms in the single-story extension of the building had a skylight (emphasis on "*had*"). They were all shattered and the water damage from the incoming rain was extensive. Once again some of the men from the congregation were up above, this time on the roof trying to cover the holes where the skylights had been, as best they could.

The hailstorm had been limited to a relatively small area, with the church and next-door shopping center at its very midpoint. Lots of neighborhood stories came out of this event. My favorite involved Hans and Gretel. (No kidding on the names—they were an older retired couple originally from Germany; they spoke with notable German accents.) When things were mostly back to normal, and most of the repairs in the neighborhood including repairs on the church had been completed, someone told me that I should really go have a visit with them.

I was invited in, given a plate of delicious German strudel and a cup of coffee, and heard their story. When the storm hit, they told me, Gretel had yelled at Hans, "Help me get my flowers inside." Hans threw aside the book he had been reading and rushed out the door to help. Gretel was an avid gardener and had many pots with flowers of various kinds. "Get the roses first!" she yelled. Hans got flustered and brought in a couple of plants—not roses. "No! No!" Gretel scolded, "The roses first!"

As Hans lugged the last of the heavy flower pots under the overhang of the garage and dashed (as fast as someone his age could dash) through the hail for the door, he noticed the BMW they had just brought home from Germany on their recent trip, sitting out on the driveway. It was too late to do anything. Hans watched as his brand new (and very expensive) car was demolished by hail—but the flowers had been saved!

Not nearly as crushing (nor expensive) was the total demolition of my older Plymouth Horizon. It was in the parking lot of the Kmart where my wife had gone to shop. The trunk lid had been pierced by several baseball-sized hailstones. in addition to the hood being punctured and several of the windows broken out. It was, like Hans's BMW, "totaled."

You can perhaps see why they hung the nickname on me: The Disaster Pastor.

Fraught Heritage

It started out like so many others.

A phone call: "Can we come in and talk to you about a wedding?" Appointment made: nice young people excited about starting a lifetime together with a church wedding. These folks were not members of our church, or of any church for that matter. But having a church wedding was important to them.

Pastors get these calls all the time—folks unknown to the pastor, who may or may not belong to or attend any church, yet they want "a church wedding" with a clergyperson as officiant. (Interestingly, over the years more and more of these requests have been for outdoor weddings rather than inside churches. Everyone pictures the beautiful outdoor setting: mountain backdrop, burbling stream, birds singing sweetly in the treetops. (Most pastors can tell you many stories about reality striking a brutal blow to that imagined pastoral setting. But I digress.)

I visited with this young couple, and went over the expectations on my part: four pre-marriage sessions, completion of a pre-marriage inventory form, payment of the church use fees, etc. This was all good with them and we reserved their date on the church calendar.

The counseling sessions went very well. They had dated for a long time, seemed to know each other well, were aware of the "sensitive areas" in their relationship, etc. In the final session I would normally go over the order of service for the wedding, make any changes that they desired (within reason), and finalize how the wedding would look. I had sent a hymnal home with them in the previous session, asking them to read through the marriage service and bring back any modifications they might suggest.

As we began our final session together, the silence in the room was deafening. They directed my attention to page 204. In a prayer on that page was the phrase, "With high praise we recall your acts of unfailing love for the church, for the house of Israel, and for your people, the church..."

They were wondering if that "house of Israel" phrase might be omitted. The groom's family might be uncomfortable with that particular phrase. Thinking little of their request, I said "Okay. We can do that." I didn't give it another thought.

The day of the wedding dawned bright and clear. Everyone in the wedding party showed up on time. They were a very nice group—mostly young professionals in their late twenties or early thirties. There were no crude jokes, no hidden bottle being surreptitiously passed around (as is occasionally the case). They were respectful of the church, of me, and of each other. The church filled and people chatted quietly. Old friends greeted each other with hugs. The wedding party lined up in the back of the church, the processional was played, and the service went off without a hitch. The wedding service was conducted in a very orderly fashion. The receiving line went according to plan. Plenty of pictures were taken from every angle imaginable with every nuance of lighting explored.

The reception was not to be held at the church, but at a restaurant a short drive outside of Denver, in the foothills. Everyone departed for the reception, as did I. I had been asked to offer a prayer before the reception dinner began, so thought I shouldn't be the last one there and hold things up.

When I got there, a number of the guests had arrived and gathered in the parking lot in groups, chatting. It was a beautiful setting and the restaurant was one with which I wasn't familiar. It had a German name and was decorated with very distinctly German details. The printing on the sign was in "German/Gothic" script. There were deer antlers and Alpen horns aplenty.

All of a sudden a large group of the guests arrived, almost in a caravan—the older generation of the family. As they got out of their cars, I saw that they were all dressed in traditional German garb: dirndls for the women and *Trachten* with lederhosen for the men. (If you are not familiar with these German terms, you should really look them up online.) It was stunning to see this German finery in Colorado. I then realized that every one of the fancy shiny cars was either a BMW, Porsche, or Audi.

These older folks clearly clung to their German heritage…and thinking back to the unusual prayer-modification request, I found myself uncomfortably wondering…perhaps some connection to Nazism as well. The grandchildren did not want to anger or offend their elders. To be praising God for divine "acts of unfailing love…for the house of Israel" would, I guessed, not have sat well with these older folks.

On my way home from the reception, my tummy was happy with the Wiener schnitzel and sauerkraut and "*bretzeln*," but my mind was buzzing with speculation about the back stories of the older relatives—what they had seen, what they had lived through. I couldn't help but wonder what they had done during those war years. Had the men been drafted into the Nazi army? Had they enlisted? Willingly? Even enthusiastically?

What might they still believe?

I found myself wishing I hadn't agreed to remove that phrase from the prayer.

Bernard's Bottles

One of the regular shut-in Communion stops at King of Glory was with a woman originally from a small town way out east of Denver on the prairie. She lived in a small, well-cared-for house not far from the church. I knew that she had two sons, but never met either of them. She was a delight to visit, full of energy and enthusiasm for life, always up to speed on the latest national and international news as well as the local Arvada scuttlebutt.

I had heard that one of her sons owned and operated a well-known local eatery, Bernard's. Once while visiting with the pastor who had been my immediate predecessor at King of Glory, he asked me if I had ever been to that particular restaurant. "Yes, a time or two," I responded.

"Next time you are there take a look at the collection of liquor bottles throughout the restaurant," he instructed. I told him I had noticed them while there—they were prominently displayed on a rack that encircled the entire place, as well as every possible nook and cranny in the several rooms of the establishment. He then explained, somewhat conspiratorially, that "Bernie" had told him one time that he had willed the entire collection to the congregation at the time of his death.

Hundreds of liquor bottles, of various shapes and sizes—I had noticed one shaped like Elvis Presley playing his guitar, another shaped like a three-masted sailing ship, and yet another shaped like Roy Rogers, King of the Cowboys—all willed to the church. I'm sure the collection could be worth a lot of money to some collector, but somehow the incongruity of a huge collection of liquor bottles...

My predecessor confessed he was glad that he hadn't had to deal with this unusual situation, and wished me well should it fall to my lot. I ended up moving on from KOG without the issue arising, and never heard another word about it.

I still wonder if that part of that will was real, and if so, what the outcome might have been.

Time for a Change

Having worked as a senior pastor with five different interns, each for a year, followed by a full-time associate pastor joining me for four years in my previous parish in Minnesota, I had assumed that there would be no problem working with another associate.

I did remember that our seminary professor for a course in Church Administration had been adamant that when a new senior pastor arrives in a congregation, the expectation is that a resignation from each of the staff members, up to and including the associate pastor, if there is one, will be on his desk when he arrives. This was, we were given to understand, the common practice throughout our denomination. It would then be up to him to decide who is retained and whose resignation is accepted.

But that seemed so outdated, so arbitrary and formal. Due to a combination of circumstances, it had been agreed before I'd arrived that none of the staff at King of Glory would have to submit resignations when I was called there as senior pastor. (And, speaking of outdated, please notice the pronouns in the previous paragraph: all masculine, reflecting the reality of ministry at that time of my life. I had graduated from seminary some ten years before the Lutheran Church had started to ordain women.)

All that being said, when I began at KOG my education in pronouns, and a lot more, had gone into overdrive.

"Inclusive language" was a big term at the time I arrived at King of Glory to serve as senior pastor; I had not heard it before. My ignorance of this term was a source of concern, naturally, for the staff members—all of whom were female, including the associate pastor. When one of the first sermons I preached was titled, "The Fatherhood of God and the Brotherhood of Man," the adverse reaction was predictable (by everyone but me!).

After I had successfully convinced everyone on the staff that the error was unintentional—committed out of ignorance rather than malice—all was forgiven. And my education sped up.

Being something of a slow learner, though, I confess that this education process into more awareness and sensitivity took me a while. And patience can only go so far, so there were misunderstandings and even blow-ups along the way.

Over time, one thing led to another and at a tumultuous confrontational meeting, called in order to point out my many shortcomings and failings, I had offered to resign. I had then gone right into the church office and called the bishop, asking if there might be another parish to which I could be moved. He refused, saying he knew he should not have made an exception to the usual practice when he had assented to the associate remaining in place, back when that request had been made before I arrived.

He told me I would be staying at King of Glory as called, and he would instead find another call for the associate. True to his word, the associate moved to her own parish, in which she was very successful. A new "fresh start" associate pastor was called to King of Glory, and we all moved on.

However, the situation continued to be somewhat uncomfortable both for me and for the rest of the staff, and remained an undercurrent even while we carried out good ministry at KOG. I'd also experienced upheaval in my personal life that had led to my wife and I making the painful decision to divorce, so after a total of four years in this vibrant parish, I accepted a call to serve on the staff of the Lutheran Church in America Foundation—and moved to California to set up an office for the Foundation there.

NATIONAL FOUNDATION WORK—CALIFORNIA

California Dreamin'

One of the most unusual chapters in my ministry lasted only about a year. I had seen a notice in our national church newsletter that there was an opening for an associate director of the then Lutheran Church in America Foundation, a national organization handling trusts, endowments, major gifts, etc. I read the notice several times and it really piqued my curiosity, so I submitted an application.

Very soon I got a phone call from New York. The director of the Foundation would be traveling west and he had a short stop in Denver. Would I be available to meet him at the airport for a brief conversation? "Of course!" was my reply, and the meeting was set. I got tied up in traffic, frustratingly, and the director's plane had already landed and deplaned when I arrived, but I had him paged, we managed to connect, and had a short but great visit.

Within a week came a request for me to fly to New York for an interview with the Foundation hiring committee. I went and did the interview, met the staff, looked around the office, was duly impressed, and flew back home. Another week went by and I was flown to California to be interviewed by the board of the Lutheran Ministries Consortium of the Southwest, a newly-formed regional organization with which the Foundation was entering into a partnership. The Consortium was formed by eight separate institutions: Pacific Lutheran Theological Seminary, California Lutheran University, and various Lutheran social service agencies, nursing homes, and camps.

Aside from my spilling orange juice all over my shirt and tie on the flight and having to buy replacements for them at the shop in the lobby of the hotel where the interview took place (have you ever priced anything in those hotel lobby shops?!), it all went well.

Before long I found myself driving to my new home in the San Francisco Bay Area to begin my new call. I was now the Director of the brand-new

Lutheran Ministries Consortium of the Southwest, and Associate Director with the partnering national organization, the LCA Foundation.

After getting settled into an apartment, I had to get an office functioning: one bedroom of the small apartment was for sleeping, and the other became the office of the fledgling Consortium. Office equipment was purchased, letterhead printed, letters of introduction sent to the people and institutions involved, and visits to each were scheduled.

My apartment was in Fremont, just south of Oakland in the East Bay. I chose that location because it was roughly equidistant from the San Francisco, San Jose, and Oakland airports. This was important since my territory included all of California, Arizona, and Utah, and I would be spending lots of time in the air.

Then began quite an educational experience, in more ways than one.

The eight different institutions of the Consortium each had their own fundraising endeavors. My job was to advise and assist their various efforts, especially in the area of major gifts. Serving also as Associate Director of the national Foundation meant that I could be (and often was) called upon to visit with a potential major gift donor on the national level, if they were located in my territory. Soon the eight institutions of the Consortium grew to eleven, and I was busier than ever.

I may not have been "living the dream" in California as most of us might envision it, but it was a good and challenging call.

That Clerical Collar Again

It was a beautiful fall day in Berkeley, California. The area around the University of California campus there was bustling with energy as I headed down University Avenue toward the BART (Bay Area Rapid Transit) station. I had gone to a photographer to have my picture taken for a brochure being printed to promote the newly-formed Lutheran Ministries Consortium of the Southwest, of which I was the newly-installed Director. So I was wearing a suit and clerical collar.

As I ambled down the hill, enjoying the gorgeous day and the bustling college campus atmosphere, I was suddenly aware of a hubbub on the sidewalk down ahead of me.

A large, gruff-looking man with unkempt appearance was shuffling up the hill towards me, with his arms around two large bouquets of flowers. He was talking loudly to no one and everyone, about nothing and everything—mostly politics and world affairs, it seemed. Seeing the reactions of the other people about on the street, I got the strong impression that he was a known figure.

The crowd on the sidewalk seemed to part like the Red Sea in front of Moses as he made his way uphill.

Suddenly he stiffened as he spotted my clerical collar. His laser focus seemed to bore right through me. With a glint in his eye he started calling out loudly, "Father! Father, help me, help me," over and over.

His formerly blank expression had now become more animated as he seemed to be enjoying the spectacle he was creating. I judged that this was not a sincere request for pastoral care. It was clear to me that some kind of confrontation was forming in his mind, and just as clear that I wanted no part of that.

When he got about six feet from me, I stepped to the side and said, in a voice as loud as his, "You'll be okay. Cut the stems at an angle and get them in some water. You'll be fine," as I went on past him.

A smattering of laughter mixed with some slight applause was the net result of the impromptu street theater. Just like that it was over.

I was glad to get on the BART train and head out of there.

New Realities

One of the first tasks as I started my new joint position with the Consortium and the national church Foundation was to attend the annual week-long Fundraising School at the University of San Francisco. There were various speakers from the world of philanthropic giving, addressing many of the fine points as well as the basic ins and outs in this new and complicated sphere I was entering.

Toward the end of the week, it was announced that there would be a special surprise guest appearance by a superstar in the field, who was the head of the development office of Stanford University. One of the reasons the Stanford development department was invited to make a presentation was that they had just announced a three-billion-dollar capital campaign—at that time the largest capital fundraising appeal of any educational institution in the United States. Ever. $3,000,000,000!! Three *billion* dollars!!

On the last afternoon of the week, we were ushered into a large lecture hall. I was a bit startled to see that the superstar presenter was a woman—my education on that point obviously was still ongoing. I now think "Shame on me," but it's where I, and too much of the culture, was at the time.

Surviving that initial shock, I became completely caught up in what she was telling us about this newly-launched, gigantic campaign.

At the end of her presentation, she asked if there were any questions. I raised my hand. "Yes?" she said, pointing to me. Struggling with the enormity of the numbers being thrown around, I said, "We just learned this week that in order to be successful, a capital campaign must have a lead gift of ten percent of the total. That would mean that you are looking for a lead gift of three hundred million dollars. Is that correct?" "Well," she replied with a sly smile on her face, "yes and no. We already have that gift. That's how we determined the total amount of the campaign."

This was 1986. Their campaign was worth more than eight billion dollars in today's money. (The lead gift they had, therefore, was equal to *eight-hundred-forty million dollars* today.) Gulp.

Fairly reeling from both the astronomical sums being discussed as well as the heady new experience of being taught by a woman expert in her field… somehow, the line from *The Wizard of Oz* came to mind: "We're not in Kansas anymore, Toto."

Senior Complex

The complex was huge. There were several buildings, each four or five stories. It was a retirement community in Southern California and I was there to meet and visit three women who had each established trusts with our national church foundation. My visits with them were to establish a relationship so that I would be a face that they could associate with "that impersonal institution" out in New York. Two of them particularly made an impression on me.

Mary was a pistol. She was ninety years old and full of energy, life, and fun. She was chair of her local Republican Party caucus. She headed up the community library in the retirement center. We had to cut our visit a little short because she was getting late and had to leave—to drive herself to her water aerobics class.

Thanking her for the visit, I headed down the hall to visit with Martha (yes, really). Martha was a bit dour compared to Mary, but just as busy. We shared some coffee and polite conversation. I can't remember all the things she was involved in, but when I was leaving I asked her, "Do you know Mary down the hall?" "Oh, sure," she said, "We play bridge." Still a little overwhelmed, I said, "She's still driving!" "Well!" was the rather huffy reply, "she should be! She's only ninety!"

"Do you still drive?" I found myself asking cautiously. "I sure do!" she replied more huffily. "How old are you, if I may be so bold as to inquire?" I asked. "Ninety-five," she replied with a very self-satisfied air, and with the biggest huff of all—one that pretty much said, *"Put that in your pipe and smoke it!"*

I thanked her for the visit and departed.

I drove very slowly out of the complex parking lot and driveways with both hands gripping the wheel, looking carefully both ways, and praying for all who drove their vehicles in that area…but also impressed and proud of the human race, that despite age or infirmity or situation, we all just "keep on truckin'!"

Continuing Education

From time to time, I would get a phone call from my supervisor in New York with the name of someone they wanted me to see. These names were of people who had contacted the Foundation with questions about charitable giving to the church—people who the Foundation assessed might benefit from a personal visit. My visit with Dr. Johnson was the result of one such call.

The address given to me was actually not that far from my office. This being in the days before Google, I got out my map and proceeded to hunt it down. Having no phone number, I dropped a note to Dr. Johnson explaining who I was and asking if there might be a time when I could stop by for a visit. I got a response suggesting a convenient time.

On the appointed day, I got out my map and headed off. The address was relatively easy to find. I actually arrived a little early, so I drove around the neighborhood a bit. It was pretty much your typical middle-class area; nothing grand, but nice homes.

At the appointed time I parked in front of the house, walked up to the door, rang the bell, and waited. I was surprised when a tall, regal-looking black woman opened the door. I then tried to hide my shock when she answered my question about whether Dr. Johnson was available with, "I'm Dr. Johnson."

I don't know for sure if it was because of my obvious astonishment, but the entire conversation was held standing at the front door; I was not invited in. It was clear that Dr. Johnson knew what she was doing, and that she had visited with a number of reps from other foundations. She asked me some questions, made some value judgments in her head, and then abruptly dismissed me, explaining that "the Salvation Army offered a much better deal."

The drive back home gave me time to reflect on value judgments of my own…and to ponder my own—no other words for it—racism and sexism.

Brush With Fame

One of the constituent members of the consortium I represented was a Lutheran Social Services agency in southern California. I had gotten to know the director, a fellow pastor, and we quickly formed a friendship. He was very capable and committed, and his dry sense of humor made him fun to be around.

On one of my visits to his agency, he talked about the large fundraising campaign they were about to initiate. His lament was that they had no celebrity to be the public face of it. In California, he explained, success is often determined by the quality of your celebrity endorsements.

On my way home from that meeting I got to thinking. A few years earlier I had met a pastor who was a professional fundraiser for a college from my home state of Minnesota, who had gone to high school with actress Lonnie Anderson and who had known her well during their school years, through involvement in the youth group at their church.

I called the struggling social service agency director and asked if he'd like me to try to arrange for Lonnie to be the celebrity face of his campaign. "Wow!! Would I ever!!" he exclaimed.

One phone call to the fundraising friend in Minnesota led to Lonnie Anderson agreeing to be the celebrity spokesperson, and the campaign went over the top in its success.

My only regret? I never got a chance to meet Lonnie.

The Joy of Giving

They were the nicest couple. He was a retired pastor, she a retired school librarian. They were quiet, soft-spoken people with a keen interest in their respective fields and a wondrous intellectual involvement in the world around them—from their southern California community, to church (locally, nationally, and worldwide), to politics, and world affairs. I loved visiting with them.

They lived in a modest second-story condo that had been their home for many years since their retirements. Now, however, the stairs to their home were becoming a problem for them. In researching possible solutions, they had made a decision: they would donate their condo to the church. It could be sold and the proceeds placed in a Charitable Remainder Unitrust for them. The interest from this trust would be enough for them to make the payments on another condo—in the same building, but on the first floor with ground-level access. At the time of the death of whichever one would be last to die, the condo would be sold and the proceeds would go to whatever charity or charities they had determined.

The arrangements had been made, the new trust established, and I was directed to make a call on them to thank them for their gift. Part of the "thank you" was for me to take them out to dinner. They had chosen a modest local restaurant, their favorite, and I enjoyed one of the most delightful evenings of my life visiting with these charming, witty, warm, and wonderful people.

This was one of the true joys in the ministry of the Foundation. There were no "losers," only "winners."

The World Moves On

This interesting chapter of my ministry came to an abrupt end after roughly a year.

In the U.S. a merger between three major Lutheran Church bodies occurred, forming what is now the ELCA (Evangelical Lutheran Church in America). Three bureaucracies were combined and needed to be whittled down. In an attempt to be fair to everyone, all staff persons were asked to resign—and then the newly reorganized church could hire back whomever it wanted and/or needed. Since my position with the LCA Foundation and Lutheran Ministries Consortium of the Southwest had been somewhat unique, I had been assured by my supervisor that I would be one of the re-hires.

However, my supervisor did not get *his* job back with the new church organization, and therefore his promises to me didn't hold. I would have to re-apply like everyone else—and, "Oh, by the way," the salary for my position was being cut by twenty-five percent.

I was infuriated. I felt humiliated. I was completely disgusted.

In a snit, I resigned not just from my position, but from the clergy roster of the newly-formed church—"Take that!"

It will be noted that the merger took place as planned, in spite of my hissy fit. A successor was hired for my (former) position. The world moved on.

And so did I. I returned to Colorado.

That triggered a boatload of life changes for me, as I both remarried and started a business. And thus began my brief stint as owner and operator of a small print shop franchise.

Evangelische Versohnungs Kirche, Leonberg-Ramtel, Germany. Striking in its departure from traditional German church architecture, it was conceived to look like a tent symbolizing "the church underway," but came rather to look like Martin Luther's "A Mighty Fortress" instead. (Photo by Manfred Gloss.)

Interior view of the *Evangelische Versohnungs Kirche* showing the metal sculpture suspended above the altar. (Photo by Manfred Gloss.)

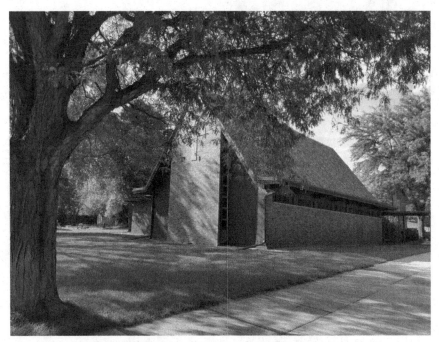

Resurrection Lutheran Church, Pierre, South Dakota. This was the
author's first call out of seminary. The building is a typical "first unit" for
the Board of American Missions in the 1960s. (Photo by Pam Faro.)

Redeemer Lutheran Church, Thief River Falls, Minnesota. A new building in
the early 1970s, it was home to the amalgamation of several smaller Swedish
Lutheran churches in the Thief River Falls area. (Photo by Dale Dillon.)

Black River Lutheran Church

Black River Lutheran Church in rural St. Hilaire, Minnesota. It was part of the Black River/Redeemer Lutheran Parish, located southwest of the town of Thief River Falls. (Photo courtesy of the *Thief River Falls Times*, Thief River Falls, Minnesota.)

King of Glory Lutheran Church, Arvada, Colorado. Jokingly referred to as "Our Lady of Kmart" because of its location right next door to, and virtually sharing the same parking lot as, the local Kmart. (Photo by author.)

Saint Matthew Lutheran Church, Aurora, Colorado, donated its building in 2017 to the Village Exchange Center, a non-profit organization formed to serve immigrants and refugees in the Aurora/Denver metro area. VEC celebrates cultural and religious diversity through its youth and adult programs and services. (Photo by author.)

Cross of Christ Lutheran Church, Broomfield, Colorado. The first unit (the central area directly under the steeple) was a sanctuary about 1/3 the size of the current one. Additions over the years led to an expanded sanctuary, offices, classrooms, a large fellowship hall, and a daycare center; the two-story classroom/choir building on the far end is the 4th and most recent addition. (Photo by author.)

Rejoice Lutheran Church, Erie, Colorado. This one-story ranch house was remodeled into a small sanctuary, with an office in the former garage and classrooms in the basement. (Photo by author.)

Pastor Keith Prekker and wife Pam Faro at a 50th Anniversary celebration of Keith's ordination. (Photo by Mackenzie Byrnes.)

SAINT MATTHEW— AURORA, COLORADO

Pastor Rudy

A visit to Lutheran Church of Hope in Broomfield, Colorado, on a Sunday morning in the 1980s would almost certainly result in a home visit during the following week from its pastor, Leonard Rudolph. Pastor Rudy, as he was affectionately known, was adamant about returning visits.

So it was, that, on the Monday night after my wife and I had attended a Sunday service at Hope, the doorbell rang and there stood Pastor Rudy. We invited him in, and my life changed.

I had resigned from the clergy roster of the Evangelical Lutheran Church in America and had returned to Colorado from my year in California. Disgruntled over a variety of things, I felt I needed a new direction in my life. I bought a Minuteman Press franchise, went to their two-week training course, and took over an existing franchise operation.

Looking for a church home, my wife and I visited several congregations in the area. Our visit to Hope was different from the others. I was especially impressed by how good a preacher Pastor Rudy was. He captured my attention right away and held it firmly throughout his sermon; peppered with illustrations from renowned theologians to Peanuts cartoons, his sermon was both easy to listen to and very meaningful. His greeting at the door was sincere, warm, and personal.

His visit to us sealed the deal. Having made countless home visits myself when I had been serving in congregations, I found his to our home to be perfect. His caring focus was entirely on us; we were the center of his attention. He wanted to learn about us, our backgrounds, our story, our needs and interests. When he left, I felt like I had made a lifelong friend—and indeed, I actually had.

Soon after joining this rapidly growing congregation, I was recruited as a confirmation class teacher. My wife and I were both enlisted as visitors to other congregation members to seek financial commitments for the new sanctuary that was going to be built. Our membership equaled involvement, and that felt good.

But Pastor Rudy was also there for us when things got tough. The print shop, in the midst of the huge revolution around computerized printing, was not going well. Plus, to be honest, printing sales was not a fulfilling task for me. As time went on, I found myself confused, dissatisfied, and financially challenged. Pastor Rudy's door was always open, as was his ear—and heart.

After one of our conversations about the print shop, he finally said, "Keith, you need to go back to parish ministry. That's where you are needed. That's where your skills are. But most importantly, that's where your heart really is."

He was right. I started the process for reinstatement to the clergy roster, and he encouraged and supported me every step of the way.

The thing about Pastor Rudy was, I was far from the only one who found his support and encouragement to be important. There were others. Many others. No, make that many, *many* others.

He was one of a kind. An open-heart surgery survivor, a two-time cancer survivor, and in his later years an ALS sufferer, he knew pain and suffering. I think he was caring by nature, but even if his incredible ability to identify with the hurt and suffering of others was learned from his own afflictions, he was, by any measure, a special human being. He had a gift for identifying with others, feeling their pain and suffering, and walking with them through what they were enduring.

Pastor Leonard Rudolph. Thank you from the bottom of my heart, and many, many other grateful hearts. Rest in peace, Pastor Rudy.

Needing a Plan B

Having found the role of business owner and print shop operator far from enjoyable, and having become very involved in the congregation I had joined as a layperson, about two years after returning to Colorado I made the decision to return to ministry.

With lots of help from my pastor and encouragement from others, I applied for reinstatement to the ELCA clergy roster. After an exhausting process that included selling the print shop, getting a psychological assessment and interview, plus an evaluation from a mental health counselor, I finally met with the bishop to discuss my theology of call—thereby getting all the required boxes for reinstatement checked.

But where I would serve was not yet clear.

St. Matthew Lutheran Church was situated in the heart of "Old Town" Aurora, Colorado, one block north of Colfax Avenue, a major east-west artery through Denver and surroundings (recognized as the longest commercial street in America). Though today the church is now closed and the building is currently serving as a busy social service center for the community, it had once been one of the largest Lutheran congregations in the Denver metro area. In its heyday it boasted a membership of fifteen-hundred-plus, but at the time I interviewed there the membership had shrunk to five hundred—on the books, that is. In reality, there were probably two hundred active members, with the two weekly services totaling around one hundred, plus or minus, in attendance.

Located in a neighborhood of compact brick homes on small lots, which had been built hurriedly for servicemen returning from WWII and their families, the church building itself was an imposing structure. The large sanctuary was barn-shaped, with classrooms and office space surrounding it on three sides. The kitchen and fellowship hall were in the basement, along with several more classrooms.

My interview seemed to go well. I would later learn that I was the sixth candidate they had interviewed. Each of the previous five had been offered the position and had turned it down. Perhaps out of either fatigue or desperation, following my interview I was invited back to "meet the folks." That meet and greet turned out to be a fun evening. Gathering in the spacious basement, fifty to one hundred of the members had come to chat with each other and with me. A portion of the evening was a group Q and A session in which my self-effacing "bald jokes" seemed to be a big hit, and not one question was raised about my status (i.e., being newly restored to the clergy roster after having previously resigned from it).

At a subsequent congregational meeting, a vote was taken on issuing the call to me, and it was affirmative.

I accepted the call, and so began one of the more challenging chapters of my ministry.

The aforementioned "one block north of Colfax" location set this congregation in a tough area. At this point in its long east-west extension through the metro communities of Aurora, Denver, Wheat Ridge, and Golden, Colfax Avenue had become a fairly seedy piece of roadway. Starting at dusk the streetwalkers were on duty. Every couple of blocks there were pawn shops and motels that catered to the one-night crowd and the "no other place to live" folks. Within one block on either side of Colfax itself, it was not unusual to see people—often young people (kids)—waving bags of pills (or worse) at you, offering them for sale as you drove by. Shootings were not uncommon.

Directly across the street from the church was a house that had been spray painted with all sorts of graffiti both before and after it had been boarded up. On a fairly regular basis someone would manage to find a way past the obstructions to "set up shop" again. The traffic in and out would increase markedly. Not only potential customers, but also the police would notice; there would be a raid, the place would be re-secured, and the process would start all over.

The neighborhood had gone from all White residents to mostly Black folks, with some Hispanics and Asians as well. Not too many Lutherans in the mix of people living in the area. Many of our regular worshipers on Sunday would drive into the neighborhood from the outer ring suburbs to which they had "fled" not too long previously.

I thought that my task was clear: Go calling on the local residents, and invite them to worship.

Somehow, the experience of a lily-white pastor knocking on the door to invite non-lily-white residents to attend that lily-white church down on the corner was not overwhelmingly well-received. Most neighborhood residents were not outwardly rude to me, but their incredulous looks told the story. My Plan A went down in flames.

There was no Plan B. We limped along, attendance holding somewhat steady. Our two Sunday morning services were sparsely attended. The sanctuary had capacity for three hundred. We generally had fifty-to-seventy at the first Sunday morning service, and usually no more than thirty-to-fifty at the second. My suggestion to consolidate the two services into one was roundly defeated. "We've always had two services."

And so we settled into a routine—a pretty discouraging one, sad to say.

Anonymous Note

I'd been at St. Matthew for a month or two.

And then there it was: ugly in its childishness and ignorance.

It was placed in the church mailbox by someone—not the mailman. There was no postage, no return address. The message on the front of the envelope was spelled out by letters cut from newspapers and magazines and glued to the envelope unevenly, like some cartoon ransom note: "WHAT DOES THIS MEAN??"

Yes, *two* question marks.

Upon opening it, I found a piece of paper to which had been glued a small article from *The Lutheran* magazine, our denomination's monthly news publication. The article was a regular feature showing pastors who had moved from one parish to another. At the bottom of the article was a category called "Restored to the Roster." I was listed in that category, with several others. Apparently, this looked really suspicious to...someone.

I had been approved for reinstatement. My name had been submitted to St. Matthew Lutheran for consideration, the interviews conducted, the call voted on by the congregation and approved, and I had accepted the new call. I had been installed by the bishop and had been functioning as pastor of the congregation.

Now this.

While the question—already asked and answered several times during the call process—was certainly legitimate, the method of delivery was clearly wrong. How best to deal with both the question and the issue of childish anonymous notes?

The next Sunday while giving the announcements, I added one final one. I held up the envelope with its silly lettering. Explaining that it was my practice to never respond to anonymous communications, I said simply that the question on the envelope had already been answered, and that I would be happy to answer it again for the questioner—but only face to face. If he or she wanted to make an appointment or just drop by the office, it would be my pleasure to sit down and explain the process and details.

No one ever contacted me about it.

Diving In

Maybe it was because I was eager, returning to congregational ministry after three years away. Maybe it was because St. Matthew was a small congregation, so it seemed doable. But at some point in getting started in my new position there, I mentioned wanting to call on every member of the congregation to get to know them on a personal basis.

One of the women in the congregation picked up on that idea and came into the office one afternoon. "Pastor," she said, "Your idea to call on each household in the congregation is great. I'd like to volunteer to help you set up those calls." A long-time member, she knew most everyone in the congregation and she was able to set up a schedule for me, giving helpful background when warranted as well as directions on how to find homes (pre-Google Maps).

Irene was an efficient organizer, not one to waste my time or the time of those being visited. Within a couple of months, I had called on every home in the parish, had learned a lot of history, both personal and congregational, and had started forming relationships that would bear good fruit in the months and years ahead. Without Irene's encouragement and organizational ability, I wouldn't have been nearly as successful, either in starting or completing such a large undertaking.

The calls were brief, and really diverse.

In some, I learned of people's past history with the church in general or that congregation in particular. I heard about physical ailments, past slights, or hurt feelings from years gone by. I learned of medical problems, current and/or upcoming. There were discussions of theology both shallow and deep. Through it all, I experienced a wide variety of people's circumstances and attitudes.

There was a visit to an older woman who suffered from glaucoma; I knew virtually nothing about that condition before getting to know her, and she raised my consciousness and awareness so that I better understood her challenges. The man who commuted daily to the Air Force Academy in Colorado Springs to teach firefighting was astonishing—it was a 110-mile round trip. A mom who had been abandoned with two young sons in a trailer court opened my eyes to a slice of life I had never encountered. A couple of retirees, both former heavy smokers now limited by the length of their oxygen tank hoses, who referred bitterly to "The Golden Years," made for a sobering visit. Another senior couple insisted to me that Black people bear the "mark of Cain" in their skin, and thereby segregation is justified (somehow overlooking the fact that that mark was to be for Cain's protection, not separation). Chatting with the former nightclub singer who now anchored the choir was a delight. A visit to a couple who showed me the pictures of their only child's grave (having died at birth) was a deeply moving experience.

Those visits, and the encouragement and facilitation to make them (thanks, Irene!), were invaluable in getting to know the members of that congregation and in them getting to know me. Though the time investment was great, so were the rewards.

This is the church. God's people.

They Say Hindsight is 20/20

It was the late 80s, early 90s, and the computerized world was continuing to grow. I suggested getting a computer for the office.

EARTHQUAKE!!

The secretary objected—She'd never be able to learn how to use a computer! The council objected—"We'd never be able to afford that extravagance!" And besides that, "We don't want someone to steal our data" (though I wasn't proposing connecting to the internet, then in its infancy).

There were some forward thinkers in the congregation who were somewhat familiar with the new world of computers, and they started a fund for purchasing one apart from the overburdened budget. Before long the money was in hand. Though some members still had misgivings and objections, we got a computer, one of the early IBM 286's.

The church secretary let it sit there for a while, eyeing it suspiciously from time to time. Finally, we had the first lesson. (I had gone through this learning process myself, in my previous position with the church Foundation in California.) After a brief introduction, she plugged away at it at her own speed, and before you knew it…she was a believer.

She mastered that thing, and one day came into my office to thank me for getting her started on it. She actually loved it!

Fast forward several years. I had left St. Matthew and moved on to another parish. Invited back for an anniversary celebration, I was pleased to visit with many good friends. Towards the end of the evening, that former secretary came over to say hello. I learned that her situation had changed considerably. She had left her position with the congregation because her husband had died unexpectedly, and she had had to seek full-time employment instead of the part-time church position. It turns out that her computer skills, early in the "computer revolution" as it was, equipped her to get a really good secretarial position. She thanked me over and over for "pushing her" into learning to use the computer.

Some earthquakes are better than others.

Room for All

It was a constant struggle to be physically located in a community but have neither effective outreach to, nor contact with, that community.

One Sunday as I and the other worship leaders for the day assembled in the narthex at the back of the sanctuary, with all of the usual pre-procession assembling and last-minute preparations going on, I looked into the church and was pleased to see that a nicely dressed Black woman, maybe sixty years old or so, had come to worship. She sat at the outside end of a pew, right on the side aisle. She took one of the hymnals and began to look through it. After checking it out, she sat back to await the start of the service.

The opening hymn began, and while processing down the middle aisle to the front of the church, I was as usual focused on what was in front of me—singing the words from the hymnal I was holding, the beautiful chancel up front, not tripping over my robe as I walked—and only peripherally aware of anything happening in the pews. I was therefore barely aware of an interaction off to the side.

In retrospect, I realized that an older member of the congregation had arrived during the hymn and walked up the side aisle. I heard a loud voice off to the side behind me say, "You're in my pew!" And a softer voice replied, "I'm sorry."

By the time I reached the chancel up front and turned to face the congregation, I saw that our visitor was nowhere to be seen.

The sanctuary would seat three hundred. A typical service would find maybe a hundred or so people in the pews. There were plenty of seats available, more than enough room for all.

We never saw her again. Of course not.

Déjà Vu All Over Again

Many churches have multiple services on Christmas Eve, to accommodate the large numbers of people who traditionally attend church on that night. In addition to the regular churchgoers, there are always many additional people who go to church only on Christmas Eve. The well-known phenomenon of "C and E Christians" (Christmas-and-Easter-only attendees) is a cause for humor in some instances and concern in others.

In planning for my first Christmas Eve at St. Matthew, I wasn't sure what to expect. The large size of the sanctuary coupled with our smallish regular Sunday worship attendance made me think one service would certainly suffice. Surely we could also accommodate any additional Christmas Eve attendees with just one service. However, the council and the worship committee were immovable that their two-services Christmas Eve tradition be maintained.

The towering Christmas tree that appeared early in Advent (somewhat to my dismay—I prefer Advent to be Advent, and save Christmas decorations for Christmas), pointed to Christmas possibly being a huge celebration there. Past attendance records seemed to bear out the need for two services. So, two Christmas Eve services it would be!

I confess I harbored some amount of secret resentment over the multiplicity of services. While everyone else was making plans for their special Christmas Eve family gatherings, I knew I would of course have to be at the church especially early on Christmas Eve, and then stay late, with my frozen microwavable dinner to gobble down between services, amidst the joyous hustle and bustle of everyone else going to and from their festive holiday meals and celebrations. But it was a familiar annual routine, and I kept my pity party to myself.

Christmas Eve arrived. It was picture-perfect, I have to say. There was fresh snow. It was cold, but not twenty below. There were no major international crises filling the headlines. Everyone seemed to be in a good mood.

Christmas and Easter are regarded by many preachers as the two hardest sermons of the year to write. What can be said that is fresh and captivating? How to make that "old, old story" come alive and be relevant? This being my first Christmas in the parish, I had worked a little extra hard to come up with what I hoped would be a good sermon.

The first service started and as I processed down the center aisle during the opening hymn, I estimated the church to be about two-thirds full. Nice. Not crowded and cramped, but with the feeling of a "nice crowd." The joy and cheer of Christmas seemed to pervade the place.

With the first service ended—greetings, hugs, and handshakes completed; everyone out the door and on their way to nice holiday meals and joyous family gatherings—it was time for *my* traditional Christmas Eve routine. I took myself down to the kitchen, popped my frozen dinner into the microwave, gathered utensils and a glass of water, and waited for the sometimes (but on a lonely Christmas Eve, never) pleasant ding announcing it was done. There was quite a long gap of time between the services, but it just wasn't possible for me to drive home in between—I lived some twenty-five miles from the church, and who knows what the holiday traffic would be. I had been tempted to try it, but my better judgment prevailed, so I stuck to my usual practice of a frozen dinner (sometimes a PB and J sandwich).

Following my Christmas Eve dinner there was quite a bit of time until the second service, so I was able to straighten up the sanctuary a bit, catch up on a little reading in my office, and run through my sermon again to smooth out a couple of rough patches and be ready for the second group of worshipers.

Hearing the organist begin her warm-up routine for service number two, I went to the sacristy. I put on my robe, fidgeted nervously as I always did, and went to the back of the church, ready to process down the center aisle during the opening hymn as usual.

Walking down the aisle, I saw the folks gathered for the second service that festive eve.

Suddenly I was overwhelmed with confusion. *Wha-a-a-t?*

What was going on?

It looked as though most—maybe all—of the people sitting in the pews at that second service had attended the first one.

The opening hymn finished. Facing the congregation from the front of the sanctuary, instead of speaking the usual liturgical greeting, I invited everyone to be seated. I then asked, what was happening? A representative of the congregation stood and explained that their tradition was to have two completely different services on Christmas Eve, and most folks would attend both.

I was shocked—I had never heard of such a practice!

No one had bothered to explain this to me, either. They assumed that every congregation did it that way. I, rather sheepishly, explained that my experience was always to have multiple *identical* services to accommodate more worshipers. Since I was operating under the only format I had ever known (or even contemplated), and so were they, I asked what they wanted to do. "Let's go ahead with the second service anyway," came the reply—and so we did.

I tried to be a little more informal the second time. I tried to alter the sermon illustrations where I could. I tried to be a little more concise.

But it was the very same service twice on that one fateful Christmas Eve. I have never forgotten my shock…confusion…panic…embarrassment.

The next Christmas Eve (with no dissenting opinions expressed) we had just one service.

Stoney

He was an older man, slender and a little hunched over, walking with a shuffle and aided by a cane. He dropped by the church one afternoon and asked to see the pastor. The secretary directed him down the hall to my office.

The first thing I noticed was the odor. The second thing was the two little dogs he had with him. But really the most noticeable thing about him was his infectious smile. I couldn't help but smile back!

I was going to invite him into my study, but didn't know if I could trust the dogs, if you know what I mean, so I suggested we sit on the steps out front and visit a little. His name was Charles "Stoney" Jackson. "Stoney" was short for Stonewall, he explained. A true son of the South, he was named for Confederate general Stonewall Jackson. He was technically, he added, "*Reverend* Charles 'Stoney' Jackson," since he had been ordained by the Disciples of Christ denomination "way back when..."

I resisted the impulse to ask to see his birth certificate to check out his story of his name. He was obviously a yarn spinner, so I settled back to listen to his tale—and what a tale it was! I will spare you the hour-plus version and go right to the highlight: He told me he had been a contestant on "The $64,000 Question" TV quiz show and had won some money. He then went on to "The $64,000 Challenge" program, and won some more. When the scandal broke about some of these television quiz shows feeding answers to eventual winners, Stoney was invited to testify before Congress.

And now, for a whole chain of reasons I can no longer recall, he was in Aurora, Colorado, in a small apartment, without a connection to a soul in the world—and wanting to receive the sacrament. I served him Communion, and promised to call to bring him Communion on a regular basis.

I only made one visit to his home before I learned that he had died. That one visit revealed a squalid apartment. The shabby furnishings were tattered and worn, dishes piled high in the sink, and an unpleasant odor suffused the place. Stoney, as he insisted I call him, really seemed lonely and desperately needed someone to talk to. We visited for a while, I served him Communion, and then took my leave.

I never saw him again. I saw no mention in the news of his passing. I don't know where or even if a funeral took place. I don't know what happened to his little dogs. It was when I returned for my second visit that the new residents informed me of his death.

I have since searched online, and found verification of his quiz show story. Charles Stonewall Jackson. Rest in peace.

Secretary to the Rescue

Over the years I've many times dealt with people who I confess made me nervous in some way—street people, con artists, thieves, people on the run, etc.—but there was one time I was really frightened: the day a young, clean-cut soldier showed up in my office.

He told me he had just been discharged from the Army. For the past few years he had been stationed in Colorado Springs (seventy miles south of Denver) with his family. Upon his discharge, he and his wife moved back to Denver as planned, but his twin seven-year-old daughters had become ill just before the move and had had to be hospitalized in Colorado Springs. One had been well enough to come to Denver with her parents at the time of the move, and now the other daughter was ready to be released from the hospital. But he had no means of going back to the Springs to pick her up. Could I help him with money for a couple of bus tickets?

The amount of money was not huge—sixty dollars or so. We had no "discretionary cash" in that congregation like many churches do, so if I chose to help it would be coming out of my pocket. I didn't have that much on me, so would have to make some arrangements to get the money if I were going to try to help.

I had learned over the years to check out the stories that people presented whenever possible. So, with this guy sitting across my desk, I picked up the phone and called the military hospital in the Springs. They had no one there by either daughter's name. Nor had they had anyone by that name in the last month.

Out of the corner of my eye I could see this ex-GI getting more and more agitated as my phone quest went on. When I hung up the phone, he slammed his hands down on my desk, pushed himself to his feet and started screaming at me. I stood up, too, so as to not have him looming over me. He continued to shout in quite "graphic and colorful" terms, and started moving around my desk towards me in an exceptionally threatening manner.

Thankfully, I had left the door to the office open—the office secretary heard the commotion and came down the hall to see if everything was all right, bless her heart! Her voice and sudden presence in the room seemed to jog him out of his fit of rage. He stormed out, not to be heard from again.

I thanked the secretary, and told her it was no big deal.

But, I was shaken.

Truly shaken.

No Words

Looking out from the pulpit, the sea of white faces was enriched by a group of four black ones.

St. Matthew, located in an area of Metro-Denver that had become predominantly African-American, had remained an almost exclusively White congregation—save for one family. I'd been there about a year when the Joneses began attending worship occasionally. They were a young couple with a seven-year-old and a brand-new tiny baby. They were at the same time a bit reserved yet outgoing, and I enjoyed my brief encounters with them.

Then I realized I hadn't seen them for a while. Then it became a long while.

I tried to call—their phone was disconnected. I dropped them a note—it was returned: "No forwarding address." What had happened? Where were they?

The mystery festered for a long time, but finally word arrived. That darling tiny baby we'd seen was so tiny because he had been extremely premature, and his early arrival had caused him to be placed in the NICU. The duration of his stay there had been nearly record-breaking, measured in months, not days or weeks.

The employer-provided insurance had run out. The bills had mounted. When mom and son were finally discharged from the hospital, the debt total was astronomical. We learned that bankruptcy and its aftermath resulted in the loss of their home. They had been evicted with nowhere to go—no family in the area—no support network around them. They had disappeared.

It was a tragedy. No, it was a string of tragedies. How could this happen, in the first place? How could it be that in this rich country—a country in which there are appeals on TV for poor homeless animals that result in donations of thousands and thousands of dollars; a country in which churches dot the landscape, churches that worship a God who mandates care for the neighbor, and for the poor and needy; a country that touts its foreign aid to struggling and developing nations around the world, but—there is no help for our own people? How could this happen?

And how could it be that we, the faith family with which they had chosen to affiliate, knew so little about them that they could just "fall off our radar" and we couldn't locate them to try to help? How could it be that there was so little trust within our community of faith that these folks wouldn't share their struggles and be open to the possibility of help?

How, indeed. We'd like to believe that they felt, and were, welcomed. But obviously there was a real chasm or barrier that we White folks, in our comfortable reality as the majority "norm," were oblivious to.

Disappointing. Eye-opening. Wake-up call.

There just aren't words.

Tears don't help.

EnKKKounter

"The Ku Klux Klan had no presence in Colorado in 1920. By 1925, Klan members and sponsored candidates controlled the Colorado State House and Senate, the office of Secretary of State, a state Supreme Court judgeship, seven benches on Denver District Court, and city councils in some Colorado towns. Mayor Ben Stapleton of Denver and Governor Clarence Morley of Colorado were also Klansmen. The Klan was stronger in Colorado than any other state."—from an online article, "When the KKK Ruled Colorado: Not So Long Ago," by Thomas J. Noel, June 19, 2013.

The former Denver airport was named Stapleton Field; it was replaced in 1995 by the current Denver International Airport. In 2020 a huge furor arose over a housing development: it too had been named Stapleton in honor of the former mayor. Residents, having been made aware of the Klan past of former Mayor Stapleton, demanded a name change. They were successful. The name of the development was changed to Central Park.

While I was serving at St. Matthew, in the late 1980s and early 90s there was a resurgence of Klan activity, both around the US and in Colorado. Emboldened by a rally on the steps of the State Capitol in Denver, a group of Klansmen announced a similar rally in Aurora, Colorado.

This rally was to take place in the neighborhood in which St. Matthew was located.

While the emotional response and suggestion by many in the community was to have a counter-rally—larger and louder than the Klan effort—cooler heads were counseling a hands-off/ignore-the-fools approach. "What they want is publicity and visibility. A counter-protest ramps up the attention." The attitude of the Aurora Ministerial Association was the same as the newspaper/ TV coverage of "don't play into their hands."

I agreed wholeheartedly with the "ignore them" tactic, and encouraged my church council and individual members to be elsewhere on the day of the rally. I wrote a letter to the editor of the local paper, adding my voice to others advocating that approach.

It was a little alarming on the Sunday before the advertised KKK rally to have a group of three leather-jacketed, skinhead, obviously-KKK-supporters noisily take their place in the back pew and demonstrably take notes on the service, the sermon, and especially my announcement encouraging people to avoid the rally area the next Saturday in order to discomfit the KKK people with low attendance and no conflicts.

The "spies" (as it felt that they were) left quietly during the closing hymn. Our member who was straightening the pews after church found a note they left, addressed to me: "You'll be sorry."

The rally?—It was a total bust for the outside agitators. They were ignored. No one showed up to counter-protest. The KKK/neo-Nazi fools "rallied" for about ten minutes, and then packed up their things and rather sheepishly left the community.

I used to require my confirmation students to take notes on sermons. (I knew what I wanted to say; I knew what I thought I said—the notes told me what they heard me say.) Never in my wildest dreams did I ever picture leather-jacketed neo-Nazi/KKK-types as the ones listening intently and recording my comments.

Walls

St. Matthew was contacted by Girls Inc. of Metro Denver about the possibility of their using some of the classroom space in the church basement for an after-school program for girls in our community. The church's basement would be an ideal location, they suggested, since there was a kitchen, a large meeting hall, and several classrooms around the central hall.

I had never heard of the program, but in doing some research I found it to be an outstanding opportunity for girls just like those in our community. So many of the kids in our neighborhood were latchkey kids: sent off to school in the morning with their house or apartment key on a lanyard around their neck. The key was sent with them because there would be no one at home after school, and the child was expected to let him/herself in, and entertain him or herself until whenever a parent got home from work.

Girls Inc. provided supervision, study space, healthy snacks, and enrichment programs—to help the girls become better educated and more fulfilled members of society. The church was asked to provide free use of the space and occasional assistance with gathering equipment (e.g., donated computers, paper supplies, etc.).

Of course, any arrangement like this has the potential for some conflict, and some conflict there was.

While some of the cabinets in the kitchen were given over for Girls Inc.'s use, there was often the suspicion among some congregation members that church supplies were being "borrowed" without permission. The Sunday School teachers sometimes complained that materials were missing, or that the rooms weren't picked up properly.

But the biggest ongoing issue seemed to be that the walls were being dirtied by little hands.

Many long discussions were held among church members concerning the "dirty walls." My contention that this was actually wonderful—the building was useful to the community!—seemed to fall on deaf ears.

The issue was never let go. Over time, I strongly suspected that the discomfort was over "our" walls being dirtied by all the little hands of "those people."

Later on, shortly after I left St. Matthew to take another call, I learned that Girls Inc. was asked to leave.

St. Matthew's congregation has since closed its doors and disbanded.

St. Matthew's building, however, is still serving the community as a center for refugees, immigrants, and cultural diversity groups and programming.

A New Chapter

Increasingly frustrated with my inability to come up with an effective strategy to reach out to our multiracial neighborhood, I was nearing the point of despair. It seemed we needed some crack in the wall, some small opening to break down the barrier between our lily-white congregation and the neighborhood that had, over time, become ever more Black/Latino/Asian. I was out of ideas.

One Sunday morning I looked out at the gathered worshipers and to my surprise there she was—a Black woman! More than that—a Black woman who appeared to be familiar with the Lutheran worship service!

After the last hymn I hurried to the door to greet the folks, anxious to meet this visitor. She was gone. She was gone! She had apparently left during the last hymn. She left no name—no contact information—nothing. "Crushed" is too weak a word for my reaction.

Two Sundays later she was back again. She was just as engaged in the service, just as attentive to my homiletical effort, just as open to greeting folks around her as I had witnessed two weeks earlier.

This time I rushed to the door before the last hymn actually began—I wasn't going to miss her again. When she came out the door we chatted a bit more than is usual. I asked if she could wait around till I was done greeting folks so we could chat a bit more. She did, and I learned more of her story.

Born in North Carolina, she grew up in the Lutheran church—quite unusual for a member of the Black community at that time. Her father was a Baptist who really loved classical music, especially the classical music of Johann Sebastian Bach. Her father loved that famed German Lutheran composer's music so much that he became a Lutheran in order to hear and enjoy it in the context of worship. Hence Marge's Lutheran roots.

We made an appointment to visit Monday afternoon and managed to chat away several hours. Marge was a newly-retired executive of a large national insurance firm. Her husband, a retired Philadelphia police officer, had recently died. She had sold their place in Philly and was planning to return to her home in Raleigh, but was making a train trip across the country to see the US and visit some relatives in different parts of the country first. From Denver, she was headed to Seattle, and then back across the country to North Carolina.

Marge had been very active in her Lutheran church in Philadelphia and in her synod's work, serving on several synodical committees. She understood church. She understood race and racial relations. She understood our situation in our neighborhood. At the end of the afternoon I had come up with a plan which I suggested to her. Why not finish her trip out west, head back home, settle affairs there—and then return to Colorado to come onto the staff at St. Matthew? We needed her to be a branch to our community. While she was completing her travels, I explained, I would be beating the bushes to find money to pay for her work in our midst. She asked for time to think and pray about it.

With renewed spring in my step and hope in my heart, I began the search for funds. The national church liked the idea and made a grant for a three-year experimental program. I called Marge. She liked the idea. Now came the final hurdle—the congregation.

I wrote up a lengthy proposal and submitted it to the church council. Hesitant at first, they finally approved the proposal to be submitted to a specially-called congregational meeting. A long background paper was prepared with a thorough explanation of what was being proposed, starting with an analysis of our community, the recent history of the congregation—its decline in recent years from a membership of sixteen hundred to its present (officially, anyway) five hundred—and expectations of what adding a person of color to the staff in our setting could mean for us and for the neighborhood.

Much lively conversation ensued before the vote was taken. The votes were counted. The motion passed with roughly sixty-five percent voting yes.

I contacted Marge. She accepted. Thus began a whole new chapter in the life of St. Matthew Lutheran Church, in Marge's life, and in my own.

What a chapter it was to be!

No Joke

Jan was my "Norwegian joke buddy." For whatever reason, Norwegians love to tell jokes about themselves. A guy named "Ole" is usually a character in these jokes; Ole's buddy "Sven" often makes an appearance; the role of significant other is filled by "Lena." Together this merry band, augmented as needed by other colorful characters, bumbles its way through one crazy encounter after another. There are a million of these jokes, and Jan knew most of them and loved to share them with me and everyone else.

I looked forward to Jan's visits with the latest misadventure of Ole and Lena, or Ole and Sven. The day that Marge began her ministry as Lay Associate at St. Matthew, I was visited by Jan. This time his demeanor was very different from his usual cheerfulness. He came into my office, declined my offer to sit down, and with a stern look on his face declared, "I'm not coming back to this church until you get that effing n***er off the staff!"

Stunned, it took me several moments to gather myself. To talk that way anywhere—not to mention in a church, not to mention in my office, not to mention to my face—infuriated me. Seeing red, I jumped to my feet, came around the desk, took hold of Jan's arm, and ushered him out of my office and to the door of the church. I said to him, more loudly and forcefully than I intended, "Jan, don't come back! We don't want you back!" And with that I pushed him out the door, slamming it behind him.

I returned to my office, went to my desk—and sat there, shaking.

In the days that followed, I had huge emotional ups and downs. I was ashamed of my knee-jerk violent reaction to Jan's declaration. I was also filled with anger again and again at that blatant racism, and the attempted diminishing of a faithful woman of God because of the color of her skin, or her background, or whatever it is that is so abhorrent or frightening or whatever to too many members of my White tribe. I struggled mightily with this whole mix of emotions and feelings.

But when members of the informal "Norske Coffee Klatch" of which Jan was a charter member started showing up one by one to tell me that I needed to go and apologize to Jan, my anger surged—not as red hot perhaps, but burning just the same. I managed to listen as politely as I could to each as he presented his case, and then, as clearly as possible, I explained that even if hell might freeze over, I would not be apologizing to any racist SOB who did what Jan had done and said the things Jan had said. In an attempt to be reconciliatory, I did say that if Jan wanted to come to the church and apologize to me and to Marge, I would be willing to listen.

Jan?—no show. Ever again.

Members of his "klatch," to their credit, stayed involved and, for the most part, came to not just accept, but genuinely appreciate, Marge and her many gifts to the congregation and the church at large.

Moral of this story? I don't know if there is one. Racism is deep-seated and it is ugly. It is in the gut rather than head-based.

It is real. It is deep. It is disgusting.

Welcoming Marge

Marge's welcome was warm and genuine from the nearly seventy percent of the congregation that voted to call her. There was a welcoming party for her, and a "care package" was assembled with basic necessities that one would not be able to bring on an airplane. A group had scouted available apartments in the area and took her on a tour to find the one she liked.

Having lived her entire adult life in Philadelphia, where her late husband had been a police officer, Marge was accustomed to always using public transportation for getting around, and expected to do the same in her new home. She was shocked to learn that the bus system was nowhere near as efficient or reliable in the sprawling Denver suburb of Aurora (and trains and light rail were non-existent there at the time). It quickly became apparent that she was going to need a car. Thus began a search for one for her. It turned out to be a very short search, because one of the church members came and told me she was planning to buy a new car, and rather than trade in her previous vehicle she would be willing to donate it to the church for Marge to use.

Marge took it for a test drive, loved the car, and presto—she had wheels. The parishioner who donated the car also picked up the insurance for the first year, and gave Marge some pointers on operating the vehicle, since Marge hadn't driven in some time.

Others were also proving to be supportive and helpful. The portion of the congregation that was in favor of our staffing experiment went above and beyond in terms of helping in the resettling and start-up phase of Marge's ministry with us. Many of those who were initially uncertain were won over by Marge's genuine warmth and sincerity. Her deep commitment to the church and its mission was evident, and her positive and outgoing nature was contagious.

Once having gained her footing in our congregation, she soon got involved with our regional church office and began representing us on several state-wide and regional committees, and a national church task force. Her commitment to the work of the church and her experience in her previous congregation were evident and greatly appreciated by these groups, and helped to bring an expanded vision to our congregation as she reported back to us.

The transition from the more formal East Coast version of the church to our more relaxed Western style was humorously illustrated one day early in her time with us, when one of our members called the church and Marge answered the phone. She was aghast when this person asked to speak with "Keith." In quite a huffy tone, she elucidated that, "Yes. *REVEREND* PREKKER is here. I'll put him on."

When the call was concluded, I explained to her that she wasn't in Philly anymore, and that I had never been called by that particular moniker in my life. I've usually been called Pastor Keith or Pastor Prekker; or just Pastor… Keith…Hey you…

"Welcome to the relaxed West. You'll come to love it." And she did.

Years later she laughed when we recalled that incident and reflected together on the culture shock of moving to a strange and different part of the world.

A Multitude of Gifts

I had no detailed plan of what sharing ministry with Marge Bailey would entail. I hoped her presence on the staff would make St. Matthew seem, and be, more open to the community that surrounded the church building. Somehow, simplistically, I guess I thought that her presence would result in an automatic influx of new Black families.

Foolish me.

Marge, on the other hand, knew better. Even though she may have somewhat shared that diversity goal for the congregation, she also knew that the real goal was to serve—to serve the community and whoever it was that comprised it. She went over to the neighboring school and started to volunteer there. She reached out and formed relationships in the neighborhood. She made herself visible as another "face" of the congregation.

She had a low-key openness and ability to relate to almost everyone. One day she introduced me to one of the Denver Broncos football players whom she had met while volunteering at the school. He would stop by the church to visit from time to time and got involved with the Girls Inc. after-school program that was using space in the church.

One day she was giving a tour of the sanctuary to a group of the Girls Inc. girls, and she popped into my office to ask if I would come and meet with the kids and tell them a little about my vestments they had found hanging in the sacristy, and about the church organ.

Marge had an easy and natural ability to connect with all kinds of folks, and she brought a real spirit of warmth and generosity as well as new energy to our congregation.

But in addition to her reaching out to the community in many and varied ways, I was most grateful to Marge for her gentle way of pointing out to me my own short-sightedness and lack of awareness in terms of interracial understanding and acceptance. Many were the deep and soul-searching conversations we shared over the gaps and misunderstandings that came from the interracial divide.

We found ourselves sharing with each other family news, joys, and heartaches, and I'm grateful to say that in addition to being ministry partners, we formed a deep and abiding friendship.

Unforgettable

The Seniors' Lunch was a highlight of the month at St. Matthew. Once a month the elders would gather at a different local restaurant for lunch and a time of "gabbing." There was no program, no agenda. It was a purely social event. Once in a while there would be a topic announced ahead of time. Very occasionally there would be some sort of community presenter. It was mainly intended to be just a fun time.

Most of the members had known each other for a long time. They had roots that went way back in the community and in that congregation. The regulars were all female, except for Emil. Emil was always glad to see me arrive so that he wouldn't be quite so hopelessly outnumbered.

Emil was a retired accountant. He seldom spoke. When he did, it was clear that he was bright, had been following the conversation, and had something of significance to contribute. He was from Minnesota, from near a community in which I had lived for a time. A lifelong bachelor, he was painfully unsure of himself with "all those women."

From time to time he and I would wander off into our own "guys'" conversation. Emil had loved to fish as he was growing up in Minnesota and we would talk fishing, some sports, and occasionally the state of the economy.

Emil followed the economy closely and had done some serious investing over the years. He said nothing specific, but I got the sense that his investments had done well. He also intimated that he had made the church the beneficiary of a couple of his investments, to be received at the time of his passing.

One month he talked a lot about an upcoming trip "back home." There was some sort of family gathering and he wanted to be there for it. He was going to drive. It would be a two-day drive, according to the plan, with an overnight in South Dakota. As a result of the trip, he would be missing the next month's Seniors' Lunch.

I had to miss that next month also, due to a conflict. About a week after the missed lunch I got a phone call from Emil's sister in Minnesota. She wondered if I had seen him or heard from him. Hearing "No" from me, she asked if I would go over to his townhouse "just to check on him." He had left to return to Colorado a number of days prior and had not called when he got home. That was unusual for him. She worried about him, because he was diabetic and he lived alone.

I found his nicely-cared-for townhouse, approached the door, and knocked. No answer. The doorbell also elicited no response. I walked across the front of the unit, looking in the windows. Nothing. Then I went around to the back. Same story. I returned to the church and called Emil's sister to report my disappointing results. She decided to call the police and ask for them to do a wellness check. At the time I hadn't heard of such a thing, but she seemed to be familiar with it.

Next thing I knew, the police called me and asked if I would be willing to accompany an officer as he performed the check. I got there first, and when the officer arrived he assumed I had more information and/or familiarity than I did. He rang the bell, knocked repeatedly on the doors and windows, kept calling Emil's name—all to no avail. Finally, he asked me to return to my car while he forced entry.

A few minutes later he came to my car looking quite ill. He had gained access and found Emil dead on his bed. According to the officer, it looked like he had gotten home, decided to lie down to rest, and died. No sign of foul play. I was not allowed into the dwelling, but I could smell clinging to the officer's clothes the awful odor of someone who had been deceased for a time.

I went back to the church and called Emil's sister, but the police had already informed her. She was crying and hard to understand on the phone. She asked about a funeral, and I assured her we could handle that at our end. "He wanted to be buried in the church cemetery back home," she said, but asked if we could also do a small service for him in Colorado, since that's where he lived most of his adult life. "Of course," I replied.

Two days later I got another call from Emil's sister. She and her husband were both on the line. They had another request. Would I be willing to go to the townhouse and try to locate some papers they needed? They thought they knew where they were and could direct me right to them. The police would have to be there to let me in because the scene had been sealed.

Once again I arrived before the police. By now the smell outside the townhouse was strong, even though Emil's body was no longer there. When the police opened the door, I was almost overcome. I hurried into Emil's study to the drawer the sister had indicated and there was the paper she needed. I snatched it up as quickly as possible and dashed for the door and the fresh air outside.

The smell of death. I had heard of it. Now I know what it is like.

They say once you have experienced it, you'll never forget it. I think "they" are right.

I'll surely never forget Emil, either. Rest in peace, my friend.

Cedric

Cedric, a seventh-grader, was an outgoing and cheerful young man who loved being around church. His grandparents were very active long-time members of our inner-city congregation. He lived with his mother and older brother in a mobile home in one of the rougher trailer parks in the area. Cedric liked being around the people of the congregation, he liked participating in church activities, but above all, he absolutely loved serving as one of the acolytes. When it was his turn he would don the robe, grasp the candle lighter (a four-foot pole with a lit wick at the end), and with military precision march down the aisle at the beginning of the worship service to perform his candle-lighting duty.

Our congregation had two morning services, with Sunday School held in between. One Sunday, during the Sunday School hour, our organist took me aside and said that during the hustle and bustle after the first service she thought she saw Cedric go up to the altar and take something from the offering plate. I decided to approach Cedric and ask for clarification. Cedric insisted over and over that he had done no such thing (in my mind, a clear case of "protesting too much").

He went off to Sunday School, but I continued to be bothered by it. On a hunch, I checked the restrooms and found an offering envelope that had been torn open but discarded with a check made out to the church inside. I pulled the church council president out of the coffee hour, explained the situation, showed him the envelope and check, and we came up with a plan.

We took Cedric out of his Sunday School class and into my study. Explaining what we had found, we asked him again if he had been involved. After at first denying any knowledge of the event, he broke down and confessed that indeed he had been the one to take the envelope, but finding a check inside instead of cash, he had ditched it in the men's room.

Amid a flood of tears, he explained that he needed money, because it was the only way he could get along at school—he had to buy candy and treats for the other kids to stop them from bullying him. The bullying centered on two things: his father had abandoned the family, and more strikingly, Cedric had the most pronounced buck teeth imaginable. His two front teeth protruded almost straight out from his mouth. His teeth had been the source of much mistreatment from classmates for years, and he had resorted to trying to bribe them with snacks and goodies to get them to stop.

Frustratingly, I had to leave for the second service, but our council president stayed with Cedric and tried to console and comfort him as much as possible. It turned out that the president had grown up in a single-parent situation after his father had deserted his family as well, so they had something of a connection.

That afternoon I couldn't get Cedric off my mind. I recalled that in a previous parish there had been an orthodontist who was quite active in the church. I called him and explained the situation. He said that he would gladly help, but that Cedric would have to be able to make weekly visits. I explained that was not possible due to the distance and the fact that Cedric's mother had no car.

The doctor then asked for a few days to check out another option. I thought maybe he had a friend whose practice was closer. Instead, this caring man contacted the state Orthodontists Society: they had a program to provide assistance in just such a situation. Cedric's case was submitted to the society, and he was accepted into this program.

The treatment was complex; it involved breaking and resetting the jaw as well as surgical intervention to straighten the teeth, and a complicated process of braces and adjustments over several years, at a location that enabled Cedric and his family to get him there easily. I left the congregation for a new call before Cedric had completed his free treatment.

Imagine my surprise some years later when I opened my mail to find a picture of Cedric, smiling ear to ear, with a picture-perfect smile, in his Marine Corps dress blues on the occasion of his graduation from boot camp.

I cried.

Following completion of his enlistment, Cedric chose to work as an aide in a large nursing care facility. He kept in touch with me for a while, and one of his notes said, "I just really like helping people because so many people have helped me!"

Morning Rush Hour

She had been declining for quite a while, and now word came that she was hospitalized. I had been serving the parish for several years and had come to know her, and the family of which she was matriarch, fairly well.

The phone call came to me at home at 6:45 a.m. "Pastor, Mom's not doing well. She is asking for Communion. Could you come to the hospital, please?"

I lived on the other side of Denver from the hospital she was in. I explained that at that hour of the day—morning rush hour—it would take me at least an hour, but that I was on my way.

"Thank you. Please hurry," was the response.

The traffic was frustrating, as it always is at that time of day. With a little zigging and zagging, lots of horn honking, and perhaps some fist-shaking and finger-wagging as well, I made it in record time. But as I got out of the car and reached for my Communion set, I realized I didn't have it with me. It was at the church. I could try the hospital chaplain's office and see if they had one I could borrow, or, I'd have to brave the traffic to the church, a good fifteen-minute drive from the hospital at best.

It seemed to me that it was unlikely for someone to be in the chaplain's office already at that hour, so I got back into the car and drove off wildly to the church. Once back at the hospital, Communion set in hand, I headed for the ICU. The family was very happy to see me, and we were ushered by the nursing staff directly to Grandma's room.

Time immediately slowed, and my rushing around transformed into a quiet and sacred pace. I greeted her. She didn't respond at all while I set up the Communion elements.

Adapting the liturgy to the solemn situation, I said the Words of Institution and then served her the elements. She understood everything, mouthing the familiar words with me as I recited them. Breaking a small piece of the wafer, which in this situation looked enormous even though it is roughly the size of a half-dollar, I dipped it in the wine and placed it on her tongue.

She nodded her head, smiled…and then she died.

We all just stood for several long minutes in stunned silence. No one cried, no one spoke. One of the nurses said, "I've never seen anything like that." The now-deceased woman's daughter said, "She was hanging on until you got here with Communion."

This was one of the most moving experiences I've ever had. The same was true for her own family, they said, and much of the hospital staff that witnessed it as well. All these years later I still get a lump in my throat telling about it.

Rest in peace, Grandma. Rest in peace.

Continuing Ed—Win-Win!

Formal Continuing Education is important in any field, but especially in a pressure-filled field like parish ministry in a rapidly developing and changing society such as ours. The importance of sharpening old and adding new skills was impressed upon us during our seminary education.

However, the reality of life in the parish, with its unending time demands, events scheduled months in advance, and rapidly changing landscapes, makes attending continuing education events such as conferences and retreats quite difficult. And even with "two weeks of continuing education time per year" written into the standard call form (essentially a contract) that is issued when called to a new parish, and the ongoing encouragement from the Office of the Bishop to keep up the continuing ed, there are not many pastors who are able to take time from the work of ministry to actually fulfill that goal.

In my first twenty years of parish ministry, there were only a handful of those years that I managed to carve out any time, and certainly not two weeks a year, for these important and refreshing enrichment experiences. This being true for many, and perhaps most, parish pastors, there has emerged the growing practice of pursuing a Doctor of Ministry (DMin) degree—somehow the requirements and structure of a degree program seem to make more sense to congregations, and to more easily justify the expenditure of continuing ed funds. Many seminaries offer DMin programs, and they often follow a basic pattern: One to two residential (and now often online) weeks of classes in each of two or three summers, several elective online classes or papers during the year, and a major paper or thesis submitted before the conferring of the degree.

I was fortunate to have the opportunity to pursue a DMin myself, while at St. Matthew. In my case, I attended two separate two-week-long residential sequences of classes over successive summers at the Graduate Theological Foundation, at that time located near South Bend, Indiana. There was significant reading required ahead of time, and when we gathered on campus for the two-week residential sessions, we had wonderful and abundant opportunity for discussion among the richly varied participants and presenters from many different fields and faith traditions.

Additionally, the program required two extended off-campus educational experiences through affiliated institutions or programs. My first was a three-week involvement in an archaeological dig in Israel. We were excavating the biblical city of Bethsaida in Galilee. My second was a week-long class on Theology in Film through the Graduate Theological Union in Berkeley, California. We viewed and discussed, from a theological perspective, two movies each day, one in the morning and one in the afternoon.

The final requirement for this degree was a major research paper. Many of the students in my group focused on worship—several compiling alternate lectionaries as their thesis project. Given my context at St. Matthew, my research and paper dealt with re-rooting in the community when a changed and still-rapidly-changing community is emerging.

All of these continuing education opportunities are so beneficial for their enrichment and educational value for a pastor. They also often provide opportunities for inter-regional and interdenominational cross-fertilization of ideas and concepts.

My research into the community surrounding St. Matthew, the ethnicities of the residents, and the socio-economic realities of an inner-city parish in a rapidly changing community, definitely helped inform our congregation's program planning and emphases going forward. Frankly, it was also life-giving for me to have had an opportunity to get a "toe in the water" of my long-standing interest in biblical archaeology!

As is the goal, the continuing education of the DMin program that I completed provided deep benefits for both me and my congregation.

Israel Dig

As part of my Doctor of Ministry program, the experience of working on an archaeological dig at the biblical city of Bethsaida was a fantastic opportunity. My wife and I flew to Tel Aviv where we met with a professor from the dig site who got us on the correct bus to transport us to Kibbutz Gadot in Galilee. As part of a group of fifteen to twenty volunteers who would be working at the dig for the next three weeks, both of us would live at the kibbutz and have our morning and evening meals there. The noon meal was served at the dig site.

This dig had been underway for several years, with the actual digging going on in the summers when volunteers, usually college students earning credits in archaeology courses, were readily available for free labor. We were picked up by a school bus at 5:00 a.m. and dug until 2:00 p.m., with a brief break for a "field lunch." We were then transported back to the kibbutz to shower and nap until 4:00 p.m., when we gathered for the "reading" of the pottery fragments found that day. This reading consisted of the archaeologist looking at, describing, and cataloging each fragment uncovered that day, its location in the dig site, and its approximate date and condition. Dr. Rami Arav was the head of the dig (see his book, *Bethsaida: A City by the North Shore of The Sea of Galilee*, Thomas Jefferson University Press, 1995), and he would conduct the daily pottery reading.

Our group was quite diverse, ranging from a retired Unitarian pastor to a number of interested volunteers, to mostly college students. Among those students was a group of "JAPS"—they identified themselves to the rest of us with that term. We had to ask about the meaning of it and they explained: "Jewish American Princesses." They had not known each other before this trip, but had become close friends while on the dig. One day on the bus back to the kibbutz from our digging, they were huddled in the back and they all burst out in uproarious laughter. After much coaxing, they finally explained that they had discovered that each of them had a grandmother who had taken them aside before they left, given them a gift, and encouraged them to find a nice Jewish boy while in Israel. The gift for each of them was the same: a box of condoms.

The archaeological site was roped off into five-meter square blocks, each of which then had the topsoil removed so that the process of careful exploration of the lower levels could begin. Since the site had been worked for several summers already, most of the blocks had been excavated to a depth of four or five feet or more. In some blocks, floors and partial walls of homes had been exposed. In other areas streets were visible.

Each of us was provided an archaeological hand pick, a hammer-type tool with a broad surface and a pointed end at the head. This was used to break up the hard-baked soil so that it could be sifted to look for pottery pieces or other artifacts. We were also given a small whisk broom. Any items or pottery pieces found were placed in one bucket, while the dirt was put into a different bucket to be taken for sifting in order to look for finer objects. All the while we were instructed to be aware of finding large stones which could be from streets, walls, or floors.

One day, one of the big, strong college guys was given a full-sized pick to go and "open up" a new area. He was to break up and remove the sod in an area adjoining that which was already being excavated. As he was working his way along the edge of the new area, a piece of metal glinted in the sun no more than six inches from where he had been digging. We had been alerted to also look out for metal, since this area (we were in the Golan Heights) had been heavily fought over in the Six-Day War in 1967. The student put down his pick and went to find the archaeologist.

Rami Arav had fought in the Six-Day War and was a high-ranking officer in the Israeli Army Reserve. He immediately identified the metal as an unexploded artillery shell and ordered us all to stop digging and go shelter behind the bus we had come in. He called the bomb squad and they arrived shortly with lights flashing and sirens blaring. The squad members suited up in protective gear and gingerly approached the shell. They surrounded it with C4 explosive putty, ran wires to a battery-powered device with a plunger, made sure all of us civilians were out of harm's way, and exploded the shell with a loud report and much smoke and scattered rock and debris.

All of us archaeological workers were quite shaken and assumed our digging would be over for the day, but to our shock (and in some cases, dismay), Rami ordered us back to work. Needless to say, there were a lot of "eyes peeled," watching for any other glint of metal for the rest of the dig!

Kibbutz Gadot

Kibbutz Gadot sits in Galilee approximately halfway between the Sea of Galilee and the Syrian border. It is about a forty-minute drive from the archaeological site of Bethsaida.

Founded in 1949 by a group of young people from another kibbutz and a group of Holocaust survivors, it was primarily an agricultural kibbutz, but by the 1990s had ventured into some manufacturing with plastics (lawn and garden furniture, etc.). It was heavily attacked during the Six Days War because of its strategic location so close to Syria and to the Golan Heights. After the war, the kibbutz had moved into the hospitality business, providing accommodations for groups of students involved in archeological digs, and evolving into a vacation destination with a lodging and meal facility, pool, and local tours.

The kibbutz was home to over four hundred people. When our archaeological dig group was housed there in 1993, there were still many clear reminders of the destruction of war. The entire residential facility was surrounded by a concrete-lined trench for defense. Still visible were the concrete storage cabinets for guns and grenades built into the trench, as well as a deeply pockmarked bomb shelter in the center of the installation. The library on the grounds had a beautiful large round window just under the eaves. We were told that was a hole from an unexploded missile. The community chose to make the ugly missile scar into a thing of beauty rather than just patching it up. In the middle of the playground for the children, a small abandoned Egyptian tank had been brightly painted with a rainbow of colors and had become one of the children's favorite playthings.

This kibbutz was a secular community. While the members were all Jewish, they were not religious. That meant that while kosher and Sabbath were observed, there were no religious worship services held and no rabbi was formally a part of the community. During our stay we were able to observe a bar/bat mitzvah class held for the youth of the facility. Instead of religious training, the participants were taught about the history of the Jewish people and of that particular community.

The young community members doing their mitzvahs were also involved in activities to develop courage and resilience. We watched as a group of ten to fifteen students formed a circle holding a blanket while each student in turn climbed to the roof of a one-story building and jumped into the blanket. They all completed the exercise except one last girl who just could not make herself jump. The group waited patiently for her to muster the courage, all the while shouting encouragement to her. After nearly twenty minutes, she finally leaped into the blanket and the group enveloped her in tearful hugs. It was a very moving scene.

The striking juxtaposition of modern culture in a biblical land, teenagers growing up in a difficult situation, and youthful energy, was powerfully exemplified by a large (five hundred gallon) gasoline tank, mounted on a stand about eight feet above ground and used to fuel the tractors and other vehicles of the kibbutz. There, emblazoned proudly on one rusty end was a carefully spray-painted slogan for the local high school: *GO GALILEE!*

Our breakfasts and dinners were served in the common food service building at the kibbutz. The morning and evening meals were the same: many trays of different shades of white stuff. I never did learn what it all was, but I assumed it was different types of yogurt, or kinds of hummus, or something akin. On the Sabbath we were served "real food" (according to my limited Midwestern American tastes and expectations)—chicken and vegetables, etc. Our field lunches were bread with honey and hard-boiled eggs. We learned (painfully) that the local hornets loved hard-boiled eggs and so, once the eggs were removed from their containers we had to eat them fast or end up sharing with the aggressive insects.

Proud as a Papa

While many of my fellow diggers at the Bethsaida archaeological dig discovered interesting objects aplenty (pottery shards, loom weights, fishing net weights, flat room floors, parts of walls, or possible paving stones), I found just one item.

When my hand pick hit a solid object, and my whisk broom revealed a fairly large piece of something, I notified Rami. He came and looked it over, took away my now-too-large pick and whisk broom, and gave me a dental pick and an artist's paintbrush. The object was broken (as is usual and expected), but as I brushed and revealed more of it, it turned out I had a real find: a unique pot with four handles around the top, instead of the much more common two.

He called over the photographer who took several photos, each of which included a placard identifying the site number, the date, and an arrow indicating the north-south axis in the picture. As I proceeded to expose more of the pot with my dental pic and paintbrush, more pictures were taken. The photographer was perched atop a twelve-foot ladder to get a full perspective.

About an hour and a half into this painstaking process, the large piece on top of the pile of pieces moved, and Rami swooped in: once a piece is disturbed, the find is no longer considered to be *in situ* and can then be taken up. The pieces were placed into a separate bucket to be cleaned and analyzed at that day's pottery reading.

Rami came and sat next to me on the bus on the way back to the kibbutz. He offered me the opportunity to wash "my baby" by myself instead of letting it be cleaned with all the other shards found that day. I gratefully accepted the offer, and when we got back I gently, carefully, and lovingly washed the pieces. At the reading that day, Rami indicated that he had looked this pot up in some of the reference books he kept on site. He thought it was Egyptian and so was an indicator of some active pottery trade in the region's commerce. He dated it to about 200 BCE.

Other than that one item, I found absolutely nothing. I was working by myself in an area that was limited by a tree stump on one side, and parts of walls on the other three sides. As I got deeper and deeper, other members of the group joked that it looked like I was digging my own grave.

On the very last day of the dig, I got to a flat surface like a floor or a street. As it came more and more into view, it looked more like a floor. As the dig was winding down, I found that one of the flat stones was ajar and looked like it had been slid partially over the stone next to it. Sliding it a little more revealed a hollow opening under the floor or walkway or whatever it was.

By now most of the other folks were on the bus and anxious to get on our way. Rami had been monitoring my progress closely throughout the day. He finally came over and said I had to now leave and get on the bus. He told me that many times in a dig they will find a loose floor tile that is hollow beneath, and that ancient people had used spaces like that as safes to store valuables. Sometimes archaeologists will find a cache of coins or jewelry in a place like that. He said we didn't have time for me to take up the neighboring stones, but that if I wanted to I could reach down into the empty space to see if I could feel something there. We had previously found a number of scorpions in the dig site so he did warn me to be careful...

I had once seen a couple of the students capture a scorpion and put it in a bucket. They threw a large grubworm into the bucket with the scorpion and we had watched the scorpion attack, strike the worm repeatedly, and the worm turn stiff as a board as it died.

I chose not to probe blindly into the little chamber.

I never did learn what may have been in that hollow space, scorpion or otherwise.

But boy was that a thrill, to have found that four-handled pot!

All in all, the whole experience of working at the archaeological dig, staying at the kibbutz, and just being in Israel-Palestine itself was fulfilling and enriching in deep and many ways. But honestly, the proudest and most exciting part was finding, excavating, handling, and cleaning that beautiful, ancient piece of pottery—a tangible result and contribution from that part of my DMin continuing education.

I returned home with a camera full of photographs, a heart full of rich experiences and memories, and a deepened understanding of both the complex history and fraught reality of that part of the world.

Blessings Abound

I remembered the young couple. Their wedding in my former parish had been very nice. Several years had passed, and I received word that they had become parents. Not just ordinary parents, mind you, but parents of quintuplets! In the meantime, they too had moved across town and were now members of another congregation, just a couple of miles from St Matthew.

Talking with the pastor of their new congregation, I got some of the details of their situation. They had been trying to start a family, to no avail. A fertility clinic was consulted. After a series of shots, there was success! A lot of success! The doctors suggested that perhaps there should be an intervention, but the mom-to-be insisted not. It was a difficult pregnancy with the last weeks including bedrest, hospitalization, and lots of concern for mom and babies, but finally they arrived—Four boys and a girl!

If you have ever been involved with a newborn baby, you know how challenging it is—especially those first days, months, years. As the grandpa of twins myself (two sets, to be exact), I know firsthand that twins make those adjustments more than twice as hard. But...quintuplets? Do the math!

In consulting with the still-dazed parents, the also-dazed grandparents, and the pastor of the expanded family's new congregation, it was decided that help was in order—lots of help. A plea for said help was placed within their congregation, and at St. Matthew's as well, since we were close neighbors. And what an overwhelming response there was!

People are great. Quintuplets are great. The urge to help is great. However, the need to *organize* was also great. Thank goodness the new mom was a wonderful organizer.

A "Quints' Volunteer Board" was set up in both of the churches, with different time slots each day for congregation members to volunteer. Grandmas, grandpas, grandparent wannabes, concerned neighbors, curious snoopers, baby lovers—in short, people of all kinds with all sorts of motivations signed up.

This very savvy new mom set up three timeslots each day—morning, noon, and night—for two volunteers to come to her door and help with feeding, changing, burping, cuddling...whatever needed to be done. Mom had mounted a large whiteboard on the nursery wall with each of the babies' names listed vertically, while the three main horizontal columns were: "Morning, Noon, and Night." Under each of the column headings were written what needed to be done for each child at each time designation. For example, my time to volunteer was Friday night at 6:00 p.m. I would ring the doorbell, be greeted by a harried mom with a child in her arms, have the child thrust into my arms, be told who it was, and then proceed to the whiteboard to get my instructions.

There was one area in the house used for supplies: diapers, powder, changing table, and formula bottles all in a row. Another area was provided with chairs to sit in while feeding. Once my charge was asleep, I would let myself out and get out of the way for whichever volunteer was to show up next. The whole routine was as well organized as possible, but also with the mayhem you might imagine in an operation of that size, nature, and complexity.

The striking, heartwarming, and deeply moving reality around all of this was the generosity and caring the community demonstrated for this young couple amidst their amazing adventure. A local grocery store had donated a year's supply of formula in single-serving bottles. There was a donation of a year of diaper service. The mom's co-workers from her previous job had chipped in to buy a van large enough to accommodate five infant seats (to replace the VW beetle the couple had driven prior to the blessed event[s]).

As time passed and I moved on to yet another parish, I lost track of the progress of this amazing family. I would hear occasionally about school adventures, learning to drive, graduation, and post-high school plans, and I can only assume that all has worked out well.

What an adventure!! And what a response from the people of these two faith communities.

A New Call

When my dear friend and former pastor, Pastor Rudy, called and suggested, strongly, that I should move to Broomfield and become the developer of the new congregation that was going to be planted there, I was faced with a real struggle.

On the one hand: a chance to tackle a new and exciting adventure in ministry near a dear old friend and mentor, Rudy. On the other hand: the chance to continue a nicely developing adventure in ministry with a dear new friend and colleague, Marge.

Ultimately, the lure of the new and unexplored, especially the thrill of being involved with building something from scratch (including a physical church structure from the ground up) won out. I submitted my name for consideration for the position of pastor-developer of the mission congregation.

It turned out that I was selected, and though I was enthusiastic about the new ministry, it was with real sadness that I tendered my resignation at St. Matthew.

I moved on to another exciting challenge.

206

CROSS OF CHRIST— BROOMFIELD, COLORADO

It Takes a Village to Raise a Church

Broomfield, Colorado, is located halfway between the cities of Denver and Boulder along the Boulder Turnpike. Historically, it had been the last stop on a small rail spur from Denver that was visited primarily for Sunday afternoon picnics in the early twentieth century. It boomed into a suburb of both cities in the mid-to-late 1900s. In the 1970s, the Board of American Missions (BAM) of the Lutheran Church in America decided that a new congregation should be planted in Broomfield, and bought a 3.75-acre piece of land for that purpose. But growth in the area then slowed, and plans for the new church were tabled.

By 1990 the growth had re-ignited, and the process for a new congregation was re-started. I became one of three candidates for the position of pastor-developer, and ultimately was selected and offered the call to the new mission start in late 1993.

My friend Pastor Rudy (Leonard Rudolph) at Lutheran Church of Hope, the Lutheran congregation closest to the Broomfield parcel of land, had been one of the leading advocates for the development of the new church, partly because his congregation did not have room enough to handle a large influx of new members from the rapidly growing area. He actively advocated for and supported the work of new church development for a neighboring congregation to serve the increasing population.

First stop for me after having been selected: BAM Pastor-Developer Training in Chicago. New "PDs" from around the country were assembled, and led through an intensive one-week course in everything from legal requirements and public relations and advertising, to door-to-door calling and dealing with existing congregations, to congregational organization and building construction…to everything else one could possibly need to know about the task at hand. It was extremely helpful—and exhausting.

As I put all that training into practice during the weeks and months of preparing to launch a new church, I worshiped most Sundays at Lutheran Church of Hope in Broomfield. I already had some relationships with people there, and because Pastor Rudy called on me weekly during worship services for updates on progress, and occasionally to help with reading lessons and serving Communion, I became a "known entity" within their midst.

Some weeks, however, I visited other Lutheran churches in the area. In those instances I would call the pastor of a neighboring parish, introduce myself, tell about the development of the new mission church, Cross of Christ, and ask to be introduced during their upcoming Sunday worship services.

In some congregations, I was welcomed. In some, I was invited to introduce myself during the service. In some, I was ignored and seen as a threat. (See the story "Good Neighbors.") In any case, our "village" of communication and support expanded.

In addition to the organizational details and Sunday morning church visits, I had begun door-to-door calling in the neighborhoods around the prospective church site. New houses and whole neighborhoods were springing up at an amazing rate. I would start calling between 5:00 and 6:00 p.m. when many people were coming home from work, and continue until dark or exhaustion, whichever came first. My goal—seldom reached—was one hundred doors in an evening. I would introduce myself, tell what I was about, offer a brochure, and try to engage in a conversation. Some people were friendly and conversational, some were tolerant, some were dismissive, a few were hostile. I would always ask if they would like to be on our mailing list. Usually there were one or two per evening who were interested in being included on the list. Seldom did I find no one to add to it. One evening there were five new additions. The village was expanding—slowly.

Finally the time came to start worship services. We had arranged to rent the gymnasium on Sunday mornings in an elementary school that was very close to the property which was to become our home. We had also conducted several interest meetings, which were publicized widely through our mailing list, in those local congregations that were willing to support, and in announcements in the community newspaper. The meetings had been small, but positive and encouraging. A steering committee from among those interested in creating the new congregation was formed, to help with decisions regarding the first worship service, etc. Our village was growing considerably.

A date was selected for the first worship service; we gathered an altar committee to plan and make arrangements for it. Preparing for worship in an elementary school gymnasium was a challenge. We had to figure out how

to turn a basketball court into a worship space. (See "Welcome to Church...
But Not in a Church.")

Finally, the appointed Sunday arrived and the new church, named Cross
of Christ Lutheran, "went live." Astonishingly, there were one hundred forty
people in attendance that first Sunday in the school gym! While we had not
speculated on a hard number, no one had anticipated that many folks. That
morning we kept adding more chairs, and more chairs!

Our village was off and running.

Endings and Beginnings

Shortly after starting as the new Pastor Developer for the East Broomfield
Lutheran Church (as it was originally called by BAM, the Board of American
Missions, before being christened Cross of Christ Lutheran), I got a note from
our bishop. Sadly, one of the most recent new mission starts in the Denver
area had failed. They were having their final worship service the next Sunday.
Since they were still meeting in a school, there was no real estate to deal with;
but they had, over their somewhat brief life span, accumulated a roomful of
"stuff"—a roomful of dreams unrealized, a roomful of hope, a roomful of
tears.

They had decided that, rather than having a yard sale or something of
that nature, they wanted to give our brand-new mission start in Broomfield
first pick of the items. However, the pastor had already sold his house, where
it was all stored, and needed us to pick up whatever we might want ASAP.

Since we were less than a month old, were just getting loose ends together
and had no place to store anything, I was tempted to demure. But after a little
thought I realized what a tremendous gift this really was. So, I agreed to drive
to the far southern extreme of the Denver metro area (from our location in the
far northern extreme) to see what I thought might be salvageable.

The trip south was filled with expectation. Would there be things we
could use? Would they be in good shape? Would the quantities be sufficient?
Too much?

Arriving at the now ex-pastor-developer's residence, I was warmly greeted
and ushered into the basement. There I encountered a mountain of church
supplies. There were music stands, chairs, hymnals, paper, and lots of odds
and ends. I tried to think of what we might need, and started loading stuff
into my car, packing it with a treasure trove of church supplies.

After thanking the pastor profusely, I headed back north. It was nearly an hour's drive and I couldn't stop thinking about that failed congregation. They had begun a couple of years earlier with all the excitement and enthusiasm, all the hopes and dreams, all the plans and projections that we were now experiencing. What had happened? Were there mistakes? Were there pitfalls that we could try to avoid?

Until then, I had never considered the possibility of failure. Did new churches really fail? After all the research and planning and studies and consultations by the national and regional jurisdictions I knew about, was failure of *our* new mission start really an option? All of a sudden, a sense of dread overtook me. All the "rah-rah," all the bravado, all the certainty and confidence I had felt came crashing down.

In addition to it all being a sober reality check, during that drive home the image of that pastor's basement—a pastor I knew and respected...all the detritus of a congregation no longer in existence—became also a real motivator. Success was not guaranteed, growth and development no sure thing. Long, hard days, incredible joys, and incredible heartaches, all lay ahead.

When I got home, it was with a heart heavy with disappointment for the failed group to the south, but at the same time buoyant with hope for what was to come for our new congregation, that I unloaded the "stuff"—the treasures.

We were just at the beginning, and I had so much to learn.

You Just Never Know

One of the tools that is recommended to use when starting a new congregation is a brochure with information about the start-up. Ideally it will be attractive, contain pertinent information, and be welcoming.

In my files I had an appealing brochure from a church in Kansas City that I had come across some years earlier. Not being a graphic designer myself, I took it, along with all the details from our own setting, to a good friend from a previous parish who was in the advertising/promotion business. He substituted our info into the neat format of the K.C. brochure, made some adjustments because of the unique nature of our situation, dressed it up with his professional eye, and presto, we had an attractive and compelling brochure to use with the door-to-door calling and other promotional opportunities.

Made from a standard 8½-by-11-inch sheet, medium-heavy stock, and with eye-catching bright colors, it was folded in a zig-zag fashion and cut diagonally so that it would stand on edge by itself. It contained the standard brief introductory information, and hopefully in a way that would be interesting and memorable.

When making door-to-door visits I would introduce myself, explain the purpose of my visit, and leave one of these brochures. When I found no one at home I would simply put one of the brochures on the step or in the screen door, and always with a handwritten note. Our visitation teams were also supplied with these brochures for their use. They were instructed to use them as I did, leaving one with a very brief personal note on it if they found no one at home.

I usually wrote something like, "Sorry I missed you. Here's some information on a new church being formed here in Broomfield," and signed it.

It was remarkable how many people, coming to visit us for Sunday worship, would reference these brochures, and very positively—commenting either on how well done they were, or how much they appreciated the concise way they presented the information about the church.

The most amazing commentary on the brochure, however, came about four years after we'd started. I was standing at the door shaking hands after church one morning, and a slightly disheveled man looking to be in his late twenties or early thirties came through the line. He smiled broadly and asked if I remembered him. Slightly embarrassed, I had to admit that I did not. He thrust a well-aged copy of the brochure at me and said, "You were at my door a while back. You left this for me. It's been on my bed stand all this time and I've been meaning to come and visit. I finally made it!"

Extending a Welcoming Hand

There were many new neighborhoods being built in the area of our congregation. The rule of thumb in new church development is to try to reach people before they have been in their new home for six months, because it seems as though by that time they have made their new contacts, found a community, a supermarket, school, and church—whatever such connections they are going to make.

When I began door-to-door calling, I had wondered what the appropriate attire would be. At first, I wore a clergy shirt with a clerical collar, thinking it would be good to be identified by "the uniform." One day I rang a bell and was confronted by a girl, probably seven or eight years old. She stood in rather stunned silence for a while, before turning and shouting loudly, "Mom! There's a 'priester-man' at the door."

Not wanting to shock any more children, I started wearing more casual attire.

It was a blistering hot Saturday morning and I was calling in one of the many new neighborhoods in the area, with only moderate success—not many people were home that day. I came to a cul-de-sac with seven or eight homes around the circle. At the very first house, I encountered a genial guy. He informed me he and his wife were still active members of a Southern Baptist church in their old neighborhood which was way on the south end of Denver, many miles away. I explained that my intention was not to "steal away" members from other congregations, but to find folks with no roots who might be looking for a church home. We stood on his porch for a bit and just chatted.

I thanked him for the conversation and headed on my way around the cul-de-sac. When I was approaching the last house on the circle, the fellow from the first house came, semi-jogging, across the street with a large pitcher of ice water and two glasses. He said it was so hot and I looked a little bedraggled, and wondered if I'd like a glass of water. Never has ice water tasted so good or been so refreshing.

I thanked him greatly and headed on my way. The next day he and his wife showed up for the worship service. Before long they joined the congregation, and he ended up serving on the church council and being a good friend.

After my usual greeting and explanation at his front door, one fellow told me he was already involved in a church. My usual response to that was to ask which one. Often people couldn't tell me the name, or if they knew the church's name, they would be stumped by my follow-up, "What's the pastor's name?" This fellow proudly informed me he was a Jehovah's Witness. I laughed and explained that I found it funny because I had been visited by JW's so many times over the years, and now here I was at his door. He grinned knowingly and said, "Maybe I'll see you Saturday." (That was his usual day to do door-to-door calling...)

One day I rang the bell at a large home. The door was opened by a boy who looked to be nine or ten. I told him who I was and asked if his mom or dad was home. He stood and stared at me wordlessly for a very long moment—you could almost see the wheels turning in his head—and then he slammed the door with such force that I feared there might be structural damage. I stuffed a brochure into the crack beside the door and went on down the street. I finished that first side of the street, crossed over to the other side, and had visited at one or two homes there when the boy came running down the street to me, in tears. He explained that his mother had insisted that he apologize for being so rude to me. I accepted his apology and thanked him for it. I then told him that it took a really big man to apologize for something like that. I gave him another of the brochures with a note of thanks to his mom so that he could prove to her that he had talked to me.

Some doorstep encounters are smooth and easy, some are uncomfortable, and a very few can be downright nasty. Quite chilly would be the best description of a Saturday morning contact I had with a man who explained I would have to speak to his wife, as she was the only one in their home who was interested in church. I thanked him for that information and left a brochure for her perusal. As I walked away from the door, I could feel his eyes on my back. I noticed a newly planted tree in his front yard. Turning to him, I asked what kind of a tree it was, since my wife and I were also in a new house and wanted to put in a tree or two as well.

"Oh, you interested in trees?" he asked, brightening considerably. "Come on into the backyard—we just planted several out there." I followed him out onto the deck of the home, we sat down with cups of coffee, and for the next half hour I got a private class on trees from a master gardener.

Neither he nor his wife ever showed up for church, however. So it goes. It was good to visit with him, and to learn about trees.

One of the cardinal rules of door-to-door calling is that you never go inside. But I broke that rule one day when I knocked on a door and encountered a woman who looked to be in her late sixties or early seventies. As always, I explained who I was and what I was about. She told me she had just moved into the neighborhood a week or so earlier. As she spoke she began to cry. She told me her husband had recently died and that her only daughter had encouraged her to move to Denver so that she would be close and would have that familial support. However, the daughter worked full time and this mom didn't know another soul in town, and was so lonely.

She invited me in and we shared a cup of coffee as she told me about her church in Wyoming, the pastor there (who it turned out I knew), and her daughter and grandkids. She was in church with us the next Sunday and immediately was welcomed by several other women her age. She got very involved in the congregation and found a new, supportive community.

And so Cross of Christ Lutheran Church was growing, bit by bit.

Good Neighbors

One of the regular tasks for a pastor starting a new mission congregation in our denomination is to visit the neighboring congregations of our "tribe." The usual procedure is to visit with the pastor during the week to get to know him or her, to explain the plans for the new congregation, offer assurances that the new start isn't trying to steal away members, and to ask to be introduced to the congregation during worship on the following Sunday.

Sometimes these visits go well, other times not so much. In one case I was told I'd be welcome to visit to attend worship, but there would be no introduction. Most pastors were more collegial than that, but certainly not, shall we say, overly welcoming. There was one bright exception.

From the beginning, Pastor Leonard Rudolph (Pastor Rudy), my former pastor at Lutheran Church of Hope in Broomfield, was one of the strongest proponents of the new congregation. Broomfield was growing rapidly out to the east and his congregation, in the heart of town, was not able to reach out effectively in that direction, nor did they have the capacity for a large influx of new members.

When I started my call as pastor developer, Pastor Rudy insisted that I be present in worship at Hope every other Sunday to give a report on the progress of the new congregation. He invited me to preach occasionally, to help serve Communion often, and to write little progress reports for his congregation's newsletter—all with his intention of actually asking some of his members to move over to the new church starting up in the local school gym, at least temporarily, to give us a startup boost once we began worship.

When the day of our first worship service arrived, there was a nice-sized contingent from Pastor Rudy's church there in the school gym with us. The big question was how many would return for Sunday number two. Once again, a pleasant surprise.

But the biggest and most moving surprise of all was that on the day of our formal organization as a congregation, a year after I had started from scratch, we had nearly twenty families from Lutheran Church of Hope as part of our charter membership—all with Rudy's strong encouragement and blessing.

There was a second large group of folks that became a part of our congregation as well. A joint Lutheran-Episcopal congregation had been trying to get off the ground a few miles south of us. Due to a complicated web of factors, that congregation didn't succeed; it was officially closed by the two denominations. However, the members had been together as a church family for some time and many didn't want to lose the relationships and friendships that had been formed: Cross of Christ "inherited" a good number of those friends and families as a group, since our start-up came close upon the heels of their closure.

And so it went. Lukewarm acceptance and even near-hostility from some surrounding congregations were tempered by good and generous support from others along the way.

Sam's Warehouse Liquors

When just starting a new congregation, the pastor-developer does everything. There is no one else.

Need a check? You're the treasurer. Need a contract signed? You're the signer. Need wine for the first worship service? You're the altar guild purchasing agent.

We were approaching the first worship service for the brand-new congregation. I needed to get some wine for Communion. Driving down a busy thoroughfare near the church, a sign jumped out at me: Sam's Warehouse Liquors. Always looking for a bargain, I went in.

Not being a wine connoisseur, and kind of recalling that I had seen big gallon jugs of wine in the sacristies of previous congregations (where someone from the Altar Committee always procured the wine,) I went for the Mogen David. I picked up a couple of gallons and went to the checkout where I was met by Sam himself, according to his large name badge.

Sam was a short Black man, a bit overeager in attending to me while at the same time businesslike—You had to like the guy from the first moment he smiled at you. Being pretty sure that this was a good price for bad wine by the gallon, I asked Sam if it was possible to set up an account for the church. Eyeing me a bit skeptically, he asked for identification. When I presented my synodically-provided pastoral identification, Sam lit up like a Christmas tree!

"LUTHERAN CHURCH?!" He exclaimed. "LUTHERAN CHURCH! Here, take the wine. Are you sure that's enough? Why don't you take another bottle just to be sure…"

After recovering my composure, I asked what that was about. "My family is from Somalia," he explained. "There was war. There was destruction. We were displaced and put into a refugee camp. We lived in that camp for over five years. Finally, we got a chance to be resettled in America. The Lutheran Church resettled us to a new life. I worked. My wife worked. I worked two jobs. We saved our money. Got a loan. Bought this store. The kids worked and went to school. They studied hard. My son just graduated from med school. My daughter is in law school. All because of the Lutheran Church! Are you sure that's enough wine?"

By the time we needed more wine, we had a functioning Altar Committee that would be taking over the purchasing of it. I told them about Sam and our account at his store. But it turned out that although Sam's Warehouse Liquors still bore that name, it was under new management. So we paid retail for our Communion wine thereafter, but Sam's excited witness about Lutheran Refugee Resettlement has resounded in my heart, and heartened my commitment to refugee resettlement, ever since.

Welcome to Church... But Not in a Church!

Announcements went out that the first worship service of Cross of Christ Lutheran Church would be held on March 26, 1994, at the Mountain View

Elementary School in Broomfield, Colorado. More specifically, it would take place in the gym of the school.

We were grateful to be able to rent a space in the community in which to meet. But we were all-too-aware that school gyms are not designed for worship services.

There were folding chairs at the school that we were free to use—but of course we had to set them all up and then take them back down again each Sunday. There was a table we could set up for our altar, which we placed right under one of the basketball hoops. The school had a piano we could use, which we had to push and roll out from its storage area and back again. We had the hymnals we'd inherited from the other mission church that had failed (gulp), and those had to be distributed and then put back into storage each Sunday. Setting up for Communion each week in a school gym setting was definitely a project, and clean-up was no less so.

As time went on, we developed a kind of rhythm to the setup and tear-down process with many willing hands to make the chore faster. One of our members was an organizational whiz, and coordinated whoever showed up to help with the setup and takedown into a well-oiled machine. Almost immediately we decided to hold two services on Sundays to accommodate more people with less commotion (easier to set up two hundred chairs and use them twice, than to set up four hundred).

We were able to hold Sunday School for the children between the worship services, which allowed for a social time for the (non-teaching) adults to chat and get to know each other. One of the school custodians was hired to come in and be present all through the morning, as per the school district rules. He eventually formally joined the congregation and became a part of the family.

There were occasional surprises. One Sunday morning we arrived to find the gym festively decorated in honor of Elvis Presley's birthday, which had apparently been celebrated the previous Friday. There were giant pictures of "The King" on the walls and hung from the ceiling. Huge guitars festooned the hallways. I can't recall ever conducting a worship service in a weirder setting!

During the week, Cross of Christ Lutheran Church operated out of rented office space just around the corner from both the school and the new church site. An insurance agent had remodeled a small older house into an office, and had a roomy addition we were able to rent. Access to our space was through the insurance office and up a half flight of stairs. We enjoyed a happy relationship with the insurance agent and his staff, with some of his staff people eventually joining the congregation and getting involved. We even joked that the mice in the old house had become "church mice!"

As time went on and we continued to grow, we became more and more anxious to move into the next phase: constructing our own permanent church building! But a lot of life and ministry, ups and downs, growth and community, were all experienced and shared together in those years we met in the school.

Next Door Neighbors

The startup for the new congregation was underway. Right next door to the church property sat a little blue house. Built of concrete blocks, it sat on a large lot with a fenced-in backyard that housed some chickens, a huge garden, and two horses.

I wanted to stop by and introduce myself as the new neighbor. Two attempts found no one at home, so I left one of our printed brochures, which had my picture on it. The third try was intimidating. I knocked on the door. A small (six inches square) window in the door was opened and I could just barely see a man's face peering at me. I introduced myself, only to hear "I know who you are—Let's just say we are atheists and we want nothing to do with you," shouted at me, followed by a slamming of the small window so loud that it almost knocked me off the step.

"Okay," I thought, "looks like no close relationship with the neighbors."

Several months went by. We were now starting to hold services in a nearby school. We even had a small youth group. One Saturday morning the teens from that group were doing a service project—picking up trash from the road that ran in front of the blue house and our future church site. The woman of the house came outside to thank the kids and ask who they were. She went back inside, and then came out with an envelope for them; inside was a thank you card and a note that read, "Thank you! This is for your next outing," and a ten-dollar bill. The kids were thrilled and couldn't wait to show me and tell all about it.

I realized that I had spoken to the wrong person that day at the blue house's door.

So, then I started to watch carefully every time I drove past their house. One day I saw the woman out in the yard raking leaves. I stopped and struck up a conversation with her, and learned some of her story. She was a retired professor from the University of Denver. She had been raised Lutheran in Pennsylvania, but the family hadn't been very active. When her father died, the funeral was in the Lutheran church back there, and there had been absolutely no follow-up after the funeral—no visits, no phone calls, no contact except multiple requests to ask for a financial commitment. Understandably, the family was turned off by that church's lack of concern for people but obvious concern for cash.

She explained that they would not be getting involved with us nor attending services, but hoped we could be good neighbors with each other. I hoped so, too, and made it a point to always honk and wave if they were out when I drove by, sometimes stopping for a neighborly chat.

Fast forward a year or so and we were getting the building under construction.

One day our neighbor came over to the temporary RV park that the builders had established, introduced herself to our crew, and said that the city water they were connected to was terrible. She and her husband had their own well, and if our builders wanted good well water they could come over and fill jugs anytime. It felt like we were building a relationship.

I had put the neighbors on our mailing list, just so they would know what was going on. It turned out she had been an English professor. After each issue of the newsletter, I would get a call or a note with editorial comments on our latest offering. I also got a phone call when I erroneously referred to the large birds nesting near our properties in connection with the song, "On Eagles' Wings." "They are red-tailed hawks, not eagles," she corrected.

One day she called and said she remembered that I had a dog. She had just baked dog treats and if I wanted to stop by, she'd send some homemade dog treats home with me for my dog. Seeing an opportunity to further our relationship, I accepted her offer. Wanting to chat a little, I said I had never heard of someone baking dog treats from scratch, and asked what was in them. She listed the ingredients and said they were edible for humans. "Here, try one," she said. Not wanting to jeopardize a budding friendship, I ate the dog treat. I went right back to the office, called the bishop's office, and told them that they owed me big time: I had just eaten a dog biscuit for the church!

That year at Christmas, our youth group was going caroling. We decided that our first stop would be at our neighbors in the blue house. Word had gotten around about the incident with the dog treat. One of the youth group members asked her if it was true that I had eaten a dog biscuit at her house.

She said yes, went inside and got another one, and insisted he try it too. I watched smugly as he sheepishly choked it down.

Several years later after I had left that parish for another call, we got word that the husband in the blue house had died. Then we heard that the professor had donated the property to the city; she moved to an assisted living facility. The blue house was torn down and the property remains open space.

It was yet another interesting chapter in the life of the congregation and in the continuing education of this pastor. A chapter with so many lessons! I'll never forget my friend the English professor.

Conflict Happens

When pastors get together to "gab" about church stuff, there are some topics that almost always seem to come up. One such topic is music—church music, to be exact. This is not because all pastors are musicians at heart. This is not because most felt the call to ministry through the influence of church music. This is not because they go around humming hymns or listening to "Christian" radio stations.

One of the reasons pastors talk together about music so much is because music is such a large and foundational part of Lutheran liturgical worship, and is also often where conflict in a congregation finds its expression. In fact, the music program—music committee, music selection, music staff and volunteers—is often referred to as the "war department" among pastors (and sometimes other church members as well). Different types and styles of music have their proponents in any congregation. But sometimes people's appreciation of certain types of music over other types can become what motivates or inhibits church involvement altogether.

We were starting a new congregation. We worshipped in an elementary school gymnasium. There was real excitement and enthusiasm within our group. Our pianist had been a part of the congregation from the very beginning. She had been a church musician from her teen years, having grown up in a farming community where she learned to play piano and accompany worship.

Our fledgling choir was led by a school teacher who kind of got the job by default. She did very well, but was filling the role out of the goodness of her heart and made it known that if someone else came along with more experience she'd be happy to cede the position.

Lo and behold, another woman came on the scene who had quite a bit of experience leading church choirs. The first director gladly "retired" and the new director was installed. All seemed to be going well for a time—a brief time. Before long there started to be signs of conflict between the choir director and the accompanist. Music choices were debated frequently. Correct tempi were contested. The overall direction of the fledgling program was questioned. Glares turned into nasty notes. Nasty notes turned into woeful words. Finally, the choir director asked for "a meeting with the pastor."

Having a copy of the most recent note sent from the director to the accompanist, I had expected this development. I invited the director to lunch where we could hash things out. In order to make things really clear, the director handed me a letter stating her position as we sat down.

After a nice cordial lunch, I took out the letter, read it aloud and, setting it on the table between us, I said, "So, basically, what I understand from this letter is that I'm supposed to choose—either you stay on or she does, is that right? It's you or her." "Yes that's about it," she replied.

Not wanting to be in a situation or set a precedent where this kind of coercive leverage was normalized, I responded, "Okay. I'll choose her." Following a stunned silence, she began to cry.

We left the restaurant in silence.

Thankfully, over all my years of ministry, this was the only music conflict that came to such a drastic conclusion. But it stands out for the pain experienced on all sides.

Modeling Career

Church, like every other group or institution, has its own jargon, its own "insider" words or language. Due to the historical influence of the Roman Catholic tradition, some of the jargon is couched in Latin. Some, however, is plain old English. An example of this is the use of the phrases "high church" and "low church." These phrases are not judgmental; they simply distinguish between styles of worship practices. "High church" refers to a more traditionally ritual or formal expression of worship practices; "low church" indicates a less ritualized way of expressing and conducting worship. Most Greek Orthodox and Roman Catholic churches are typically rather high church, while Pentecostal or non-denominational "community" churches generally reflect a low church worship style.

Within the same denomination, there can be both low church- and high church-leaning congregations. My mother grew up in the Lutheran Free Church, an example of low church practices. The pastors in that group usually led worship in a suit and tie, nary a robe to be seen. Lutheran congregations can, however, be quite high church as well, with multiple clerical vestments, processions, and liturgical rituals. Venturing in to worship in one of those congregations could even make one think that they are in a Roman Catholic Mass.

Full disclosure: while not as "low" as the Lutheran Free Church of my mother, I tend towards more low church sensibility and worship practices, myself.

When we had started up Cross of Christ, a group of folks who had been part of the recently closed Lutheran-Episcopal mission joined us. As the new Altar Committee was planning our first worship service, one of the members had suggested the use of the "Bishop's Closet" at the Episcopal bishop's office; this was a repository of lightly used worship items that had been discarded by Episcopal congregations for one reason or another, and that are offered, free, to any other congregations that might be able to use them. In fact, she had informed us, she had been at the bishop's office recently and had seen the perfect chasuble for me.

A chasuble is a formal liturgical vestment, a robe in the color of the church season (Easter, Advent, Christmas, Lent, etc.), worn by a minister on top of the usual plain white clerical robe (alb) for the celebration of the sacrament of Holy Communion.

I had never in my ministry ever chosen to own or even wear a chasuble, and my "low church" sensibilities wanted to cry out in pain at the thought of wearing one on top of my plain white robe. But I managed to control myself; I thanked her, but demurred. She persevered with her suggestion. I did the same with my declination. Finally, we had a clarifying discussion of the "height" of church practices and preferences (high church versus low church).

I didn't wear a chasuble.

I did, however, get a phone call one afternoon from a pastor I had known for a long time. He was wondering if I had ever thought of doing any modeling. More than a little taken aback, I asked if he was okay. "No, no, no," he protested. "This is legitimate." Turns out his wife had her own business as a weaver of church vestments and paraments. She was putting together a picture catalog and thought I might be a good model for some of the vestments (stoles, chasubles, etc.) she was producing for sale. Kind of sheepishly I agreed (although inwardly I could envision a whole new career path—someone had finally recognized my photogenic qualities).

I arrived at the photographer's studio and was ushered into the room where the shoot was to take place. Inside was a photographer's set-up with bright lights, several cameras, and a white backdrop that rolled continuously from floor to wall to ceiling to prohibit shadows from forming at the junction of different planes. Also present were my friend, his wife, and a very young-looking woman who was wearing one of the newly designed vestments created by my friend's wife.

Suddenly it hit me like a flash. I wasn't there for my charming good looks, but rather as a marketing counterbalance to this good-looking young female clergyperson. I was there because they needed an old bald clergyperson to demonstrate that even old guys should consider buying these beautiful works of art.

Just as quickly as I realized the true nature of the situation, both my friend and his wife realized that I had realized, and the apologies and reassurances and some rueful chuckles and more apologies ensued.

I went ahead and posed and smiled and smiled and posed. I never did see a finished copy of the catalog (and don't even know if there ultimately was one) but my friend, his wife, and I shared many laughs over the adventure. The irony of this embracer of low church sensibilities and practices (me) modeling high church attire for a catalog was not lost on us.

"And a Little Child Shall Lead Them"

Lisa was a young mother. She was active in our congregation, serving on the Service Committee, the unofficial forerunner to a church council. (Since we were not yet formally "organized" nor legally incorporated, we were governed by this group.) Lisa's preschool daughter, Nicole, was in church with her mom every Sunday in the school gym. One Sunday, Lisa asked if she could make an appointment to come into the office to talk. The appointment was set.

Arriving in the office, Lisa wanted to talk about our practice for including children in the sacrament of Communion. The national church recommendation at that time was that children could start receiving Communion when they were in fifth grade. This was an arbitrary suggestion—nothing written in stone. Some congregations across the country were welcoming children younger than that, some started older. Our default practice was to welcome kids fifth grade and up to receive the Communion elements. We encouraged parents to bring younger children to the altar when the parents came forward, and the pastor would place his or her hand on the child's head or arm or shoulder and say, "Jesus loves you." Each year we would conduct a four- or five-week class for the fifth graders to go over the meaning of Communion, what practices we observed in our congregation, the meaning of the elements of bread and wine, etc. We would often have the class bake some bread to be used by the congregation for Communion on the following Sunday.

That being our practice, Lisa astonished me when she said, "I know Nicole is only four years old, but I think she is ready to start taking Communion." More than a little taken aback, I asked why she thought that. She smiled and said, "I was hoping you'd ask that. Last week I was baking banana bread. Nicole was 'helping' me, like she always does. The baking was done and the loaves were cooling on the counter. Nicole went to the counter, broke off a small piece of the bread, and gave it to me saying 'Jesus loves you.' She then broke off another piece of the bread, smashed it ceremoniously on her head, and said 'Jesus loves me.'"

Nicole started receiving Communion the next Sunday, and the general announcement was made that our Communion practice for young children was being changed.

Thank you, Lisa. Thank you, Nicole.

Sometimes Things Go Just Right

It was a huge announcement! The national church had made some money available for grants to newly established congregations to help them to grow.

As with all grants, there were requirements and guidelines etc., etc., ad nauseam, but our regional office called and suggested we might consider applying for one. We had been growing well. We were still meeting in the school gym but were holding two services each Sunday to accommodate the crowds. Plans were underway for our own building. It was an exciting time, and now this possibility!

We applied for and received the grant—so much per year for three years, the amount decreasing each year as we (hopefully) grew and were more able to handle the costs ourselves. Now came the rub. The national church encouraged each congregation receiving one of these grants to use the money to hire several part-time people (maybe a music person, a Christian education person, and a youth ministry person, for example). I didn't like that idea. The thought of trying to organize and plan with that number of part-time folks—each, most likely, with another part-time job and a different schedule and different employment needs—seemed difficult at best and totally unworkable at worst.

I insisted, through several layers of bureaucracy, that I wanted to be able to call an associate pastor—one who could divide up all the various areas of responsibility with me. That way "staff meetings" would be simpler, time would be utilized better and more efficiently, and things could move more swiftly.

And, I didn't tell anyone this yet, but I knew who I wanted that co-pastor to be! Remember Pastor Ann? That youth director from back at King of Glory?

Excitedly, I called her and asked if she would be interested in moving back to the Denver area. She said yes. A few more hurdles were encountered. We were required to interview four candidates of which she was one—but, no surprise to me, the interview committee was impressed with her. The congregation was impressed with her. They voted.

She and I became a pastoral team.

Our previous friendship and a similar outlook on life and church were a real plus when it came to serving a congregation together. Our positive collaboration was a big factor in the rapid growth and development of a strong and vital church.

The Biggest Fan

They were the cutest couple. A second marriage for both, he was a retired Kansas farmer, and she a pastor's widow. They had moved from Kansas to be close to her daughter and family. Excited by the prospect of starting a new church, they had been involved from day one. And when I say involved, I mean involved. All in. Totally. "Never missed a Sunday" and pitching in wherever possible all in.

When the time eventually came for us to be able to build the physical church structure, Oscar was at the site almost every day. With his background on the farm, he was a real asset. He was able to understand the principles of construction plus actually do it. From framing the ceiling structure in a bathroom to sweeping up at the end of the day—Oscar was there. His positive attitude was a joy to all with whom he came into contact.

Elizabeth, too, was a positive force. Among other helpful contributions, when we had Vacation Bible School in the local park because we had no building yet, she memorably supervised the wading pool from which the little kids could try to "fish" prizes and treats.

But she had some strong opinions. When we came to the point of calling a second pastor, she was adamant that it should be a male because "women have no business in the ministry."

She came into my office one day to express this opinion and with a list of four or five male pastors that she thought would be good for our setting. When the Call Committee announced the four candidates that were finalists and that would be interviewed, Elizabeth was dismayed that two were women. I got an earful.

When the interviews were completed and the choice announced, Elizabeth was angry to learn that it was one of the women candidates. The procedure for calling a pastor in our denomination has one more step—the congregational vote. Elizabeth worked hard to make her concerns known, but despite her efforts, the congregation voted overwhelmingly to call the candidate recommended by the Call Committee.

When Pastor Ann arrived and began her ministry, Elizabeth and Oscar were in church as usual, but sitting much further back in the worship space. The new pastor was a young mother. During her children's sermons, her daughter always came forward and sat in her lap. People found that endearing. When visitors came on a Sunday morning, the image of male and female leading the worship together was powerful. The new pastor was warm and welcoming, and people responded enthusiastically. I found one of the most noteworthy features about the new pastor to be her preaching—it was outstanding. Our congregation, which had already been growing rapidly, started to explode.

We started getting weekly phone calls in the office from Elizabeth asking who the preacher was going to be the upcoming Sunday. I was disappointed in her, figuring that she was trying to avoid "that female pastor." I finally realized what was really happening, though. Elizabeth wanted to know the Sundays the new associate was preaching so she could invite all her female friends "to hear a really good preacher."

Elizabeth had become her biggest fan.

Seldom have I been prouder of a parishioner—or a fellow pastor.

Not So Typical

It fit the pattern: young couple, two young kids. Typical visitors on a Sunday morning in our new and rapidly growing congregation. They attended several times. In the crush of people, schedules, and obligations, I hadn't gotten to visit with these folks yet, but on their attendance card they had marked: "Desire pastor to call."

I was finally making that follow-up call on a chilly evening. I had visited with two families already and was now searching out this third address. I wasn't familiar at all with their neighborhood. It turns out the address was in a mobile home court. We didn't get many visitors from this area since it was quite a distance from our church building.

Finding the address, I went up the steps and knocked on the door. The welcome was warm and sincere. "I didn't expect you to come to our home!" she said. I was invited in and seated in the warm and welcoming living room. Two elementary-aged kids were busy with homework, and the dad came up to me with a warm handshake.

The family had recently moved from my home state of Minnesota, and so we bonded a little over that. We chatted and I learned that they had recently moved to Colorado and were getting settled into a "new beginning." The wife was a beautician and had just bought her own shop. Her husband worked in a pre-stressed concrete manufacturing facility.

They had changed the traditional order of things a little and had started their family before going through the formality of a wedding. On moving to their new home, they had formalized their status by getting a marriage license and being "united in marriage." That having been done, in keeping with their familial traditions they went to the local priest to have their children baptized. The priest informed them that he couldn't baptize the kids because they had been born "out of wedlock."

Dismayed, they started exploring alternatives, the wife explained. She showed me a stack of books she had gotten from the library. Several of them were about Martin Luther. They liked what they read about and by him. After attending services at our church for several weeks, they'd decided they'd like to have a conversation with the pastor. We talked for quite a while that evening.

The conversation ranged between Brother Martin, theology of baptism, church history, rigid institutionalism, Jesus' teachings versus church doctrine, etc. It was delightful. In the course of the conversation, I made a joke about being somewhat uncomfortable in the presence of a hair care professional in light of the obvious absence of hair on my pate. I was informed, laughingly and non-judgmentally, that the wife's salon catered not just to women, but also men, and that she offered a "Bald Man's Special"—a fifty percent discount on a haircut.

My first visit ever to a beauty salon was daunting. The strange smells were overwhelming. The chatter was unnerving. The sidelong glances and snickers were irritating. However, the price was well worth the discomfort. After all, I had to look good for the baptism of those two precious kids the next Sunday.

Time passed. Among other things, this family became very involved in the building of our congregation's first facility. They moved to a suburban home quite a distance from our location but continued to worship with us. The wife sold her shop and opened a business in her basement.

I drove the distance to the new location for my half-price haircuts—but the best part was continuing the great conversations and thriving friendship.

Wood Working

Starting a congregation from scratch involves the hard work and dedication of many, many people. It is impossible to name, and thank, each and every one individually.

There were the teams of callers who worked tirelessly to visit door to door to invite folks to "come and see" what was happening at the new church. There was the team that was there every Sunday morning early to transform the elementary school gym into a worship center, setting up (and, of course, taking down) hundreds of folding chairs. There were all the volunteers needed to print and fold and assemble and distribute the worship bulletins, fill the Communion glasses, set out the hymnals, make the coffee, clean up and return the gym to a gym—all the things normally done by a church staff, now done by volunteers.

There are, however, two volunteers who truly stand out in my memory, not only for their particular contributions, but for the remarkable contrast they provide—even while both described themselves as cabinetmakers.

John had a cabinetmaking business on a commercial scale. On a visit to his facility, I was amazed at the projects underway. Huge saws were cutting pieces of wood as directed by computers to form very large-scale cabinets. Much of the cabinetry for Denver International Airport had been built in this shop. It was mesmerizing to watch those computer-guided machines cut and shape such large-scale projects.

The second cabinetmaker invited me to visit his shop as well. It was located in his garage. He had many of the power tools I was familiar with from my dad's home shop, although his were much older and well-worn. On this visit, I learned of Paul's growing up and being trained in his trade back in his native Yugoslavia. At the conclusion of my visit, he showed me a special piece of oak wood. He told me it was one of the most beautiful pieces of wood he had ever seen and that he had never used it in a project because he had wanted to save it for something special. When he had learned of our new church being formed, he offered to use that beautiful wood to build an altar.

We were nowhere near the point of starting a building project—that would be years in the future, if at all. We were still struggling just to survive. But I assured Paul that when the time came, we could talk about the altar.

The congregation took off. There were many new neighborhoods springing up in our area. The door-to-door calling continued in the new neighborhoods. Soon we had two worship services in the school gym each week.

One Sunday when I got to the school, Paul was already there with a mischievous smile on his face. "Come here, Pastor, I have something to show you," he said. In the parking lot, in a trailer behind his vehicle was a truly beautiful wood altar. "Remember that piece of oak I showed you? I couldn't wait any longer," he said.

Paul had created an absolute masterpiece of an altar. It was a thing of beauty.

He had taken care to measure the narrow passageway from our storage area at the school into the gym where we held our worship, and had calculated the dimensions and built the altar so that we could easily transport it on its wheels between the storage and worship areas. And he had put doors on the back of it so we could use the space inside for storage of small items, as well.

The altar was a work of art. It was also a work of love.

The newly developing congregation absolutely loved it. No longer were we worshiping in front of a folding table covered by a flimsy cloth. We had a real ALTAR! And a truly beautiful one at that.

Years down the road when we finally were able to build our own facility, the first item in the planning was to make sure that "Paul's altar" would be used. In fact, we were able to tell the architect, "Don't worry about designing chancel furnishings or cabinetry for the building. Our two cabinetmakers will take care of that."

Every one of the kitchen, office, and classroom cabinets in our new building was built in John's amazing shop.

And in addition to the beautiful altar he had provided while we were still in the school, Paul crafted a matching oak baptismal font and other chancel furnishings.

All used and appreciated to this day.

Mission Builders

Finally, the time came for Cross of Christ to construct a church building!

Our national church body, the Evangelical Lutheran Church in America (ELCA), has a program called Mission Builders. This program enlists volunteers from across the nation and matches them up with church groups that are planning to build. They travel to a site and build a church (or church addition, or camp, or any other building project that a congregation might have). We explored using Mission Builders for the construction of our building as a cost-saving tool, and decided to proceed.

Our basic building plan had been developed by an architect who worked for the ELCA. It was then sent to us to submit to a local architect of our choosing to flesh out and adapt to our site. The "one size fits all" plan was five thousand square feet. But in our situation, being located in an area experiencing swift and massive growth, we knew that we needed much more space than that. After much yelling and screaming on my part, the national church relented and allowed us to build…six thousand. Our local architect adjusted and twisted and turned it into a workable, albeit way too small, facility.

The national church recommended to us a particular Mission Builders construction manager. Our building committee interviewed him by phone and approved his hiring, so Don then flew in to Denver for a brief in-person conference with us. Our church building committee drove out to meet with him in an airport alcove between his turn-around flights.

Tall and fit, his long fringe of gray hair gathered into a ponytail, he cut right to the chase, outlining in oral bullet points the Mission Builders program: He was recently retired. He'd sold his nationwide business building large lighted signs for several national companies. The volunteer builders were all recent retirees. They and their spouses would arrive in their RVs. They would set up a "campground" which we would provide on the building site. State law required that they be paid minimum wage in order to be covered by worker's comp insurance. "Any questions?" he asked.

We sat, somewhat stunned by the onslaught of information, and totally silent. With that, Don got up, said "I need to catch my flight home," and was gone.

We wondered if we might have made a mistake. It all seemed so cut and dried...and overwhelming.

But we took the plunge.

Several months later in early May, a loud horn sounded in the parking lot of our rented office space near the church property. It was Don and his wife in their Wanderlodge RV. The rest of the Mission Builders crew wasn't due for a month or so, but Don had arrived to get started on the planning. First project? A spot to park the Wanderlodge.

As I wasn't familiar with RVs at all, Don insisted I had to have a tour of the "WL." A huge RV built on a Greyhound bus chassis, a WL is the "Cadillac" of the genre. This one had every upgrade you can imagine. All leather upholstery, granite countertops in the kitchen, full bath...you name it, it was there. Don walked around the little house that had been converted into an office building in which we were renting our church office space, and announced that he could just park in the grass behind that building and plug into the electricity from the office. I suggested we might want to request permission from the owner, and while I was doing that Don had everything plugged in, hooked up, and turned on. Good thing the building's owner gave the okay.

First order of business: Start getting bids from suppliers and subcontractors. Don was literally a pro at this, and in a few days had the various options lined up for our building committee to review. He had clear, strong recommendations on each decision, and made them known along with the reasons for each. The big snag came with the reveal of the total price tag, which was well over the approved budget from our lender (aka the Mission Investment Fund of the ELCA). Frenzied calls to Chicago ensued with no budging on their end. It looked like project cancellation was in order.

Finally, Don said, "I think I have it figured out. The plan is drawn with ten-foot ceilings. If we just cut two feet off the height of the building all the way around, we can save enough to bring us under budget." He showed the calculations. He was right. Much to the chagrin of the architect but the delight of the financiers, we voted to proceed with a "lower profile" building.

Next order of business: Build an RV park. With the Mission Builder volunteers set to arrive in their RVs in only a couple of weeks, we needed a place for all the vehicles. Don, using his experience reading building plans, staked out exactly where the church building would be on the lot. He then staked out the parameters of the planned parking lot. Somehow he got the parking lot company to show up on short notice, grade, prepare, and pave the parking lot, complete with curb cuts for the entrance and exit. It was truly amazing! Then he got plumbing and electricity installed so that the Mission Builders would be able to just hook up their RVs and "be at home," while they built a church. Two days after those preparations were completed, the first of the builders arrived. Seven volunteer couples took up residence in their RVs on the future parking lot of Cross of Christ Lutheran Church.

Before Our Very Eyes...

The hole for the foundation had been dug, and as the forms were being placed and the concrete poured, Don had the builders construct eight-foot-long wall sections. All the volunteers were "handymen," some on a smaller scale than others. A couple of them had never handled commercial air guns. The first day of work included a trip to the local hospital to patch up a hand that had been nailed to a two-by-four with a compressed-air-powered nail gun. (Not real confidence-inspiring, I have to say...)

Air-powered nail guns having eventually been mastered, the eight-foot sections of walls were assembled. They were nailed together and lying down on the newly-surfaced parking lot. Each was different, due to the placement of windows and doorways, of course. They were marked with a code to designate where in the building they would ultimately be placed.

The concrete of the foundation having cured, the cap having been put on the foundation, the steel skeleton of the sanctuary walls and pyramid-shaped roof in place, and the wall sections assembled around the exterior of the (future) building, the time came for the "wall raising." On a beautiful Saturday, everyone in the congregation was invited to come to the site and help to raise the walls. How exciting to see the building take shape as wall section after wall section was set up and secured. The final wall that was hoisted into place was the large east wall, which took the effort of everyone present. A loud cheer rang out when it was finally in place and the outer shape of the structure, with all of the exterior walls in place, was evident.

Then Don had a surprise up his sleeve. A large crane showed up on site, lifted the steel pyramid frame of the sanctuary roof off of the completed walls, and set it down on the parking lot. Stunned, I asked what in the world was happening.

Don calmly reminded me that all of the Mission Builder volunteers were retirees. Though the steel roof frame, to ensure that it fit properly, had had to be constructed in place as part of the whole building skeleton, "I don't want us older guys climbing up that high on ladders and scaffolds to work on the roof and ceiling," he said. "We can complete it on the ground and then hoist it back into place when it is done." And that's just what they did.

In the meantime, it was rather confusing to passersby to see the large pyramid-shaped roof sitting on the ground. Not recognizing what it actually was, several people stopped as they were driving past to comment on how beautiful the almost finished structure was, all shingled and angled and such. But they all wondered where the doors were—how were people supposed to get inside?

Then the problem was how to get the finished roof back up on the building. One crane had been easily able to lift the steel roof skeleton from the walls and place it on the ground, but after completing it with all the rafters, decking, and shingles, the finished weight was much greater. But Don had calculated this too, and on the day the completed roof was to be placed back onto the building, two huge cranes arrived to work in concert to pick it up and install it on the building frame. It was amazing to watch!

By early fall we had a completed shell of a church building. Walls were up and insulated. Windows were installed. A fully shingled roof was in place. One by one the Mission Builders packed up and headed home. The last to leave was Don. As his Wanderlodge drove away, he hit his air horn...which was programmed to play "Amazing Grace." We were filled with gratitude.

But along with the gratitude, a deep feeling of apprehension that had been slowly growing as the summer of building went on started to overwhelm me. It was up to *us* to now finish the project.

The Baton is Passed

Don from Mission Builders had interviewed and signed contracts with all the various subcontractors we would need to finish the building. Plumbers, heating and air conditioning specialists, sheet rockers, painters, and flooring specialists were all contracted—but needed to be scheduled and coordinated. We needed to find someone with the skill and knowledge, and availability, to oversee the completion of the complex ongoing project. We had a retired pastor who might be available time-wise, but he knew absolutely nothing about construction. A retired farmer had been very involved over the summer, but he too was lacking in the needed type of construction experience.

Suddenly, the problem was solved. We learned that a congregation member was a recently retired sales executive from the communications industry. He was savvy in constructing and installing electronic systems. He was really good at organizing and supervising people to get a job done. He was a dedicated churchman and he was committed to our project. With a bare minimum of coaxing, he agreed to oversee the completion of our building! And as an unpaid volunteer!

The following months were incredible. Dennis was on site every day shepherding the stream of subcontractors, volunteers, city inspectors, nosey sightseers, etc., through the myriad tasks that needed to be accomplished. As the weather turned cold, the problem arose that there was not yet heat in the building. The nice space heater that helped a little with that problem for a while got stolen. While at the site, Dennis ended up donning so many layers of clothing that he appeared to be twice his size.

There were scheduling difficulties. There were problems with the city inspectors. One day, it was clear to one inspector that "according to code" there couldn't be drop ceilings in the bathrooms; the next day, with a different inspector, "code" required that there *be* drop ceilings. Well into the process one inspector insisted there had to have been a fire sprinkler system installed. The architect found a loophole in the code that allowed for double sheetrock instead of the sprinkler system; we could do that. Expected weeks became unexpected months.

But by the next spring, the project was completed. The first Sunday to have services in our brand new building arrived.

The wholly-inadequately-sized sanctuary—designed, over my strong protestations, by the national church architect to hold just seventy-five chairs—was packed with as many additional chairs as we could squeeze in. The overflow seating area was also filled to capacity. With our two services set up to accommodate roughly two hundred people, the two-hundred-ninety-five who showed up overwhelmed us.

Within a week after our very first use of the building, we had to establish a new building committee to start planning the enlargement of the building… and in the meantime, we added a third Sunday morning service.

Wonderful! But at the same time totally frustrating. Had we been able to build the larger facility we begged for in the first place, we could have saved a lot of time, money, and frustration along the way.

Nevertheless, the vision and commitment of those first attendees in the school gym, of the volunteers who came from the neighboring congregation of Lutheran Church of Hope, plus the group from the closed joint Lutheran-Episcopal mission, and many more who saw the need and promise of a rapidly growing community of faith—helped immensely by the concrete, tangible work of the Mission Builders—paid off in a powerful mission-service center helping make the world a better place.

That building (now having been added on to *four* different times since its initial unit) has served the congregation and community well for over twenty-five years, and Cross of Christ Lutheran Church is still going strong in its witness and service to the Broomfield community and the world beyond!

Same Song, Second Verse

Frustration with bureaucracy may well be universal. The church is no exception.

Our fast-growing congregation had a beautiful building that was way too small.

In spite of our begging for more space, our national church bureaucracy, which controlled the loan funds, had approved only enough to build a six-thousand-square-foot building. Right away, our two Sunday services were overflowing and we immediately had to add a third service. Our building committee had been officially disbanded the first Sunday in our building, with heartfelt thanks for a tough job well done—and the very next week a second building committee had to be formed to plan the immediately-needed expansion.

Following extensive study and planning, we decided it was best for our setting to expand the first unit in every direction. This would consist of new construction in five separate areas. The project cost included the necessary demolition of five different exterior walls of the building we had just completed. We had to borrow money to destroy walls we were still paying for having built—grrrr.

These expansions more than doubled the size of our sanctuary, doubled the size of the fellowship hall, added several desperately needed classrooms, and added more office space. The cost was enormous, but not as enormous as the frustration directed toward the bureaucracy that had denied our request to build large enough in the first place.

The ongoing growth of the congregation meant that after just a few years we needed even *more* classroom space. Another building committee—number three, but who's counting?—was formed, and plans were drawn up to add a wing to the building. These were submitted to the bureaucracy for approval in order to obtain the loan.

Same tune: We were approved, but for only half the number of classrooms we so desperately needed. We built the half-sized addition.

At the dedication of the addition, I asked the architect what it would cost to add the rooms that had been removed from the plan, as a hypothetical addition to this wing we were dedicating that day. He got out pencil, paper, and calculator. "A little more than double what you saved by removing them," was his response.

Frustration with bureaucracy may well be universal. In many cases, the frustration is based on direct experience.

What the…?

It was a little unusual—a photographer showing up at the church unannounced and uninvited, with a request to come in and take some pictures of the interior. He had driven by often, he said, and had always wanted to come in and "take some shots." I was surprised, but a bit proud of the beauty of our newly-completed sanctuary, and as usual, was in the middle of doing several things at once, and so I said, "Sure. Go ahead."

Later in the morning as I started to head out to the hospital for a couple of calls, I noticed someone moving around in the sanctuary. Having forgotten my previous conversation with the photographer, I stuck my head in to see what was happening. What I found caused a rush of emotions.

On the first row of chairs (we had chairs instead of pews), I found complete outfits of clothing laid out on each chair. The first chair had an adult male's pair of pants set out so the seat of the pants was on the chair with the pant legs hanging off the front. Each of the pant legs touched a sock that had been placed in a shoe. The back of the chair had a shirt draped over it with the buttons facing the front.

The next chair had the same sort of arrangement, but with a woman's outfit spread out. The next two chairs had children's clothing similarly arranged.

There was an empty chair next to the first four, followed by another "family" of empty outfits draped on chairs.

"What the heck are you doing?" I asked incredulously.

"I'm taking pictures of what the sanctuary will look like after the rapture," he calmly explained.

(A word of explanation here: "The rapture" is a theological position that is not found in historic Christianity; rather, it is a relatively recent doctrine devised by American Evangelical Protestants. It is conceived of as an end-time event when all Christian believers who are alive, along with resurrected believers, will rise "in the clouds, to meet the Lord in the air.")

My denomination is not one which teaches this notion.

The idea that this photographer would come into a Lutheran church to use it as a backdrop for a belief Lutherans not only don't teach but actively oppose, made my blood boil.

I suggested he gather up his stuff and get the heck out! NOW!

Growth and Grace

Many are the times over the years that I have thought back to my second intern back in Thief River Falls, Minnesota, and my initial hesitant and judgmental attitude toward him because he had been divorced.

You see, I came from a family where divorce was almost unheard of "back then." I lived in an environment where it was definitely frowned upon, if not outright decried. I remember clearly as a teen, my mother coming home from a women's meeting at our church where one of the women had told the group that she had sought counseling from our pastor, and he had suggested divorce because of her husband's alcoholism and his resulting serious physical and mental abuse of her. My mother was aghast—not at the abuse and suffering as much as that the pastor would suggest divorce. This was what was taught and modeled for me.

So it was painfully difficult for me to accept that I also had failed at marriage, and not once, but twice—my second marriage having come to an end during the early COC years. My trust in God's grace and forgiveness was severely tested, as was my confidence in my ability to be a partner in a loving relationship.

One of the strong emotional helps that I leaned on was a weekly text study group for pastors in our area; we met to look over and discuss the assigned texts for the upcoming Sunday's worship service. Much more than a study group, over time it had developed into a powerful support group for all of us.

Each week the leadership of the discussion was passed from person to person. With busy schedules and many time demands, sometimes it happened that the pastor scheduled to lead on a particular week was called away, or forgot the responsibility, or otherwise missed his/her commitment to lead. Such was the case one particular week. We sat and looked around the room, and no one had prepared a study guide nor was taking the lead. I volunteered to step in to lead our discussion through the day's texts.

What you need to know is that earlier in the year, and with the assent of the group, one of the pastors had invited a member of his congregation to attend the weekly text study. She was thinking seriously of attending our denomination's seminary in Chicago with the goal of pursuing ordination herself, and he had thought that participating in our pastor's text study for a time might help her in her discernment process. She had been attending regularly for a few months, and I was frankly drawn to her because of her attractive appearance and vivacious personality; I'd been thinking of asking my pastor friend a little more about her, outside of text study.

Well, as I had just volunteered to lead that day's discussion, I launched into it by stating some arcane fact about the text, followed by the offhand and droll comment, "as any fool who's been to seminary would know."

Immediately there were several eyebrows raised toward her among all the pastors and a subdued chorus of "uh-ohs" and laughter. Looking around, she responded, "Well, since I haven't gone to seminary, I guess that means I'm not a fool!" There was louder laughter all around the table followed by a hasty apology on my part; I thought she might have felt I was calling her a fool. When the laughter and apologies ended, I stammered on with leading the study.

That afternoon, I was still kicking myself for my foolish comment and clumsy attempt at humor. As the afternoon wore on, I formulated a plan. I called my friend and explained my uneasiness with how I had handled the situation. I asked if I could get the woman's phone number from him so that I could call and apologize even further for my comment.

I did call her, apologized again, and asked if I could take her to dinner sometime to "atone" for offending her. She told me she wasn't offended, and that that wasn't necessary. But I insisted.

I'm so glad I did. Pam and I have been married now for more than twenty years. We've worked together on the establishment of another new congregation, and are enjoying retirement, grandparenthood, and new adventures together.

I'm thankful that consciousness CAN be raised—that there ARE new beginnings—and that forgiveness and grace can be a lived reality.

The Deep Privilege of Accompanying a Family's Journey

"Hi, Pastor," the phone call began. "We have a tough situation here and I was wondering if our church could help?" The caller was a member of the congregation. I didn't know her all that well, but certainly knew who she was. She went on, "A co-worker of mine is in a bad place. Her twenty-one-year-old daughter was killed in a single-car accident just up the street from our church. Their family is Catholic, but they have just recently moved to Colorado and haven't transferred their membership here yet. They went to the local priest but he won't do the funeral for their daughter, because they aren't members of his parish. Do you think we could have the funeral at our church?"

I was stunned. I didn't know the details, but I was aware that there had been an accident near the church. As terrible as that was, that wasn't what stunned me. I was stunned that a pastor or priest would turn down anyone in such a crushing time of need. "Of course we can do that," I replied. Our member then said she would talk to her co-worker. She hadn't wanted to suggest our church as an option yet without checking first.

A short time later she called back: she had explained to her friend that our church would be available if they wanted, and told me that her co-worker had been grateful for the offer. Would I please go see the grieving family? And so it was that I met a family that would come to be very good friends.

The scene was difficult when I arrived at their home. Mom and dad were there with a high-school-aged daughter. They talked about the older sister, the daughter who had been killed—about her life, what she was like, her hopes and plans and dreams. There were tears and anguish. After a time, we started to talk about the service. I explained that the Lutheran funeral service would be familiar to them, but probably not identical to a Roman Catholic funeral. They understood that, they said.

I explained that we could host a luncheon following the service if they would like. They thankfully accepted that offer. I suggested that the co-worker who first called might be willing to coordinate the luncheon and that was agreeable, so that co-worker started to plan and enlist help and all the things that are necessary for a post-funeral reception.

There was one factor to consider that was a bit unusual for the planning of this reception, however. The younger daughter was already a basketball standout at the local high school, and it was possible that some of the kids from the school might come to support her.

I don't know if anyone counted the students from the high school, but there were *a lot* of them who came to support. The funeral was one of the largest I have ever done. For people new to a community, the response of love and support was tremendous.

These good folks became regular worshipers in our community of faith. I felt, and I think many in the congregation felt, a close bond with them because of the profound situation they had experienced and the grief and loss they were dealing with. In any case, I deeply appreciated the friendship that formed between us.

As time went on, the basketballer graduated from high school and went off to the University of Denver on a scholarship. She sometimes had complimentary tickets to her games that she would share—lucky me!

Then came a second unexpected blow. The father came down with cancer. He fought hard but died very quickly. There was a second funeral for this poor family at our church. It was doubly gut-wrenching, to say the least.

The reason for the family's moving to Colorado having been the dad's job, and with a large extended family still on the East Coast, the draw "back home" was very strong. Following graduation from DU, mom and daughter moved back East.

A year or two after these now-good friends had returned to the coast, my phone rang. It was the hoops star. "Pastor, I'm getting married. I was hoping you'd come out here and do the wedding. You've been through so much grief with our family, we wanted you to come and be a part of a happy family celebration."

Pam and I flew to New Hampshire and had a chance to celebrate with this family. It was wonderful. The bride's former teammates were in her wedding party—I think I was the shortest person in the pictures.

But I certainly wasn't short in the joy department!

LEARNINGS FROM ALL OVER

Indispensable

If "lifelong learner" is an appropriate description of a parish pastor, among the chief and best instructors would be "church secretaries."

The second set of quotation marks is there because the term "church secretary," though long-used and still common in many places, is rather outdated, not wholly accurate, and has been evolving over several years. Most congregations have a position that handles the administrative details of parish life. In smaller parishes, this central figure might be a volunteer. In very large congregations there might be multiple paid staff to handle the many duties. Increasingly this position has been more accurately called "office manager" or "parish administrator." These essential figures are and always have been a key part of the ongoing education of pastors.

My first parish was so small that there was no designated secretary. (The term "secretary" IS the word that was used at that time, and at most of the parishes I served in my years in ministry; the evolution of the title of this administrative position is ongoing.) There was one volunteer there who would type the weekly bulletin—no small feat since back then before digital printers and copiers it had to be typed on a plastic film-like stencil which was placed on a mimeograph machine to ink-print the bulletin. With incredible patience, this dedicated volunteer taught me how to place the stencil that she had typed on the machine, how to place the paper into the feeder tray…and how to clean the huge puddle of ink up from the floor when I incorrectly left the ink drum down instead of up when done printing.

Another volunteer member of that congregation wanted to keep her stenographic skills sharp, so she volunteered to take dictation on any correspondence I had. I marveled at how she could translate all those scratches and squiggles of shorthand script into words and sentences, and I learned how to be more succinct in expressing my thoughts.

From the two of them, I learned early on the importance and practice of clear and concise communication, both within the congregation and in dealings with the world outside the church walls. Good lessons to learn so early in my ministry!

All of the other congregations I have served have had someone in this important position—and all who served in this central role were, in my opinion, "saints" in their patience and forbearance.

They are a part of a pastor's education, understanding, and shaping of what a pastor is and does. Most of them are gracious people who really want to help—and they do. Each one is different, but they can play a large part in forming the atmosphere of a congregation, and sometimes provide valued continuity—not uncommonly serving in their position long before a given pastor arrives, and remaining there after the pastor moves on to another call. In my experience, they also generally provide a wonderful face of the congregation to the wider community. As in all relationships, there is wide variety when it comes to pastors and office administrators, but when it's working well it can be a truly wonderful team.

I've experienced a few pretty memorable situations with some I've worked with over the years. A couple of them are related elsewhere in this book—see "Sorry, Not Sorry" in the King of Glory section, and "The Wild West Indeed" with the Interim Ministry stories.

One of my top favorite memories is of one who was not even working at my own church. On a visit to a local care center, I realized I had forgotten my home Communion set. Being quite a distance from our church building, I decided to go to a nearby congregation for help. I had been to this church many times previously for meetings, etc., and knew the secretary to be warm, friendly, and helpful. I explained my situation, and she assured me that she could help. She disappeared into the sacristy and soon reappeared with a makeshift kit for me of several Communion wafers and a small vial of wine.

See what I mean?—*Saints!*

Whatever their official titles might be, these central figures in the life of any congregation enable efficient and effective ministry both to members of the congregation and to the larger community. They help to determine the congregation's personality, and contribute to a pastor's ongoing education in uncountable ways.

"Mixed Marriages"

My mother and father were in a "mixed marriage." She was a Lutheran Free Church (Norwegian) Lutheran. He was an American Lutheran Church (German) Lutheran.

The LFC was a pietistic group that felt "everything" was wrong—dancing, drinking, smoking, not to mention swearing. The ALC was not so strict and would usually have a keg of beer at the church picnic. It was something of a scandal in those years in their small southern Minnesota town when one of those "nice Norwegian girls" started dating one of those "beer-drinking Germans." This social pressure was one of the reasons my parents eloped and even kept their marriage secret for a time. They ended up moving to the big city of Minneapolis, where their "mixed marriage" was more readily accepted (and where I was born).

The first "mixed marriage" I performed as a Lutheran pastor caused a huge furor. A young lady from our congregation was marrying a Roman Catholic young man. They were a great couple—deeply in love, both committed to their faiths, gregarious, and loved by their friends. I had previously been collaborating with the young priest from the big Catholic church in town on a class for student nurses at the local hospital, and he and I had gotten to be friends. In an effort to make both sets of parents happy, I invited him to participate in the wedding. We had several families leave the congregation over the fact that a Catholic priest would be invited to take part in a service in our church.

When I moved to my second parish, a young man came into the office to arrange for a wedding. He was marrying a girl he had met in high school. She was a Native American from a local reservation. They were the nicest kids and really were a cute couple. A big flag went up for some in the church because I was going to perform a "mixed marriage." Several families left the congregation because I was going to officiate such an event.

A few years later, a young woman from our congregation fell in love with a basketball player from the nearby junior college—a Black basketball player. He was from a Southern Baptist background and for one reason or another had never been baptized. The three of us met several times to discuss weddings and church and baptism, and after some months the groom-to-be was baptized in one of the Sunday services at our church. I'm not sure if it was the baptism or the "mixed marriage" that caused several families to, you guessed it, leave the congregation.

I have never yet been asked to officiate at a gay or lesbian wedding. My sorrowful guess is that in some instances the reaction to an "unmixed" (same-sex) marriage could be as strong, and foolish, as the strident reactions to the "mixed" marriages. It's worth noting and celebrating that that has been changing, however, and that my denomination now officially recognizes, conducts, and celebrates same-sex unions.

May we rejoice in and support all committed, loving relationships!

There Are Interviews...And There Are Interviews

Interviews for new positions are an inescapable part of being a pastor. While some pastors do spend their entire careers in the same parish, the norm for most would seem to range from seven to ten years in one place.

When a pastor has the need or feels the desire to relocate, or if a congregation desires a change in pastoral leadership, the bishop is usually contacted. Functioning as a "matchmaker" of sorts, the bishop's office tries to facilitate these requests if reasonable, or work out some other arrangement if they are not.

While most of the interviews I went through were fine and good parts of the call process, a few were more "interesting" and memorable than others:

My first interview, when I was still a seminarian, was with a congregation that had been functioning for a full year with just the lay leadership from within their group. I was told, point blank, by one of the council members, "We don't think we really need a pastor. We can do everything that a *pastor* can do, and do it better."

In another setting, I'd been interviewed but time had passed without hearing anything from them, so I called the chair of the call committee to see where things stood—and I learned they had called the other interviewee and had neglected to inform me. He told me that my "trial sermon" was outstanding, but "every pastor has one good sermon in their file, and we think we got yours. And, by the way, the other candidate, who had much more experience than you, was willing to come for $1,000 a year less than you."

Another congregation proudly showed me their new yellow hymnals.

(This happened to be at the time that our denomination had just come out with a new hymnal—which wasn't yellow; neither had been the previous one.) Their new hymnal came from a publishing house in Utah, as had their new Sunday School materials. When asked what my first priority would be if I should be called as their pastor, I said, "To get rid of the yellow hymnals. I am a Lutheran pastor being considered for a call to a Lutheran congregation. If I were to serve here, it would be with Lutheran worship materials and Lutheran educational materials." Upon returning home from the interview I sent a letter to the bishop of that synod, with a carbon copy to that call committee chair, explaining my decision. A week later I was surprised to get a call from the committee chair asking if I would reconsider. Of all six candidates they had interviewed, I was the only one who had challenged their materials. It turns out they appreciated that, and if I would reconsider, they wanted to extend a call to me. However, I declined. It just wasn't the right fit.

Another time, I was interviewed by a wealthy congregation just outside of the Twin Cities. They wanted to know if I would be willing to "defend" their wealth to the rest of the synod. Defend their wealth? I asked, "Why? Did you steal your money?" No call was extended to me there, big surprise.

Once, I was interviewed for a two-point parish position by a call committee made up of forty-eight people—twelve council members from each of the two congregations, plus their spouses. (A more typical number would be eight to twelve members.) Forty-eight was about the average attendance of the congregation I was serving at that time!

Then there was the interview that was as if it had never happened—not only did I not hear back from them, but they didn't respond to either of my two direct inquiries as to where they were in their process.

Like I said, "interesting!"

Door-to-Door Calling

In starting any new endeavor, be it a business or a school or a church or anything, one of the key tasks is to get the word out.

Radio, TV, billboards, internet, whatever—get the word out.

It may be that the most effective form of communication is face-to-face, personal contact. In the case of starting up a new congregation, that means calling on people: going door-to-door to introduce, explain, invite. For many reasons, this is difficult for most people to do.

In the training for pastors who are about to try to launch a new congregation, which I went through at the beginning of my ministry at Cross of Christ in Broomfield, this type of visitation—both to introduce oneself to the community and to invite neighbors to "come and see" the new congregational presence—is somewhere between strongly-encouraged and mandated.

Like most people, I found this task to be difficult at first. But I gradually warmed to it, and even rather enjoyed it. While there were definitely difficult moments, and some outright dismissals and/or rejections, most people I called on were friendly and open. I continued practicing door-to-door calling all through my time at COC, and of course when I started another mission congregation, Rejoice Lutheran in Erie.

A few of my experiences especially stick in my memory...

With Cross of Christ in Broomfield, we were in the right place at the right time! As the new church building was under construction, so were literally hundreds of houses in new developments around us. The challenge was to try to visit the new families moving in within the first six months of their arrival. (Studies have shown that after six months most of the new residents' decisions are made as to schools, churches, etc.)

Often people would show up to visit our church without having gotten a visit or a formal invitation. Many of the invitations were from other newcomers who invited their new neighbors to "try us out." It seemed that many of the young couples who came to visit had young kids about the same age—often two in number. I tried to greet new visitors either before or after church, but was aware that I was able to see only some of them.

One Sunday I went over to greet one such young couple (with the "requisite" two kids). Upon asking their names, I told them I had seen their names on a sheet that we always made up on Monday, showing the visitors from the previous day. I asked if it would be okay for me to stop by during the coming week.

An awkward pause was followed by: "Sure, I guess so. You know you were at our house last Wednesday..."

"Mortified" is too weak a word to describe my feelings at that point. I mumbled and stumbled and apologized the best I could. The family joined our church in spite of me.

Fast forward about two years. I had left that fast-growing congregation to develop another one ten miles to the north. One day I was loading my purchases from Costco into my car trunk when I sensed someone walking up behind me. I turned and saw that very same fellow I felt I had insulted so badly by not remembering my home visit barely a week after its occurrence. "Hi, Pastor Keith!" he brightly chimed. "How's it going with the new church?"

I gave a quick rundown on the progress we had made. "Have you started doing door-to-door calling yet?" he asked. I told him no, we were not quite at that stage just yet. "When you get to that point," he said, "if you need a little help, let me know. I'd be happy to give you a hand with that."

I almost fainted. Door-to-door calling can be grueling and difficult. Most people would avoid it like the plague, but here he was volunteering to help. He said, "You'll never know how much that meant to us that you would come to see us. I'd like to do that for others!"

One experience I'll never forget was when we were starting the congregation in Erie, Colorado. We had been able to hire a summer intern, a student who had completed three years of seminary study at Iliff School of Theology, a Methodist institution in Denver, and would be starting her "Lutheran year" at one of the Lutheran seminaries in the fall. She had grown up in South Dakota and was half Lakota Sioux and half Norwegian. I told her it would be good for her to get some experience doing door-to-door calling. She was extremely nervous about this prospect. Hoping to allay her fears, I suggested we go together for her first experience.

As we drove to the neighborhood in which we were going to make our calls, she asked some anxious questions. She wondered what to do if we would encounter a Buddhist. (There is a fairly large Buddhist presence in the area.) I assured her it was unlikely, but if we did we'd converse with them like anyone else.

The very first doorbell we rang brought us face-to-face with a woman who identified herself as a Buddhist. We chatted a little and left. When we got to the sidewalk, our intern looked at me with a sly grin. "Unlikely, huh?" was all she had to say.

The second door produced a young man who got a rather smug look on his face as we announced our purpose. "Well," he proclaimed, "I belong to a Lakota Sioux sweat lodge in Denver." "Wow!" I replied, "Let me introduce you to Inga. She is Lakota Sioux."

I don't remember whose eyes were bigger, hers or his.

Another time I bumped into a young man at a wedding. He said, "Do you remember when you came to our door when the church was starting?" I confessed that I didn't recall. He said, "Your visit really made an impact on me. It really did! In fact, I'm starting a new dental practice, and I'm going to go door-to-door to introduce myself to the neighborhood where the practice will be located. Your visit meant so much to our family. I want to do the same with my new practice."

Thought-provoking, isn't it, how something seemingly so ordinary—chatting with people at their door—can make such an outsized impact.

Lutheran-Catholic Relationships

On October 31, 1517, Martin Luther posted his Ninety-five Theses on the door of the Castle Church in Wittenberg, Germany, and the Protestant Reformation began. Ever since, the relationship between Catholics and Protestants, and Lutheran Protestants especially, has been fraught.

There have been theological disputes, mutual disagreement, even armed conflict, and suspicion and dislike and misunderstanding through the centuries. Relationships have improved in recent years, but the rift is not erased, mutual distrust continues, and real reconciliation is still a dream.

In the US, the divide is evidenced in very public ways, as well as in more local personal situations. President Joe Biden is only the second Roman Catholic to be elected president of the United States in the entire history of the country. The first, John F. Kennedy, wasn't elected until 1960, one-hundred-sixty-four years after its founding. This was not by accident, but because of suspicion, distrust, and fear of "the other," as the majority culture of the US was Protestant.

I can recall my good Protestant Lutheran family explaining to me as a child, that if a Catholic were elected president, the Pope would be "running the country." These same parents were convinced that Catholics were collecting guns in the basements of all the Catholic churches for the violent overthrow of the country. When my Norwegian Lutheran grandmother heard the Polish surname of a girl I was dating, she asked suspiciously, "Is she Bohemian?" followed closely and in hushed, horrified tones by, "Is she *CATHOLIC*?"

My family had these fears about "the other" because their peers, their culture, and their community taught them to have such concerns. Meanwhile, "the other" had similar apprehensions in reverse about "us."

When I began seminary in 1965, we were four-plus years past the election of JFK, not quite two years past his assassination, and still experiencing real mistrust and fear between Protestants and Catholics. Imagine my shock when a professor from my Lutheran seminary left on sabbatical, and a Roman Catholic priest, a professor from a local Catholic seminary, was selected to fill in. The shock was compounded by the fact that the class was Sacramental Theology, an area of bitter dispute between our denominations and traditions.

But perhaps most shocking to me was the fact that that class ended up being one of the highlights of my four years of theological education, both in the depth of its content and in the integrity with which the positions of "both sides" were presented and analyzed. It was an eye-opening, mind-broadening experience for me.

My education in interdenominational relations continued in my first parish in Pierre, South Dakota. The assistant priest at the large Catholic church in our town was a young man about my age. He was active in the local Ministerial Association and we struck up a friendship. After several months of occasional cups of coffee after the ministerial meetings, he asked if I would help him team-teach a course for student nurses at the local Catholic hospital. The course was to introduce the future nurses to the various faith traditions they might encounter when they were out of school and serving in various hospitals and communities. He and I taught the core of the course, and we invited various pastors in our community to come and explain their particular denomination's understandings and practices. This way the student nurses could learn directly what assistance various clergy might appreciate and/or supplies they might need in the case of an emergency baptism, Communion, pronouncement of last rites, or other religious needs that might arise in their contexts.

This cooperative effort between the young priest and myself blossomed into a real friendship, within which we could and did share some of our experiences both within our ministry settings and our personal lives. Father Don seemed to enjoy being invited into our home for an occasional dinner, and especially delighted in rocking our baby in the squeaky rocking chair. When he handed her back to me one evening, I noticed a tear in his eye.

When I was in my second parish, the local priest was elected president of the local Ministerial Association and I was elected secretary-treasurer. In working together, we also became friends. One year, none of the other clergy in town wanted to observe the "Week of Prayer for Christian Unity" as had been the practice in that community for quite some time, so Father Jim and I decided the two of us would trade pulpits on the Sunday within that week for our own "mini-commemoration" of the important concept. (He obviously got the better deal, since he only had to preach at our three Sunday services while I had to preach at all six of his Masses.)

Also, while at this parish I had the opportunity to work with Sister Janice, a young nun who was serving as the leader of an interdenominational campus ministry at the local community college. She and I had become acquainted through the Ministerial Association, and she asked if I would serve as "clergy support" for her ministry at the school. She did not wear a traditional nun's habit, and with her youthful appearance and guitar-playing skills she was hard to distinguish from one of the students. This all made her very popular with them and very effective in her work there.

At the end of one academic year, Sister Janice went to a month-long continuing education course at a seminary in Wisconsin, and left the key for the campus ministry room with me. When she returned and came by to pick it up, she asked if I had a minute to talk. In a tearful session, she told me of her struggle: she had met a young man, a teacher at a Catholic parochial school, and they had developed deep feelings for each other. She was torn between her vows to her order and her feelings for him. Over the next several months she and I met fairly frequently to explore the meaning of her vows as contrasted with a possible calling to serve as a marriage partner, and potentially in a parental role. After many anguished discussions, she finally told me she had decided to honor her vows.

The next school year was another success story for the thriving campus ministry program she led—numbers were up, enthusiasm among the students was through the roof, and service projects were many, varied, and extremely successful. At the conclusion of that year, Sister Janice stopped in to our church one morning and asked if she could leave the key with me again over the coming summer; she was going for another continuing ed course. I asked if she was going back to Wisconsin. "Yes." I asked if "he" was going to be there, too. "Yes," she answered with an embarrassed smile. At the end of the summer, Sister Janice came back—and asked if I would hold on to the key for her replacement. She had revisited her decision, and was now planning a wedding. The last word I had of her was several years later: she was a happy homemaker, very involved with her husband and kids in their parish in the South, and, I'm sure, a tremendous asset in her congregation and community.

Several other very positive relationships with Roman Catholic brothers and sisters, both lay and clergy, have helped me see the fallacy of the worldview I was raised with. While official relationships between Lutherans and Catholics may remain somewhat contentious and theological disputes may remain unresolved, "on the ground" cooperation, respect, and getting to know each other may yet overcome organizational suspicion and disagreement, to the benefit of all.

Tense Situation

Some situations a pastor encounters in his or her ministry can be especially sensitive, tense, even dangerous. This story is an example of one such situation I experienced, and I wanted to share it in this book. To protect the privacy of the individuals involved, it's located in this section of "Learnings from All Over" rather than in its specific congregational context.

"Pastor, can you come over right away? John has locked himself in the family room in the basement and I'm worried about him. He's talking about hurting himself."

They were a great couple with two teenage kids. They were very involved in the life of the church on many levels.

I drove hurriedly over to their home and found lots of confusion and tears. John had become extremely upset over something, and had stormed out of the room and down to the basement.

"And Pastor, one other thing. He has a gun," Martha said. On his way to the basement, he had detoured out to the camper in the driveway and retrieved a handgun.

Martha stayed upstairs and had been communicating with him by yelling down from the top of the stairs. This was awkward, tense, and ineffective. Over her objections, I went downstairs to talk to John.

It was only slightly less awkward, and significantly more tense, to be in the basement talking to him. There was still a door between us, but at least we didn't have to shout. Obviously embarrassed by the situation, he told me I shouldn't have come to the house, but at the same time thanked me for coming.

We talked about what was upsetting him just then—about challenging things at work, about the disturbing national political situation, and more. As we talked, he seemed to settle down a bit, the edge left his voice. After quite some time, he started to talk about how embarrassed he was over his actions—storming out, locking himself in the family room, the gun. Then he was into analyzing what his actions meant in terms of the dynamics within the family—long-term fallout, embarrassment, shame, guilt, etc.

When he was all talked out, I suggested he come out and move on.

He eventually assured me I could "go on home and be with *your* family." I went back upstairs. John's wife and I talked a little, shared a prayer, and at her insistence I left.

My follow-up phone calls seemed to be almost as reassuring to her as they were to me.

I Could Tell You Stories...

The cassowary, sometimes referred to as the world's most dangerous bird, can be found in northeastern Australia. That's where we found one. Slightly smaller than an ostrich, with a large bony crest and bright blue and red on its head and neck, it has the appearance of a prehistoric version of that huge flightless bird.

My wife, Pam Faro, and I were on a vacation trip there after she had completed a month of performing and teaching workshops Down Under, culminating in serving as the keynoter for the Network of Biblical Storytellers (NBS) Australia National Gathering. Driving (on "the wrong side of the road," mind you) through the Daintree Rainforest north of Cairns, we came across a male cassowary tending to two chicks. The papa was taller than our car, and the chicks were the size of large geese—quite a thrill!

Pam has been involved with NBS International for many years. As the origin of most of the biblical writings—both the Hebrew scriptures and the Greek New Testament—was oral composition and transmission, storytellers in antiquity passed on the stories orally from person to person and town to town. NBSI works to help present-day storytellers refine their understanding and skills in the oral transmission of biblical stories for today's listeners. With a worldwide membership and the deep involvement of noted scholars, NBSI brings to light the significant research on the oral generation and communication of biblical stories in the ancient past, as well as the impact of that orality on the written form of the Bible we have, and on listeners today.

NBSI is at the core of the development of a relatively new field of biblical study that explores the oral performance of the biblical texts both in antiquity and today. It is called Performance Criticism (not criticism of someone's performance; rather a methodology of analyzing, understanding, and interpreting the texts through critical thinking that recognizes that the vast majority of these stories were originally embodied and then performed in community). Performance Criticism is increasingly taught in universities, seminaries, and theological schools. It is contributing both to academia and to the formation of preachers and pastors.

This fascinating exploration of the oral nature of biblical stories, and the actual experience of biblical storytelling, has the power to enrich people's understanding of the gospel message, my own included.

In each of the interim settings in which have I served (please see the stories under "Interim Ministry"), I invited Pam to tell the Passion Narrative from Mark's gospel (Mark 14-15) on Palm Sunday. According to congregational members with whom I spoke following Pam's by-heart tellings, the experience of hearing the story told directly to listeners from memory, as opposed to having it read, was deeply moving, and added new appreciation for and understanding of the powerful narrative.

One of the many additional benefits of Pam's involvement with NBSI is the personal friendships that have developed with people from other countries. After Pam stayed with them a couple of times while working "across the pond," an English couple, both priests in the Church of England, then came and spent some time with us at our home. Not only did we have the pleasure of their company, but one of them told by heart the lectionary gospel text during a service at the church I was serving at the time.

Another NBSI friend, a Roman Catholic educator from Australia with whom Pam had stayed while "down under," has also visited us a couple of times. Among the many joys of our cross-cultural friendship was seeing her pure delight in watching the squirrels in our backyard perform their acrobatic tricks on our fence and in the trees. I was amazed to learn that there are no squirrels in Australia!

But they definitely have cassowaries, and we were blessed to see some in the wild!

For more information on the Network of Biblical Storytellers see their website: nbsint.org.

To learn more about storytelling in general, see Pam's website: storycrossings.com

To Name a Church

It's challenging to name a church. I had the opportunity to do so twice.

In 1993 I had been called to develop a new congregation in Broomfield, Colorado. In uncreative bureaucratic fashion, the ELCA dubbed the prospective congregation East Broomfield Lutheran Church—with the full knowledge and expectation that, once formed, the new congregation would select its own name. Since, as the pastor developer, I was the only one around at the time and I was doing all the legal necessities like incorporation and registration with the state, etc., I'd had to name the congregation.

There were some guidelines provided by the ELCA, developed over time: Don't use a theological doctrine (such as atonement, sanctification, absolution, redemption, etc.), no saint's names (most people aren't conversant with saints anymore), no numbers anymore (First Lutheran, Second Lutheran), no duplicating a name already in use in the area, etc.

It was hard. Every time I came up with a name I really liked, it was already in use.

Finally, in total frustration, I called our synod office. I explained my frustration to my supervisor. With only a moment's hesitation, he said, "How about something old-fashioned, like Cross of Christ?" And so it was named. Not ideal, maybe, but what is? It was long and hard to put on a letterhead... we put "COC" on the chairs and tables. Doesn't really roll off the tongue. But that was the name chosen—and it has become beloved over the years.

Roughly ten years later I was called to develop another new congregation ten miles to the north in Erie, Colorado. This time there was a group of people from COC to go along and help with the new start. We gathered one evening to work on a name, along with other planning. With a group dynamic involved, and real excitement and anticipation in the air, we bandied about many possibilities.

Erie was an old coal mining town, so someone suggested using the patron saint of mining. No one knew who that was so we googled it: "St. Barbara Lutheran Church"—um, no. Several people from Cross of Christ remembered and brought up a very well-received little sign we had made when getting started, that had been set out by the driveway on Saturday nights. It said simply: "Come and See!"—but somehow, "Come and See Lutheran" didn't seem to fly. There was a popular series of books by some conservative pop culture theologian making the rounds at the time, and it had a catchy name—but no, "Left Behind Lutheran" didn't sound like a winner, either. So I suggested: "Right Behind Lutheran" instead. Lots of laughter, but no cigar (and probably not even close, either.)

With all of the laughter in the room that night, and all the joy and excitement and enthusiasm in looking to the future of this congregation, someone said, "How about Rejoice Lutheran?"

A name was born.

REJOICE—ERIE, COLORADO

Teamwork

Within the Lutheran church there is an ongoing debate over the best strategy for starting and developing new congregations. Some things are clear, such as to go where there is new population growth and development, and there's a need for a new congregation to serve those folks. Other parts of the strategy are less clear, such as whether to buy land first (as had happened with Cross of Christ in Broomfield), or let the new congregation form and then select their own site; whether to send one person or send a team…

In the case of Rejoice Lutheran in Erie, the approach was to send in one pastor (me) and hope for the best. Thank God "I" was for all practical purposes a team of two. Turns out my wife, Pam, a graduate of Luther College in Decorah, Iowa, willingly brought a huge basket of skills to the task.

Having been a music major and then a professional musician, she had years of experience in planning, organizing, and directing choirs and worship experiences. In previous congregations, she had also worked in church offices and was familiar with administrative functions and needs in congregations. At the time, she was also in the process of earning an MDiv degree at Iliff School of Theology in Denver, and her theological insights and understandings were being honed and sharpened. That, plus her extensive background as a professional performance storyteller, provided perspectives to me that enriched my preaching.

In those first "start-up" days it was just our team. Pam organized and typed the weekly worship service bulletins. I took them to a helpful neighboring congregation and ran off copies. Every Sunday we arrived early at the school in which we rented space, and with some dedicated volunteers set up the dividers and chairs in the cafeteria for our worship space. The team grew—gradually we were able to involve and train other willing and capable folks to take over many of the responsibilities of making a mission congregation vital and viable.

One of my fondest memories is being recruited by the choir director (yes, my wife) as the only male voice in our fledgling choir. As one of the worst singers in the world, this was thrilling for me. At first, I was flattered to have the director's eyes so often intently on me—until I realized that it was because I sang out of tune. On almost every long note, she would look directly at me and then with her index finger motion urgently for me to sing either higher or lower.

Years later now, it is thrilling to see those early endeavors bearing good fruit. Rejoice has grown from our initial little team into a functioning congregation now serving its community faithfully and effectively!

Chicken Ranch

It is common for congregations in the start-up phase to rent space in a local school. Nearly ten years earlier in Broomfield, my previous parish, Cross of Christ, had done that. It's likely that many churches, in researching their histories, would find that they met at first in a school building. The school that had provided an initial home for Cross of Christ had been right near the church property, and a newer facility, still "shiny and fresh." Such was not the case for our new mission start in Erie.

There was no school in Erie that would work for us to meet in; we ended up renting space in Pioneer Elementary in neighboring Lafayette. It is one of the older schools in the area, and while the facility lacked the sparkle and shine of a newer building, the staff was very accommodating. Worship was held in the multipurpose cafeteria/gymnasium, which was down some stairs and through a corridor from the front doors.

Sunday morning's first task at Pioneer was to take the folded-up lunchroom tables (they lifted up in the middle to fold and form structures approximately eight feet tall) and push and pull and wheel them into place, to act as ungainly walls that defined a smaller area for us within the cavernous multipurpose room. Folding chairs were set up and placed in rows inside the two boundary walls of folded cafeteria tables. With a smaller table as an altar at the front, donated secondhand Communion ware filled and set upon it, and the school's slightly off-key piano in place, we were ready to roll.

At first, most Sundays we gave an update on the search for land, which everyone was eager to hear. With lots of open spaces around the town, I thought it would be easy to accomplish land purchase. "Not so fast," reality came screaming.

Between an abundance of land that was unusable for any kind of building due to subsidence from unmapped mine tunnels, the presence of a very small airport (with expansive state safety regulations about building anywhere near it), and competition from developers who were buying everything in sight ahead of Denver's continued explosive growth from the south and Boulder's from the west, the price of land was through the roof! Sellers with sites near well-traveled roads were asking five million dollars per acre, and up.

Because they were so depressing, these weekly updates became less and less frequent.

At long last, we discovered Chicken Ranch. This was an area of five-acre parcels that had been owned by a company that sold eggs. Each of these parcels had been sold to an individual at a much-reduced price with the stipulation that a dwelling be built and a chicken coup also be erected on the property. Chickens and feed had been provided and the eggs produced were sold commercially. Once a year the chickens were shipped off to a soup company and new chickens were provided.

The egg company was now long gone but the parcels and homes remained, along with a rusting structure that had once dispensed feed. Two of the homes happened to be for sale. Our church council looked at the area and chose one of the homes on which to make an offer. An architect had reviewed the large home and felt it could be converted into a small church. The commercial real estate consultant we were working with agreed it might be our best option.

At the council meeting where we were going to make the final decision, one of the members said, "Have we really looked at all the possibilities? I drove by the site. It's sandwiched between two other large homes—there could be difficulties with neighbors, having a church built right in the middle. I drove to the end of the street and saw a cute, newer-looking home of log construction. It's at the end of the lane. I think that might be a better site."

With all the patience I could muster, I explained that, yes, it would definitely be a better location—but (and I emphasized "but") it wasn't for sale. The response: "Come on—anything and everything is for sale!"

So, having been encouraged—no, make that directed...no, make that forced... So, having been "forced" by the council, a couple of days later I rang the bell of the log cabin-looking structure on 4.78 acres of land on the very outskirts of Erie, Colorado, in that development called variously by different locals "Chicken Ranch," "Chicken Acres," "Chicken Egg Ranch," "Soup City," or "Chicken Estates." The door was opened by an older, cheery woman, who, upon learning who I was and why I was there invited me in.

We sat at a large table in the great room of an 1800-square-foot, two-bedroom log home less than ten years old. With a full basement and an attached garage, it was a very comfortable space. The covered porch on two sides of the house offered a welcoming place to sit and gaze at the mountains in the not-too-far distance.

My hostess, an active Episcopalian, seemed intrigued by the idea of her home becoming a church. Before long she was describing where she envisioned the altar and pulpit. It was interesting…exciting…confusing, all at the same time. She asked for some time to think about it, to talk to her son, etc.

I, in turn, asked if I could bring our council for a visit. With her approval, we scheduled a group visit with our real estate agent as a part of the group.

There would be twists and turns—loan issues, county issues, fire protection issues—but it seemed that Rejoice Lutheran Church may have found a home.

Couldn't Have Done It Without Him

Have you ever met someone you will never forget? Jerry was one of those people.

He was retired from a career as a commercial real estate broker. He had had his own business and had done quite well. He was a very active volunteer with our bishop's office, donating his experience and expertise to help with the sale and/or purchase of real estate for new congregations like ours, and/or congregations that were at the other end of their life span.

He was a tall, rather gaunt man with the deepest speaking voice I think I have ever heard. He had an infectious smile and great sense of humor—but when it was time for business, he was all business. His lifetime of experience in commercial real estate was an invaluable asset for our little start-up congregation as we tried to navigate the incredibly murky waters of land acquisition for a home for our "baby."

Jerry and I logged many, many miles in his pride and joy: a several-years-old PT Cruiser. We scoured the area in and around the town of Erie looking for something, anything, that might provide a site for us. He and I visited countless possible sites, to no avail. Every time either one of us got a lead, we would call the other and schedule a "look-see." Potential sites were becoming more and more sparse. One exciting possibility was finally ruled out because it was within the strangely far-reaching legally-defined safety zone of the small local airport; several others because of the fear of subsidence from the unmapped coal mine tunnels. Jerry maintained his low-key, cheery manner throughout the countless trips he made from his home to the south of us in downtown Denver up to our location on the far northern reaches of the metro area.

When we finally found a real possibility in the Chicken Ranch development, Jerry handled the negotiations completely. On what turned out to be the last day of the process, he had been in and out of the log house we were trying to buy, talking to the woman who owned it, and her son. He would be in with them for half an hour or more at a time, while I waited outside. I could only hear voices—couldn't make out actual words. Then he would come out to the lawn where I was anxiously waiting, to give me a report. Each report followed the same pattern: "They're at (x number of) dollars. I explained the tax benefits (or the inheritance issues, or the—fill in the blank—other arcane issues) to them. They're discussing it."

Finally, he emerged from the house with a broad grin. "It's done! You folks are now the proud owners of this house and the 4.87 acres it sits on!" he beamed, waving the signed contract in the air.

When everything had closed, the check delivered, and paperwork signed—Rejoice Lutheran Church was finally going to have its own home, there with the log house.

After that, Jerry said what I had been feeling: "I'm going to miss working with you on this." He also made one of those offers that often actually go unfulfilled—"My wife and I would like to take you out to dinner sometime."

But empty promises were not a thing with Jerry. A couple of months later he called. "Are you free next Tuesday evening?" One of the most highly regarded restaurants in Denver was having some sort of a special that day, and my wife and I were invited to be guests of Jerry and his wife for dinner. It was a great meal and a fun time.

But it wasn't like riding around in that PT Cruiser—just me and Jerry and that amazingly deep and resonant voice.

Rejoice...or Not

The ELCA is one of the largest mainline protestant denominations in the United States. Headquartered in Chicago, it consists of thousands of congregations across the country. To administer such a sprawling organization, there are several focus areas. One of these areas is new congregation development, and part of that work is facilitating loans to new congregations when they are ready to build a facility.

Having thoroughly enjoyed my previous experience as mission developer at Cross of Christ in Broomfield, I had jumped at the chance to repeat it when the announcement was made of a new congregation to be formed in Erie, Colorado, a small former coal mining town ten miles north of Broomfield. All the necessary steps were taken, space for services in a local school was rented, a congregation assembled and growing as per plan, and finally land was found and purchased for Rejoice Lutheran Church.

With the acquisition of the ranch house and its parcel of land, Rejoice was ready to build. An application was submitted for a loan. It was rejected. "Too much money! You can't afford that big a loan," we were told. The building plans were revisited, cuts were made here and there, and revised plans were resubmitted. The response was quicker this time, and still the same. "No."

A day or two later the phone rang. I answered and was greeted by a sweet voice. She introduced herself and explained that she wanted to talk to me to make clear why our loan request had been declined.

"Pastor, you are sixty-five years old. We like to know that the pastor will continue with the congregation for four to five years after a building is completed, and we don't think you'll stay that long."

I was crushed. I had no intention to retire at that point. But it was crystal clear: my presence was impeding rather than assisting the congregation. I wrote a resignation letter, delivered it to the congregational president, notified the denominational headquarters of my retirement, and filed for Social Security.

I wondered if I should start shopping for a rocking chair.

Little did I know…

The very next day I got a call from a pastor I knew who had just accepted a call to a new congregation, and he was wondering if I'd be open to serving as an interim pastor in the congregation he was leaving. I accepted.

And…turned out I worked in interim ministry for the next ten years.

INTERIM MINISTRY

Continuing Education of a Different Kind

Interim ministry is its own unique "breed of cat."

In Lutheran congregations, whenever a pastor leaves for any reason—moving, retirement, whatever—the congregation itself selects its own new pastor, as contrasted with having one assigned by a bishop or some central authority. There is a "call process" which includes assessing the needs and wants of the congregation, and then interviewing candidates to find a pastor who best meets the needs in that particular setting.

Some pastors are specially trained to lead congregations through discerning and evaluating the specific situation, and helping them through the process of selecting the best pastor available for them. Often these interim pastors are more-experienced (older), recently retired pastors, which was my situation.

I ended up serving as an interim pastor in nine different congregations, each of them being between pastors and needing to go through the process of calling a new one. With each interim position I served, I stepped into a different set of circumstances, ranging from calm and well-functioning to deeply troubled and fraught. My stints ranged from a few months to a year-and-a-half; most of them about a year. I was sometimes chosen by the congregation, sometimes appointed by the bishop.

Whatever the specific circumstances of each setting, I found interim ministry a challenging and satisfying "final chapter" in my lifelong pastoral education.

You Learn Something New Every Day

The first Sunday in a new parish is stressful. This Sunday was doubly so since it was my first Sunday in my first interim ministry assignment. The people of the congregation were great. The sanctuary was beautiful. Everything had been set up in a way that was familiar and functional.

There was one new thing for me. There was a small plate of Communion wafers on the altar. I asked about this and was told that these were the gluten-free wafers. Unfamiliar as I was at the time with this practice, I asked how that worked. The assisting minister explained that when I was distributing the "regular" Communion wafers at the altar rail, someone might ask for a "gluten-free" wafer instead. The small plate on the altar held the gluten-free wafers for those who needed them.

The service proceeded. Time came for Communion, and people came and knelt at the altar rail to receive the bread (in the form of a wafer) and the small glass of wine. I was moving around the Communion rail distributing the wafers, and the assistant followed me with the wine. As I held out the wafer to one individual, he demurred and asked for a gluten-free wafer. Now fully informed about the procedure, I went to the altar and picked up one of the gluten-free ones. Returning to where this member was kneeling at the altar rail I said, "The body of Christ, given for you," and placed the gluten-free wafer in his hand. As I moved on, I saw him take the wafer and put it in his pocket.

There wasn't time for me to go back to him and ask what was going on. I continued on around the Communion rail distributing the bread to the others as I went.

Standing at the door at the end of the service to greet those who were on their way out, I noticed the fellow who had requested the gluten-free wafer waiting to the side for me to be done. When I had finished, he came over and said he wanted to explain what had happened.

I had never heard of celiac disease before, a condition from which this man suffered. He was so very sensitive to wheat, that for him to eat a gluten-free wafer from my hand which had been also handling regular wafers made from wheat would have made him sick. (What he needed—and what I had neither been informed of nor had thought of myself, was to be offered the plate of gluten-free wafers from which he could take one himself.) Though he was concerned about even touching a gluten-free wafer touched by my gluten-contaminated hands, he had taken it when I'd offered it to him rather than refuse it—but handling it gingerly, had placed it in his pocket for disposal after church by emptying his pocket without further touching the contaminated wafer.

Years later I was serving another interim with a congregation that shared their building with an Ecumenical Catholic Community. I learned that the priest there was also a celiac disease sufferer.

My education about gluten-free wafers stood me in good stead.

At the Ready

An interesting thing happened in nearly every one of the interim positions I served.

At some point very soon after I began, a member of the congregation would take me aside, introduce themselves, and say, "I'm an alcoholic. I want you to know that I am available to aid any others you may encounter here, so that they may have some support and encouragement to get the help they need."

The first couple of times this happened I was a little surprised. For whatever reason, in all my congregational positions throughout my ministry career, it had taken a lot longer to find out this kind of important and extremely helpful resource. Maybe in these interim situations it was the knowledge that I would be a "short-timer" that prompted the quick introduction.

Whatever the reason, I found it invaluable to have that information available and to know I had the support implied in that announcement.

Thankfully, I never had to actually call on these individuals for their assistance during my stints in each congregation, but the awareness of their willingness and openness and genuine concern for others was reassuring and inspiring in its own right.

Words to the Wise

Estes Park, Colorado, is a tourist town par excellence. It sits at the gateway to the main entrance of Rocky Mountain National Park, one of the most visited of all the national parks in the US. In the summer its streets bustle with tourists on their way to the park or to the many other attractions in the area.

Shepherd of the Mountains Lutheran Church is a relatively new congregation with a building built in 2008. Small in size, but large in power, the congregation consists of many folks who have retired to this beautiful area, along with many locals who are still working and who enjoy living amidst the mountain scenery and wildlife.

I was somewhat familiar with the town prior to being called to serve as interim pastor there. Estes Park, with its gorgeous views, is in demand as a setting for outdoor weddings. My first professional encounter with Estes Park had occurred some years before when I had officiated at a wedding that took place in the Stanley Hotel, famous for being the inspiration for Stephen King's novel, *The Shining*. A gorgeous facility and location for a wedding, it was a bit disconcerting when, just as we were about to start the ceremony, a herd of elk wandered through the hotel yard and all of the wedding guests rushed to the windows to watch and take pictures. Order having been restored and the guests having returned to their seats, the wedding went on with no further interruptions.

As is always the case, once an interim pastor gets moved in and acclimated, the realities of the parish gradually become apparent. One of the realities in this congregation was the fact that there were eight retired clergy who were members. Gulp!

You see, among the unspoken (no, make that spoken, but usually softly) words of advice given to pastors early on, one of the more common is, "Beware of any retired pastors in your congregation, especially if they served the congregation to which you are being called immediately prior to your arrival." Sage advice born of real-life experience, I'm sure. If a dearly loved predecessor is still in the parish, anyone who disapproves of or disagrees with something you are trying to do can always seek to have their opinion validated by the previous pastor, setting up uncomfortable dynamics.

But so much for words of advice!

For I was immediately greeted by, welcomed, supported, and encouraged by these fine retired folks. "Anything I can do to help, just let me know." "I really appreciate your sermons and look forward to them week to week." "You have been a real help to us here in our interim." "Thanks so much for coming to help in this 'in-between' time."

When my yearlong interim stint with them was done, I not only had greater respect and appreciation for my retired colleagues, but vowed to try to emulate their gracious reception of me, as I myself moved further toward full retirement and might deal with pastors younger than I. They had taught this old dog a new trick in terms of support for and encouragement of younger folks coming along in one's footsteps.

Another caution often offered among pastors has to do with people who come up with wonderful ideas for the parish—ideas for *you* to carry out. This was in my mind when one of the members of the congregation approached me with an idea for a service project. Since the tourist season for Estes Park is primarily the summer—there are no ski resorts nearby—the community becomes quiet over the winter. Up until recently, the service workers—hotel staff, restaurant staff, seasonal park employees, etc.—would return to their home communities once the season was over. But that was changing. Many of the folks in the tourist service sector were remaining as year-round residents, and struggling to make it with no work in the off-season. The suggestion to me was that the church open its fellowship hall and kitchen for a weekly free meal for these formerly seasonal, now permanent, residents and their families

Being no novice at this point in my career, I had a picture of where this might go: "Here it is, Pastor. We've set it all up and have it running—now all you have to do is keep it going." As an interim pastor, I didn't feel it was right for me to saddle a new incoming pastor with that kind of commitment. So, I hemmed, and I hawed, and I tried to discourage the idea.

Good luck with that! The folks in that congregation took the idea and ran with it—and to my knowledge, it is still going today. Another great service to the community and to people in need.

Yet another great lesson learned for me: "Words to the wise" may not always be as wise as they purport to be.

An Unexpected Shared Memory

While serving as interim pastor in Estes Park, I made a follow-up call on a visitor from the previous Sunday morning's worship service. Shepherd of the Mountains is a small congregation, and Estes Park is a small town, and there are few non-tourist local visitors, so I was anxious to meet this guy. I knocked on his door and was greeted by a friendly man who looked to be about my age.

He invited me in and we sat down for an amiable chat. In the course of that chat, we discovered we were both from Minnesota…not just Minnesota, but Minneapolis…not just Minneapolis, but Northeast Minneapolis…not just Northeast Minneapolis, but nearly the same neighborhood! Well, you know how that is—*OLD HOME WEEK!*

We had attended neighboring grade schools and high schools, but remembered many of the same landmarks, etc. Suddenly my new/old friend got quiet. "Do you remember the plane crash?" he asked. I knew immediately what he was talking about, and recounted my experience to him.

In 1957 on Memorial Day, there was a "flyover" by the Minnesota National Guard Air Squadron at a large cemetery on the border between Minneapolis and the northern suburb of St. Anthony Village. My Boy Scout troop was participating in the memorial service at Sunset Memorial Gardens. I had been involved in the service, reading Logan's General Order establishing

Memorial Day. There were a couple of speakers—a pastor and a politician—and then everyone went outside to gather around the reflecting pool while the formation of four jets roared over. We all watched in horror as two of the planes clipped wings and crashed in flames and smoke—lots of smoke. One plane had gone down into a gravel pit, the other into a Northeast Minneapolis neighborhood.

The scout leaders quickly decided that our troop should go to the scene of the crash to see if we might be of assistance. We got there as quickly as possible, ten minutes at most, and were immediately pressed into duty by the authorities, holding a rope line to keep onlookers out of the way. We witnessed things that we were probably too young to see. The pilot had stayed with his plane too long, apparently trying to keep it from hitting any houses (which he succeeded at). However, his attempt to eject, coming as late as it did, got him and his chute caught in the branches of one of the large trees that lined the streets in that part of town...

As I recounted my experience to my new acquaintance, he shared his with me. He had seen the crash and the smoke, also from a distance. He had gotten on his bike and ridden to the scene of the crash, following the smoke rising from the scene. He must have arrived just a few moments after our scout troop did.

We sat in silence for a few moments, each reflecting on that horrific event and the fact that we had both been there and both been affected so deeply by it. It was a deeply moving time of remembrance. Finally, sensing that the visit was over, I thanked him, excused myself, stood, and left. He accompanied me to the door. He never returned to a church service in the few short weeks that I had left in the parish. I don't know if he ever went back to Shepherd of the Mountains once I had gone. But for that brief time, I felt a bond of belated grief and shared horror with him that is hard to explain.

Another Chance

Arriving for work one weekday morning at the suburban church just north of Denver where I was serving as interim pastor, the office manager encountered a tall man, mid-twenties or early thirties. He asked, politely, if the church had any food available. She took him down the hall to the food pantry that the church sponsored and got him something to eat. She also invited him back that evening for a hot meal. It happened to be a Wednesday during Lent, and the tradition in that congregation, as in many Lutheran churches, was for a brief midweek service to be held, preceded by a soup supper: various families would bring pots of soup and a meal would be served for all to share.

She told me about this encounter afterward so that I could watch for a possible visitor that evening. The soup supper began, and as I entered the fellowship hall I saw a man, fitting the description provided by the office manager that morning, standing and looking rather uncertainly into the fellowship hall. I went over, introduced myself, and invited him in.

He came into the room and with a little coaxing went through the line for soup. With his plate and bowl, he went to a table and sat by himself. I filled a bowl and went to sit with him. We talked a little as we ate. His was a tough story. As we visited, a member of the congregation named Dave, an older man, came over with his soup and sat down with us. Sizing the situation up perfectly, after a bit he said to the visitor, "You sleepin' in the bushes?"

It turns out, there was an undeveloped area near the church that was referred to as "the bushes." It was known among the homeless population as a safe place to sleep. When the visitor's answer was yes, Dave said, "I have a cot at my house. Nothin' fancy. If you want to sleep inside on my cot you're welcome to." At this point, I had to leave to get ready for the service. When church was over, they both had gone before I could find out what happened.

The next day I learned that the visitor had, indeed, accepted the invitation to sleep at Dave's house, and that Dave felt sorry for the guy and extended the offer until his visitor could find work and get his own place. I kind of let it slip my mind and got busy with other things as the week went on. The next Sunday Dave wasn't in church, even though the choir was singing, and Dave was a member. After the service I asked around about Dave. "Anybody seen Dave?" Nope. No one had had contact with him.

All Sunday afternoon I had an uneasy feeling. Monday was my day off, and I couldn't get Dave off my mind. Tuesday morning I told the office manager about my concerns. I didn't have a phone number for Dave at my home, but she did at the church and we tried calling—no answer. The office manager knew someone at the police department and called to request a welfare check. The police called back a little later: no sign of life at the home.

After a good deal of fretting, the office manager and I drove over to Dave's house ourselves. Everything was dark and locked up—shades drawn. We knocked on the doors of neighbors. No one had seen Dave or any sign of life for several days.

Wednesday night—another soup supper—no Dave. What to do now?

The police were unwilling to force entry to the house. I was busy with a dozen other tasks. A few more days passed.

Sunday morning, there was Dave. He had gone to visit family for a few days. Whew, our worst fears were unfounded! But it turned out, sadly, that his visitor had actually stolen some of Dave's tools to pawn for drug money. Dave had "evicted" him—without incident.

Dave said, "We gave him a chance. That's all you can do for someone is give them a chance. I was in a tough spot one time. Someone gave me a chance. I took it. Hopefully, he'll get another chance and by then be ready to take it. That's all you can do—give 'em a chance."

God bless you Dave, and all the other "chance givers" of this world.

Scaling Questions

The interview was at a local restaurant. The interview team was the entire church council. The interviewee was me.

The congregation was in turmoil. Their two pastors were in the center of the upheaval. There had been a long, drawn-out, messy conflict in the congregation. There had been flurries of hateful email exchanges. There had been in-person meetings with shouting and tears. It had gone on and on and on for far too long. Efforts by the bishop's office to address the issues had been made. Nothing seemed to work. Finally, the pastors both had left, and now there needed to be a "time of healing" to enable moving forward.

I was appointed by the bishop to be the interim pastor to facilitate that healing, in addition to then helping with the process of calling the next pastor. After my appointment, there was this initial interview with the church council. It began with the council president giving a somewhat sanitized version of events leading up to the present.

He then said, "We're afraid that we could get a bad reputation in the synod, and that this could make it harder to call a new pastor."

I replied with a little "tough love"—"You don't have to worry that you 'could get' a bad reputation. You already have one."

I went on to explain that there is, of course, informal communication among pastors just as there is, I presume, among workers in any other segment of society, and that the situation in their congregation was widely known among the pastors in our five-state-wide synod.

The silence was deafening. After a long pause, the council president said, "Where do we go from here?"

We laid out a strategy of sorts. It included six months of an intentional healing process, during which there would be no movement toward issuing a call to a new pastor yet. Regular congregational functioning was to continue as much as possible, followed by a re-evaluation of the situation at six months, and a then subsequent move into the call process if advisable. That was the plan.

At the end of six months, the re-evaluation showed that the council felt we could go ahead and start the process of calling a new pastor. Many steps are involved in this process; the first one was a series of "cottage meetings," small group meetings held away from the church building, usually in a member's home. The purpose of such cottage meetings is to discuss a topic—in this case, "What are we looking for in a new pastor"—in a low-pressure informal setting.

I was a little worried about these sessions. I was expected to lead each of them, keep them under control (in light of the recent difficulties in this area for this congregation), and produce a report that might be helpful for an eventual Call Committee, those charged with the responsibility of interviewing candidates and recommending one for a congregational vote. My task seemed daunting if not downright impossible. In fact, I was scared silly. This was different from my previous interim positions.

Out of the blue, someone, and someone else, and then a third someone, said, "You need to talk to Deb." Deb was a social worker for one of the large counties in the Denver area. She had most recently been helping with families trying to deal with the aftermath of the Aurora Movie Theater mass shooting that made national headlines. Her primary focus, however, was dealing with families whose children had been removed from them by the county social services department. Wow! Talk about someone used to working with people in delicate and emotional circumstances. In my eyes, Deb was a gift from God.

I called her and she readily agreed to come in and talk to me. In our conversation, she suggested the use of "scaling questions." I wanted to nod wisely, agree, and then when she left go and look up what the heck "scaling questions" were—but instead, I swallowed my pride and said, "What the heck are scaling questions?"

She explained: Gather people in small groups of no more than ten. Set up a large tablet on an easel. Ask a question that requires an answer on a scale of one to ten. (For example, "How would you rate the worship services in this church?") Draw a line on the board with 1 at the left end and 10 at the right. Go around the room and ask each person to answer. Mark their score on your rating line and put their name next to it. Go around the room until everyone is listed on the board.

Now, go back to each person in the same order and ask, "What would have to happen to move your rating number up by one point?" When everyone has responded, open the discussion for a brief period.

Flip the sheet over and ask another question, following the same procedure. Try to have significant questions from each program area in the congregation, or any areas of concern.

Brilliant! The conversation flowed freely. It was controlled and (mostly) respectful. As each comment was made I wrote it down on the appropriate sheet. We had a written record of all that was said. People talked to and with each other, respectfully, thoughtfully, and constructively.

I am so grateful for Deb. For her wisdom and experience, for her willingness to apply her professional experience to our delicate and difficult situation, and for her help in sorting through and making sense of all the responses. I have found this process of scaling questions really useful over the years.

After that good start, and thanks to the hard work and commitment of so many in that congregation, we worked through the healing and restoration that was needed. A Call Committee was finally formed, and they went through the call process, interviewing candidates, and ultimately calling a pastor who is still serving outstandingly in that congregation after many years.

Youth Director, and More—Much More

Back in that initial interview with the church council (see "Scaling Questions"), I had been told that "the only thing we have going for us right now is Kayla." "Kayla? Who's Kayla?"

Previous to being appointed as their interim pastor, I had been part of a Listening Team that had been sent by the bishop to interview members of the congregation regarding the conflict there. Our team had conducted over one hundred twenty interviews of individual members and member families about the life and struggles of this congregation, and not one mention of a Kayla. Now in this interview with the council, I suddenly hear, "The only thing we have going for us is Kayla."

On my first day in my new role, I met Kayla. Young, bright, enthusiastic, she was bursting with excitement and enthusiasm. Her energy was infectious! I found myself infused with positive vibes and really looking forward to working with her to face the problems in the parish. And we did.

Always with a positive approach, we began a nearly two-year-long journey—a journey of healing and restoration for that community, and a journey of focus and direction for Kayla.

Kayla's job title was "Youth Director," but she was so much more than that. She was a powerful force for positivity, sound judgment, and reason. She was a down-to-earth embodiment of the gospel of love and care. She was joy and enthusiasm and excitement wrapped up in a forceful package of life-giving grace.

Kayla's "let's git 'er done" attitude produced some wonderful results. Vacation Bible School had grown to over two hundred and fifty children during Kayla's ministry. And the youth ministry was outstanding in its involvement and enthusiasm, but also its depth and commitment. One favorite, exuberant memory: On one Sunday the youth became a "flash mob" that unexpectedly invaded the sanctuary at the start of the service and got people on their feet and (sort of) jiving to a lively gospel tune. LUTHERANS!—(sort of) Jiving!—Gospel tune!

Those eighteen months in that congregation were one of the highlights of my ministry. The congregation ended up calling a young woman pastor with depth, commitment, and enthusiasm. The congregation prospers today.

As for Kayla, as time passed she discerned a call to full-time ministry and entered seminary. Wherever she lands to carry out ministry will be a lucky institution indeed!

I was blessed to have had her as a ministry partner.

More Than Cowboys and Tumbleweed

Laramie, Wyoming, was to me the stuff of "Wild West" lore. I had heard of it in print, on TV shows, and in the movies.

I drove the 135 miles north from home to the interview for the interim position there. As you drive up I-25, the land is spare and harsh, but rolling and beautiful. Turning west at the intersection with I-80, I was immediately aware of the almost continuous cross-wind. (There are electronic signs warning of the wind speed, which is normally over 60 mph, often 75 mph.) I was not aware that I was climbing and gaining altitude until I began the unexpected descent into Laramie. Its elevation: 7,200 feet. Even though a "Mile High City" (Denver) resident, I found myself winded during the shortest walks there. The old TV shows hadn't depicted Laramie as a mountain town.

The dearly loved pastor I was following had died suddenly and unexpectedly just short of his retirement. I had known him from interacting at our annual assemblies over the span of many years. The congregation was still in shock and mourning his loss.

The interview went well, I was hired, and settled into the role of Interim Pastor in the life of another faithful congregation.

Laramie is home to the University of Wyoming, and so there were a number of professors and other staff people from the university that were a part of the congregation, along with other community residents, and some students. There was also a former seminary student who had not completed the seminary curriculum but was very active in the congregation's life.

I had been there nearly a year, and we had nearly completed all the steps necessary in the process of calling a new pastor. We had journeyed as a congregation through the season of Lent, and now Easter was upon us.

I awoke on Easter morning and literally could not get out of bed. The pain seizing my lower back and radiating down my right leg was crippling. I managed to roll onto my stomach and slide off the bed and into a kneeling position on the floor. From there I somehow managed to wriggle into my clothes, hobble out to the car, and drive to the church. The pain was excruciating.

Thank God the former seminary student was there helping with the services that morning. She was able to lead both services. I preached the sermon I'd prepared, standing hunched over in the pulpit. I blessed the bread for the Communion, and sat in brutal pain for the rest of each service.

After church, I drove to my townhouse, somehow managed to load up what I could of my stuff, and drove a painful 130 miles home. Without the powerful help from the faith community and the seminary student that day, I don't know what would have happened.

I ended up needing a microdiscectomy and spinal fusion. Thankfully, the bishop found a replacement for me for the congregation while they finished their process for calling a new permanent pastor.

Laramie remains the stuff of "Wild West" lore to me, but with a whole new twist.

Oh wait, don't say twist…

The Wild West Indeed

Laramie is situated right on Interstate 80, one of the main east-west routes across the US. Since the church I was serving is about two blocks away from the highway, it was not unusual to get visits from stranded travelers needing assistance to continue their journeys. Some of these travelers were hitchhikers who had hitched a ride with one of the truckers, and then left on their own when the truck that had been their conveyance stopped in Laramie for the night. Some were a pretty rough-looking lot.

The layout of the church building was a little unusual. Built on a hill, the sanctuary and offices were on the upper level, as was the large outdoor entrance to the sanctuary that was open on Sunday mornings; classrooms were on the lower level. The "office entrance" to the building that was used for access during the week was on that lower level, near the parking lot. Once inside, there were interior stairs (as well as an elevator) that ascended to the offices and the sanctuary. The secretary's office on that upper level had an interior window overlooking the stairs and the entrance below.

Our church secretary was extremely competent, quiet, and unassuming. And also very short and slight. Unless she would position herself standing at that window—which was not the case while she was working: sitting at her desk, working with the phone, the copier, other office equipment, etc.—she had no view of the stairway below.

With the combination of the physical setup, the possibility/likelihood of dubious strangers showing up, and her diminutive size, I used to worry that someone could come in the front door, climb the stairs, and accost her before she even knew that they were in the building. She often worked alone, if I was out making calls, or if it was a day that I wasn't in town (I was usually back home in Denver on Mondays and Tuesdays).

One day I broached the subject of keeping the door locked and installing a buzzer/intercom system on the door for safety. Someone desiring entrance might buzz the office and the secretary or whoever could glance through the window and buzz the visitor in, if appropriate. As I was explaining my brainstorm, the secretary told me in no uncertain terms that it was not only unnecessary but also foolish. "I'm not at all worried about my safety," she emphatically exclaimed. "I pack!"

It took a moment for that to register—a long moment. Then a chill ran down my spine. The headline started to form in my head: *"Church secretary shoots intruder—'I pack!' she states triumphantly."*

I guess this still *is* the Wild West.

Christmas Grace

Christmas Eve can be a strange and difficult time for pastors.

Typically, churches offer multiple services on that day, often at unusual times. (Anyone up for a 5 a.m. Swedish *Julotta* service?)

Sermons on familiar texts can be difficult to write for many pastors because of people's acquaintance with the material—and what is more familiar than the Christmas story?

Christmas Eve services are usually packed with visitors, many of whom are technically members of the congregation and expect the pastor to remember them even though they only show up once a year at Christmas and maybe Easter, causing the pastor embarrassing silences, awkward attempts at cover-up, or painful admissions of guilt when they can't remember names.

All that having been said, and even with the cheer and joy that is surely part of Christmas as well, Christmas Eve is an even stranger time for interim pastors. All of the aforementioned factors are in play, but add to them the complicators of unfamiliarity and uncertainty.

Christmas fell on a Wednesday in 2013, the year that I was serving an interim in Laramie, Wyoming. This congregation had been host to a series of seminary students who had served their year-long internships there. The townhouse which the church owned for the interns to live in during their internship was vacant that year of my interim ministry, so that's where I stayed during the work week. I returned home to Denver after church each Sunday for my "weekend" break, and returned to Laramie on Tuesday to start another week.

All that meant that I would be driving 135 miles north on Tuesday to lead two Christmas Eve services that evening in Laramie, and then turning around and driving the 135 miles south to have some semblance of Christmas with my family at home the next day. (Thankfully, the church didn't hold Christmas Day services, and I could spend that day at home.)

That particular Christmas was special, because my wife's sister and her husband had come to be with us. My brother-in-law is a retired physician and a good friend, and when he heard the schedule of services and the plan for me to go up and then return home late that same night, he was concerned about me driving that many miles alone. He graciously volunteered to come along to keep me company. What a guy!

Christmas Eve arrived. About noon my brother-in-law and I jumped in the car and headed to Laramie. It was snowing lightly. The wind, always a concern on this drive through the mountains, was blowing, but only lightly. The holiday traffic was steady, but not overwhelming.

The first service went well. Everyone stood around and visited a bit following the service, but didn't linger. There were festivities and dinners and family time, etc., to get home to. There was a two-hour break between the first and second services, so I suggested to my brother-in-law that we go get a bite to eat.

Now, Laramie is not Denver, and Christmas Eve is not every other night. What was I thinking? There was not an open eating place in town! We scoured the community, to no avail. Finally, we found a little corner establishment, kind of a combination grocery store and pizza place. The owner was just closing up.

I'm not sure if it was the profit motive, or our "hang-dog" look of desperation and hunger, or just what motivated him, but he took pity on us. He unlocked the door and let us in, locking it behind us. He put a frozen pizza in his microwave, opened a couple bottles of Coke, and my brother-in-law and I shared Christmas Eve dinner.

Now, I've been through a lot of Christmases—all special, some strange, some stranger than others—but this one was extra special *and* strange. The kindness of the pizza place proprietor coupled with the caring and friendship of my brother-in-law was deeply heartwarming.

I know it wasn't Bethlehem and babies and inns, but it was certainly caring and concern and generosity.

I'll never forget Christmas Eve of 2013.

The Governor's Place

Cheyenne is the capital of Wyoming. A city of 60,000-plus residents, it is the home of Warren Air Force base, the NCAR (National Center for Atmospheric Research) supercomputer center, and the 120-plus-year-old Frontier Days rodeo and celebration of the Old West. It sits at the intersection of I-25 and I-80, so is a busy transportation hub as well.

After completing my interim in Laramie to its west, I next found myself at a congregation in Cheyenne, serving as interim pastor at a medium-sized church with a very nice newer building and a very involved membership. As with many, if not most, established congregations, over a period of time there gets to be a "regular" seating pattern. People sit in the same area week after week, if not the same actual seats.

Two of the active members of this congregation were the immediate past governor of the state and his wife. The former governor and wife had seats where they usually sat, and due to their visibility and "fame," their regular seats were informally "reserved" for them.

One particular Sunday the church was quite full. The former governor and his wife were running a little late. A visitor couple entered the sanctuary, saw two empty seats, and innocently and unknowingly sat in "the Governor's place."

An audible gasp went up from everyone in the sanctuary. The gasp was followed by an equally audible chuckle when everyone heard the gasp, realized the cause, and saw the humor in the situation.

No sooner had the gasp/chuckle subsided than the governor and his wife arrived. Totally unaware of the preceding drama and totally gracious as always, when they saw that their accustomed seats were occupied they found another place, and the service proceeded.

I'm pretty sure that no one heard a word of my carefully prepared sermonic masterpiece that morning. Minds remained on the seating *faux pas*. After the service, the scene was recounted and replayed over and over through everyone's eyes—including both the "First Family's" and the visitors'.

Somewhere in the US, there may be a couple who delights small gatherings of people by telling the story of their visit to Cheyenne, Wyoming, and sitting in "the Governor's place" during worship.

Heavy Snow

Wouldn't you know? The big snowstorm came rolling in on Christmas Eve—snow measured in feet, not inches.

The church in Cheyenne where I was serving as interim pastor had an arrangement with a local temp worker agency for shoveling our sidewalks, and with a local snowplowing service to clear the parking lot. But many people had already left town to be with family for the holidays. Snow removal was always a problem, and the Christmas holiday only compounded it.

There was one shoveler who showed up alone on Christmas Eve, early in the afternoon, after it had been snowing awhile. I went out to talk to him—but "he" turned out to be a "she." She was an older woman, looking to be in her late sixties or so. But she was bundled up against the cold and obviously in good condition to be shoveling like she was.

The church sat on a corner with sidewalks all around the building. There were two parking lots, one on each side of the building, with sidewalks leading from the lots to the church. She was gamely attacking the whole maze of sidewalks all alone. I asked why not wait till it was done snowing, and she replied that if she could "stay ahead of it a little, she wouldn't have to shovel so much at once." When I left, mid-afternoon, she was still working.

I went to my apartment to change clothes and get ready for the Christmas Eve services. When it was time to head back to the church, there were almost two feet of snow on the ground and it was still snowing. I pulled on my boots and started slogging through the drifts, thankful I lived only a couple blocks from the church as I trudged past my buried car.

When I arrived at the church, I found the snow-shoveling woman hard at it. The snow was so wet that she had been soaked after a couple of hours, so had gone home to put on dry clothing and had just gotten back. She had kept the walks as clear as possible, and since the plowing service for the parking lot had not yet arrived she had started on the edges of it, explaining that if she could clarify the outline of the lot it would be much easier for the plow once it arrived.

I went into the building absolutely astonished at this woman's commitment, strength, and resolve. I hunted around the office, found a Christmas card, put some money in it, and went out to give it to her and say thanks.

As I thanked her verbally and extended the card to her she said, "Is there money in there?" "Uh, yes," I replied, somewhat taken aback." I won't take it!" she stated firmly. More than a little surprised, I asked why.

"My mother was from Poland," she explained. "She was pregnant with me when WWII ended. She fled Poland and walked to Germany to escape the Russians. The camp that had been set up to house the refugees was run by the Lutheran Church. I was born in that camp. Later, we were moved to a resettlement camp further west, also run by the Lutheran Church. After some time, we were transported to the US by the Lutheran Church and resettled here in Cheyenne. I owe the Lutheran Church a lot. I won't take that money."

I had much to think about that Christmas.

I thought about the biblical story of upheaval and travel and caring. I thought about the 1940s story of upheaval and travel and caring. I thought about today's many stories all around the world of upheaval and travel, and the never-ending need for caring.

Political upheaval…people displaced for political reasons…women pregnant in the midst of everything else…caring strangers willing to help.

It was profound. It was powerful. On that Christmas Day, it was sobering and heartwarming at the same time.

Lived Experience

Of course a pastor brings his or her experiences and lessons learned from life, not just the seminary education, to their work. The good and the bad, the challenging and the uplifting, the sorrowful and the joyful—all of it contributes to the formation of a pastor, and to him or her being able to minister effectively. And the longer one serves, hopefully, the more insights one has to offer.

This was brought home powerfully to me in one particular way, while serving in my final interim position.

As I wrote previously, I have experienced divorce firsthand—not once, but twice. After my first marriage of nearly twenty years to the mother of my children, a second marriage also ended, that one after more than ten years. Divorce, rather than something to read about, study, and imagine, became something very real and personal. The pain and agony, the self-doubt and loss, the loneliness and feelings of unworthiness that entwine and torment a person, became real in a way I never wanted nor dreamt possible.

(Thankfully, that's not "the end of the story" for me in this regard; see "Growth and Grace" in the Cross of Christ section.)

In the last parish in which I served as an interim pastor, with fifty years of parish experience behind me, one day a woman made an appointment and came into the office. She wanted to discuss several difficult issues she was experiencing, mostly relating to her divorce and her ex-husband.

Then she said something deeply meaningful to me. She said something to the effect of, "Thank you, Pastor, for listening and REALLY hearing what I had to say. To know that you have been down this road yourself means so much. You're not one of those 'perfect' people in their 'perfect' little marriages.

You've been there and you understand how difficult and gut-wrenching this all is."

I thought of that second intern back in Thief River Falls, Minnesota (see "Eye-Opening").

And I was so grateful my lived experience proved helpful to her.

Education Never Ends

Iliff School of Theology is a United Methodist seminary in Denver, located adjacent to the campus of the University of Denver. My wife, Pam, earned her MDiv degree at Iliff, like many Lutherans from Colorado and other Western states who complete most or all of their seminary coursework there, because the nearest Lutheran seminaries are in Illinois, Minnesota, and California.

When I started my next-to-last interim at a church in Lakewood, a southern suburb of Denver, I learned that a Lutheran student at Iliff had been assigned to do field work at the congregation I was serving. The demands on an interim pastor being quite overwhelming, I was glad for the help. The student was older than most interns generally are, quiet, competent, a great guitar player in the congregation's praise band, and required little supervision or guidance from me. He interacted easily with many of the musicians and other congregational members. He worked so independently that often I was hardly aware of his efforts.

Toward the end of his term, he asked to meet and go over the report I would have to write on his involvement at the church. We met for lunch, and in our conversation I got one of the biggest jolts of my life. I learned that this student had been convicted of attempted murder at the age of sixteen and had spent over a dozen years in prison in upstate New York. While incarcerated, he had completed high school and much of the college coursework toward a degree.

His job in the prison had been working in the chaplain's office. He later went on to work in the prison hospital ward caring for patients dying of AIDS. As a result of his close contact with the chaplain who was a pastor of the African Methodist Episcopal Church, and the encouragement and support he received from this caring and nurturing man, after he completed his sentence he decided to go to seminary.

His Lutheran roots and some of the reading he had done in prison led him to a Lutheran seminary, then also to classes at Iliff and fieldwork with us. His warm and wise presence was a powerful witness to all he came into contact with in the congregation, and beyond. He has since been ordained and is now serving in a congregation, doing outstanding and effective ministry.

Even as retirement knocked on my door, my education continued.

CLOSING THOUGHTS

I'm sitting here in my study, nearly sixty years from that first unnerving day of being interviewed by the faculty of Northwestern Lutheran Theological Seminary.

I'm retired.

It's been a trip.

No, it's been much more than a trip. It has truly been a lifetime journey.

I've had the privilege of being invited to share in the lives of many different people in many different circumstances and junctures of their lives. I've been invited to this role not as me alone, but as a representative of God's church here on earth.

Like all who have been afforded this privilege, I am grateful for the chance to serve, but also awed by the trust, love, guidance, and compassion of those I have encountered along the way.

"Blessed to be a blessing" is a phrase Harley Swiggum uses in his Bethel Bible Series. I know I have been blessed by so many people over the years. I hope and pray that I have been a blessing to others as well.

ABOUT THE AUTHOR

Keith Prekker has worked as a Lutheran pastor for over fifty years. Born and raised in Minneapolis, Minnesota, he served in congregations and organizations in South Dakota, Minnesota, California, Wyoming, and Colorado. He holds degrees from the University of Minnesota, Northwestern Lutheran Theological Seminary, and the Graduate Theological Foundation, and he served his pastoral internship in Leonberg-Ramtel, Germany. Now retired, he lives in Broomfield, Colorado.

Printed in the United States
by Baker & Taylor Publisher Services

Printed in the United States
by Baker & Taylor Publisher Services